society and **SCIENCE**

society and SCIENCE

CHANGING THE WAY WE LIVE

BERNARD DIXON

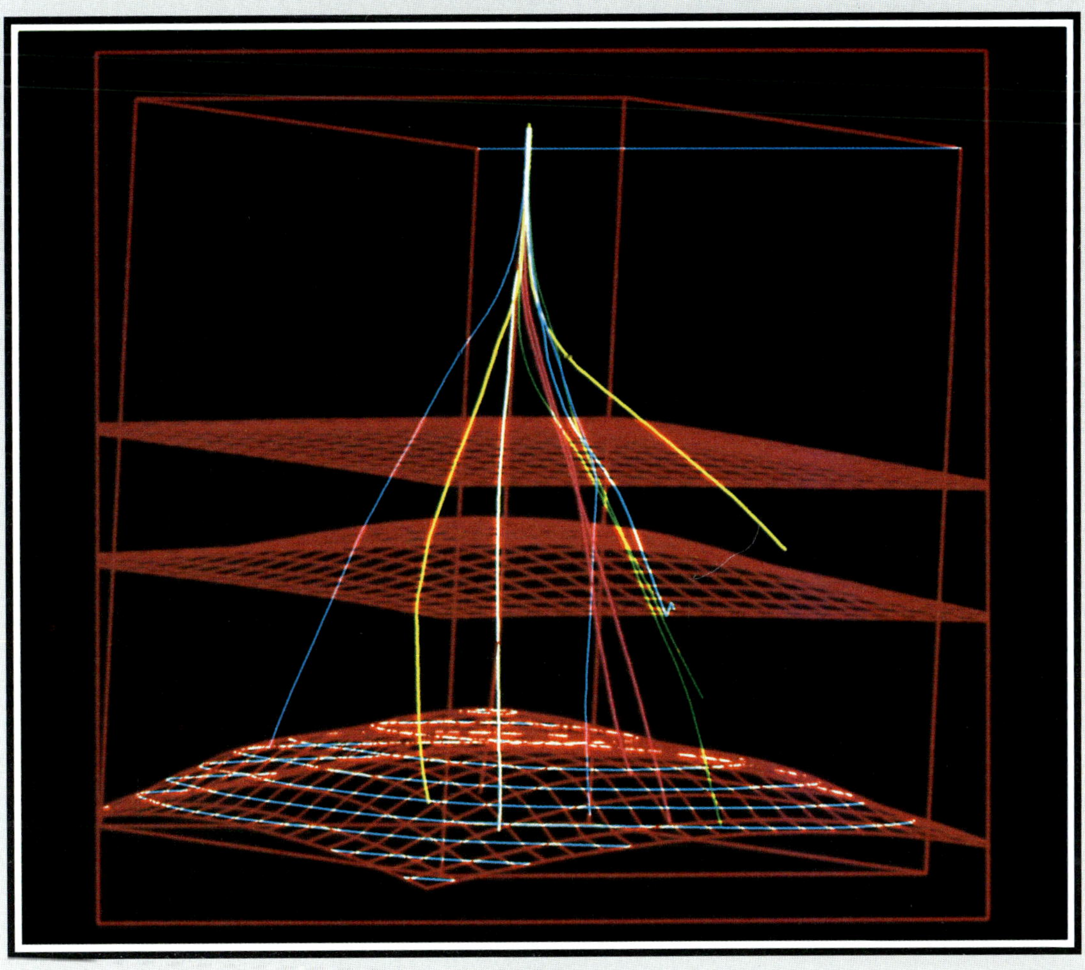

CASSELL

Editor Bill MacKeith
Designers/Art Editors
Frankie Macmillan, Chris Munday, Niki Overy
Picture Researchers Mary Fane, Alison Renney, Rose Taylor, Menna Williams
Design Consultant John Ridgeway
Project Director Lawrence Clarke

Contributing Editor
Dr Bernard Dixon (chapters 1, 2, 4-6)

Principal Contributors
Professor A.J. Meadows (chapter 3)
Lloyd Timberlake (chapters 7, 8)

Advisors
Eugene Garfield, founder and president, Institute for Scientific Information, Philadelphia
Professor John Ziman, H.O. Wills Professor of Physics, University of Bristol

Other Contributors
Michael Allaby, Susan Blackmore, Paul Davies, Robin Holloway, Anthony Martin, Zhores Medvedev, John Newell

AN EQUINOX BOOK

Planned and produced by:
Equinox (Oxford) Ltd
Musterlin House,
Jordan Hill Road
Oxford OX2 8DP

First published in the UK 1989 by Cassell, Artillery House, Artillery Row, London, SW1P 1RT

Distributed in Australia by
Capricorn Link (Australia) Pty Ltd
PO Box 665, Lane Cove, NSW 2066

British Library Cataloguing in Publication Data Dixon, Bernard Society and Science; changing the way we live 1. Science & Technology. Social aspects I. Title 306'.45

ISBN 0 304 31785 3

Cover picture

Main picture: Science Photo Library/Malcolm Fielding, The BOC Group PLC.

Corner picture: NGS

Printed in Spain by H. Fournier, S.A.

Contents

Social Relations

1

Scientific research as a Pandora's Box?...The "pull" of society on science...PERSPECTIVE...Opponents of new technology...Development and impact of the Pill... Science shops...Impact of science on society...Forensic science... and its validity...How gunpowder changed the course of science...The mysterious story of television... Scientists and the Bomb...Development of a drug

Countless magazine articles and learned papers have been written about "the impact of science on society". UNESCO even has a magazine with that very title. Such publications invariably portray a continual, one-way movement of products, processes and ideas from the domain of research and development into the rest of the world. Whether beneficial or otherwise, the fruits of science – from the steam engine and weaving machines of the industrial revolution, the chemical explosives of World War I and the nuclear bombs of World War II, to today's microprocessors and far-reaching techniques of genetic engineering – are portrayed as arriving, often unheralded, in a society that may be unprepared and which then has to work out how to respond.

Some of these "impacts" are more conceptual than practical, as when the sun-centered picture of the Solar System replaced the geocentric version and thereby altered our intuitive understanding of our place in the universe, or when Darwinian evolution undermined the notion that Man was the pinnacle of divine creation. Many "impacts" are blatantly obvious – for example, the introduction of penicillin, which vanquished many potentially fatal but previously untreatable infections.

Some end products of applied science, such as the explosion at the Bhopal chemical factory in India, in December 1984, or that at the Chernobyl nuclear power plant in the Soviet Union in April 1986, are accidental. Others have caused particular consternation because they have been widespread but initially unrecognized – as with the damage caused to wildlife by pesticides, as first highlighted in Rachel Carson's 1962 bestseller *Silent Spring*.

The notion that science, pure and applied, always causes one-way reverberations and consequences in the world also seems plausible because science does indeed have a greater impact on society than in the past. Heavily centralized, interdependent, and evolving at a far greater pace than in the pastoral past, developed countries are inordinately sensitive to technological change.

Nor is the Third World insulated from these effects. The second "green revolution" promises freedom from famine or social disruption for peasant communities. Satellite dishes in remote villages purvey educational enlightenment or subversive propaganda. Across-the-counter antibiotics cure dread diseases or create the drug-resistance that disarms such nostrums of their power in future.

Such examples appear to confirm that scientific research is akin to a Pandora's box, spawning products which society may or may not welcome but over whose genesis and deployment it has little or no influence. The real world, however, is more complex. Science does impinge on society. But society also has multifarious impacts upon the scientific community and the industrial world.

"Luddites" in the Industrial Revolution

Britain's industrial revolution, the first, is often portrayed as a one-way process, relentlessly transforming the landscape and people's lives. During the years 1811-1813, however, groups of so-called Luddites were operating in England, opposing new technology with violence. One group of weavers, supposedly led by "Ned Ludd", broke into weaving sheds in Nottinghamshire and Leicestershire to smash up the wide frames that had been introduced to manufacture cheap "cut-up" stockings. The attacks spread to Lancashire and Yorkshire, when cotton weavers attacked factories containing new steam looms, which were thought to threaten employment. In some places "croppers" led the action. They were skilled, well-paid men involved in the finishing of woollen cloth, but the hand shears which they used with strength and dexterity were being supplanted by labor-saving shearing frames. As described in Charlotte Brontë's "Shirley", these increasingly violent campaigns to smash the frames culminated in the repulsed attack on Cartwright's mill and the assassination of the Huddersfield "Committee for the Suppression of Outrages".

◀ An early 19th-century cartoon shows Ned Ludd, probably mythical, after whom King Ludd was named. Usually masked, the machine-smashing Luddites tended to operate at night.

▼ The care of premature babies, saving many who previously would have died, is an activity based on many technical advances, from the science of materials to our modern understanding of respiration.

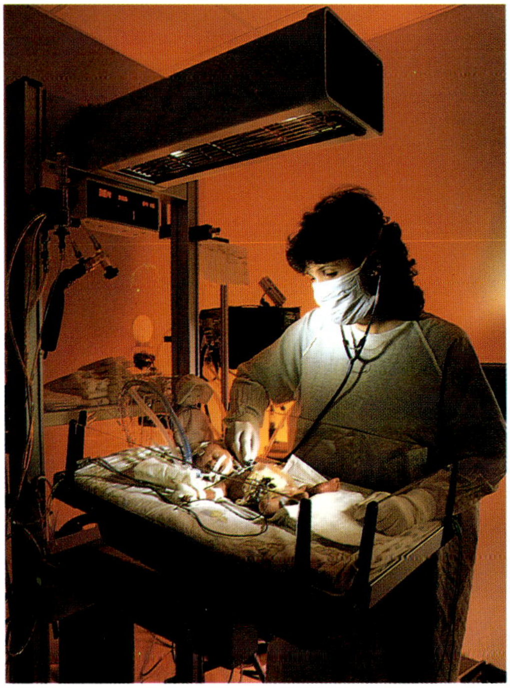

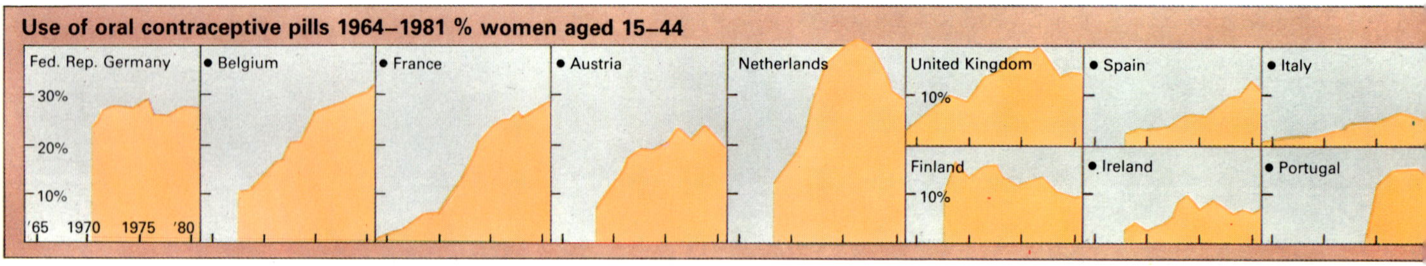

Priorities of the wider community

Opposition of the "Luddite" sort (◆ page 5) has its modern counterpart in attacks on laboratories where animal experiments are conducted and is the most blatant way in which the wider community affects the course of science and technology. The funding of research is another powerful channel of influence (◆ page 21). Choices made by societies and institutions regarding the fields where investment is considered desirable have a profound impact on the evolution or stagnation of different disciplines. Certain communities at certain times decree that they should plow more resources into one type of research as against another.

One example is high-energy physics, which is dependent on the construction and use of huge particle accelerators. When Britain found itself facing economic difficulties during the mid-1980s, the government appointed a committee to consider whether it should continue to subscribe to CERN, the subatomic physics center at Geneva in Switzerland. Britain's domestic program of work in this field had already been curtailed, and the committee concluded that continued membership of CERN would be possible only if the country's membership fees could be renegotiated. Although this kind of "pure" science is international, results usually accruing to the world community, such developments clearly affect the pattern of scientific discovery. In 1986, for example, when there was a further financial threat to continued British involvement in CERN, particle physicists faced the prospect that their country would opt out of this entire speciality of science.

▲ Within ten years of Gregory Pincus's historic announcement of his first successes with oral contraception, ten million women had taken the Pill. There was an extensive trial in Puerto Rico in 1957, and in 1960 the first trials began in Britain, where 44,000 women were on the Pill by 1964. Over five million women in the USA were using oral contraception by 1966. Factors affecting its adoption in different countries (shown here as the minimum percentage of women aged 15-44 supplied through commercial channels) include religious and social attitudes and information about the benefits and side effects of the Pill.

The impact of the Pill

No other substance has ever been consumed so widely so soon after being put on the market, or aroused so much controversy, as the Pill.

Beginning with the work of the Roman Catholic Dr John Rock, a member of the team working on the Pill with Pincus, the Roman Catholic Church was shaken by one of its biggest rows ever, over the morality of "artificial" contraception. Nonetheless, the introduction of the Pill has had a momentous effect on millions of human lives bringing release from the fear of unwanted pregnancy, particularly in those families and those parts of the world where the creation of new life is not a joyous experience but a costly burden. Coincidentally, the Pill has been blamed for its contribution to the decline of standards of sexual behavior – just as an earlier product of science and technology, the cheap mass-produced car of Henry Ford, allegedly led to an increase in "promiscuity" by making mobile seclusion available to the young in the United States of the early decades of this century, and as the availablility of penicillin reduced fears of venereal disease.

▲ Margaret Sanger, pioneering spirit of the Pill.

◀ For Roman Catholics, here greeting Pope John Paul II at Wembley Stadium, London, in 1982, oral contraception has posed one of the greatest moral challenges this century to the church's teaching.

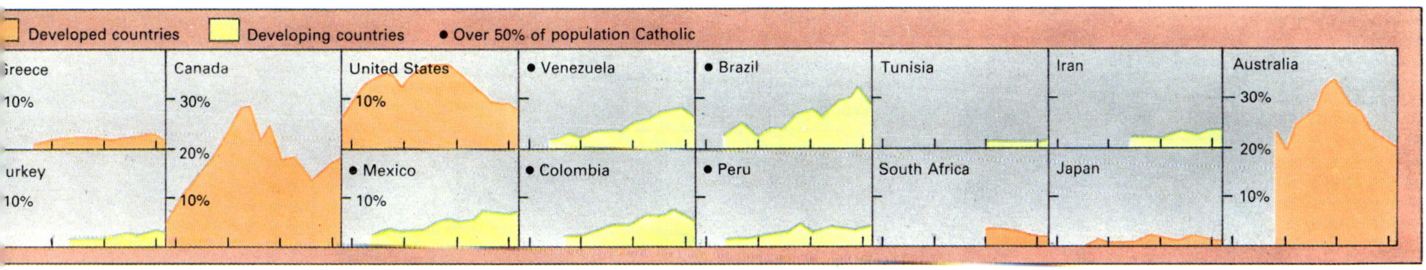

The development of the Pill

Lobby groups and particular individuals often play crucial roles in altering the pattern of research, as in the case of the contraceptive pill, a unique product in the speed with which it was developed and brought into practical use by millions of women all over the world. During the early 1900s, physiologists had discovered that the ovaries played a central role in regulating a woman's sexual cycle, and in the 1930s they began to learn something of the hormones responsible for controlling the process. Then they discovered that injection of the steroid hormone progesterone inhibited ovulation in the rabbit. It seemed unlikely that progesterone would have the same effect in women. In any case, steroid hormones were prodigiously expensive to manufacture.

There are, however, steroids in plants which can be grown cheaply. Perhaps these substances could be converted into others which would be effective in controlling fertility in humans? The American chemist Russell Marker was the first to develop the necessary chemical technique. In 1943, he offered his services to a company in Mexico that was later to become the Syntex Corporation, a major world concern in the fertility control business. Marker is said to have presented as his credentials two jars filled with 2kg of progesterone – worth about $160,000 at the then market price. By 1950, steroid hormones were available at one-hundredth of their price a decade previously.

A nonscientist's key role

Still, no one had developed a steroid that exerted a contraceptive effect when given by mouth. Then the Syntex chemist Carl Djerassi synthesized a steroid that was effective by mouth, as a possible means of preventing habitual abortion. At this point in the story a key role was played by someone who was not herself a scientist: Margaret Sanger (1883-1966), the American pioneer of birth control, who had opened the first family planning clinic in the United States in 1916, in Brooklyn. In 1951, she went to see Dr Gregory Pincus of the Worcester Foundation at Shrewsbury, Massachusetts, and persuaded him to slant his current research on mammalian fertility toward the possibility of an oral contraceptive for human use. Pincus decided to pursue this line of research, and in 1954 reported that a number of synthetic steroids related to progesterone inhibited ovulation in the rat. One of them, norethisterone (or norethindrone) also proved effective in women, and in 1955, at the Fifth International Conference on Planned Parenthood, held in Tokyo, Pincus described his first successes. The only apparent problem was occasional "breakthrough bleeding", but Pincus and his colleagues overcame this by using a mixed pill containing other substances, which they introduced in 1957. Since then a number of modified formulae have appeared on the market, each dependent upon the original work of Pincus and his team.

▼ Gregory Pincus was the physiologist whom Margaret Sanger visited in 1951 and persuaded to work toward chemical contraception.

Political and consumer "pull" on science has increased in recent decades

"Science shops"
Universities in the Netherlands have pioneered a simple and direct method of making scientific expertise available to the wider community. They run "science shops" which provide information for citizens on food additives, radiation risks and similar topics, as well as more local issues such as pollution. Science shops emerged during the 1960s, when left-wing students and staff tried to "radicalize" science in the Netherlands (and other countries). After an initial period when the shops were ill-organized and staffed by part-time volunteers, the University of Amsterdam was first to found one with a fulltime staff member, in 1977. Today, other European countries are experimenting with similar schemes, and all Dutch universities have a science shop with 2-7 paid staff.

A key part of science shops' work is to translate customers' often ill-defined requests into specific questions that can be answered immediately or researched. Clients are expected to make use of the information they receive from the shop – through trade-union activity in the workplace, for example, when an alleged occupational hazard is at issue. Facilities provided by the shops range from literature surveys, together with help in interpreting technicalities found in research papers, to the collection of samples and the conduct of sophisticated laboratory analyses.

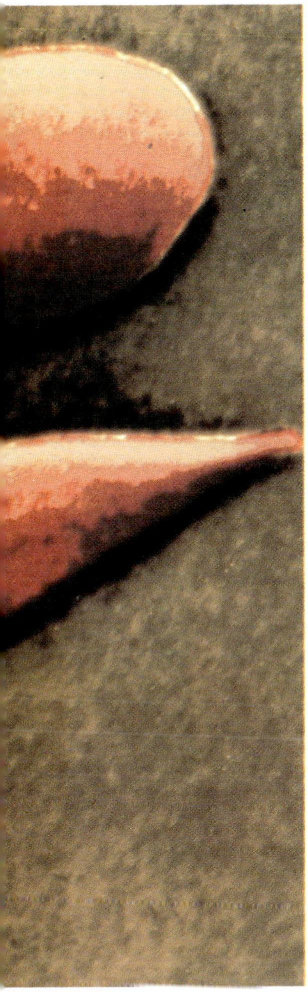

◄ Additive-free preserves are one commodity being produced in increasinng quantities in response to consumer demand. But public attitudes toward more or less wholesome foods and beverages do not always square with a scientific analysis of what they contain. In recent years, for example, there has been a boom in the sale of bottled mineral waters. Yet the labels and advertising for these products often boasts of the absence of the same salts – minerals – which were formerly considered to be valued health-giving constituents.

◄ Sickle-cell anemia is so-called because the victim's red blood cells contain an abnormal form of hemoglobin, which fails to carry oxygen as it should, and which causes the cells to assume sickle shapes. During the late 1960s and early 1970s, the Black Panther Party in the United States – seen here in a courtroom demonstration – made the disease into a major political issue. The party argued that sickle-cell anemia, which preferentially affects blacks rather than whites, had been seriously neglected as a research topic. The result was a considerable increase In federal funding – to such a degree that scientists now protested that they had more money than ideas.

Changing the course of science: the "pull" of society

The relationship between science as society is often characterized in terms of a contrast bettween push and pull. Sometimes, the products and even ideas spawned by research push outward from the laboratory bench, causing ripples and reverberations in the world outside. On other occasions, there is a pull from the community at large, when social demands impinge upon scientists and their institutions, shaping the work they do.

Social "pull" has increased considerably over recent decades, so that few if any researchers today can now lead the sort of monastic professional life, insulated from external pressures, which was possible in times past. There are now two sets of forces acting in the affairs of science: external forces representing the aims of society, and internal forces representing what would otherwise be the "natural" development of science. On occasions the internal forces – the inherent logic and concepts that propel investigation and speculation forward – are so compelling that they push science beyond our immediate capacity to deal with either the social or the practical problems which are produced as a result of scientific progress (➧ page 16). Social, political and commercial pressures *within* the scientific community may add momentum to the bandwaggon too.

Funding for research in sickle-cell anemia

On other occasions, an ill-informed public (or enthusiastic politicians on its behalf) make unrealistic demands of scientists, which cannot be met. A typical example was epitomized by the initiative taken by the United States Senate in December 1971 on the subject of sickle-cell anemia. Approximately one in ten American Negroes carries a sickle-cell gene – the hereditary determinant of a severe disease in which the red blood cells are unable to carry oxygen properly to the tissues of the body. Such individuals do not themselves suffer from sickle-cell anemia, but anyone who inherits the defective gene from both parents develops the crippling disease, which invariably shortens life.

As a research topic, the condition was surprisingly neglected until President Nixon, in his annual health message in February 1971, announced that an extra $5m would be allocated for research and treatment. Not to be outdone, Democratic senators mounted a campaign to increase spending still further, and by December had persuaded the Senate to vote some $142m over three years for research, screening and treatment.

Meanwhile, the Black Panthers had publicized the disease as "black genocide" and boxer Muhammad Ali had sponsored a screening program. The Negroes had begun to feel angry about the lack of cash support for research into, and treatment of, sickle-cell anemia, while losing their former sensitivity about a condition that differentiated them from their white countrymen.

However, the newly-attained social judgment that sickle-cell anemia merited far greater attention by scientists could not, immediately, be matched by a commensurate increase in research activity. Shortly after the Senate vote, scientists concerned with blood disorders were writing to the journal *Science* to point out that, while grateful for heightened support, they were unable at once to find appropriate uses for their new-found funds. There simply were not enough unexplored conceptual "leads" upon which to begin planning new investigations. Internal "push" and external "pull" had got severely out of balance.

Forensic Science

Expert testimony of scientists in the lawcourt
The lawcourt, particularly in the United States, is one forum in which science plays an increasing role in the resolution of conflicts arising in society – and in which, in turn, judges and juries are called upon to adjudicate on the rival merits of scientific evidence. On February 27, 1982, photographer Wayne Williams was convicted of murdering Nathaniel Cater and Jimmy Ray Payne, whose bodies had been found on the outskirts of Atlanta, Georgia. Although Williams' conviction was later reviewed and affirmed, it remains controversial – in part because the outcome turned upon purely scientific evidence.

Using a spectrophotometer and several sophisticated types of microscope, scientists had compared textile fibers from the victims' bodies with two other sorts – those removed from a carpet in his bedroom and those taken from his Chevrolet station wagon. After identifying the fibers from the bodies and bedroom as originating in a type of carpeting manufactured by the West Point Pepperell Company in Dalton, Georgia, they were able to argue that the statistical odds against such a coincidence were exceedingly low. Based on an analysis of the company's distribution chain, an expert witness called by the prosecution claimed that only one in every 7,792 homes in the Atlanta area would have been likely to contain carpet of that particular brand and color. He then added that figure to the one in 3,225 which he calculated for the proportion of cars in the Atlanta area that were Chevrolet station wagons containing carpeting with the other type of fibers found on the victims' bodies. Almost entirely on this evidence, the jury accepted the prosecution's plea that Williams must have been in contact with Cater and Payne before their death, and that he had killed them.

Although by no means the first to involve scientific evidence, the Williams case symbolizes a rapidly increasing trend in the use and abuse of expert testimony in the lawcourt. So pervasive is this trend in the United States that many prosecutors, mindful that judges and juries will invariably expect to hear scientific "proof", now call fingerprint experts to the stand to explain why such evidence is not available in a particular case.

A homicide investigation

▼▶ As techniques of forensic examination become more extensive and complex, so the range of expertise needed to deploy them has diversified. Scientists from a broad range of disciplines are now called upon to assist the forensic pathologist. Analysis of trace elements, combined with the expert assessment of evidence can confirm and quantify circumstances that are suspect.

Identifying body

Finding cause of death

Tracking killer

Convicting suspect

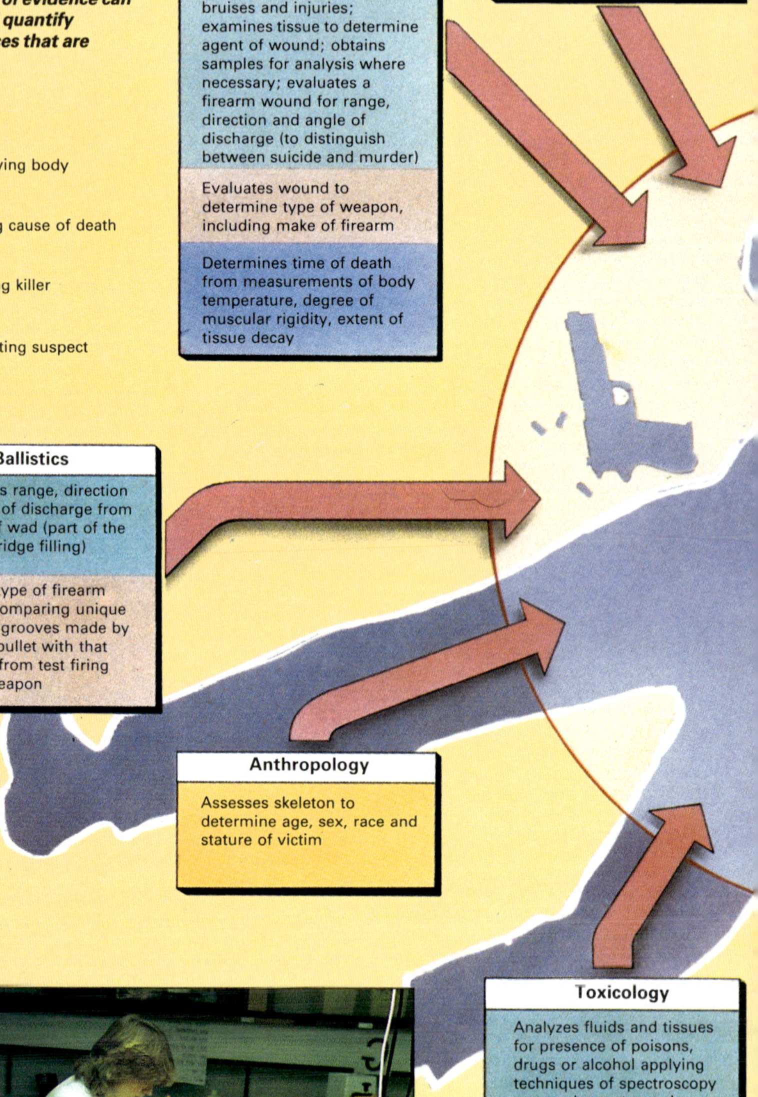

Pathology

Obtains samples from victim and circumstantial evidence for analysis; compares evidence of deformities, surgical operations etc. with medical records

Performs autopsy, noting position of body and any evidence suggesting particular cause, including bruises and injuries; examines tissue to determine agent of wound; obtains samples for analysis where necessary; evaluates a firearm wound for range, direction and angle of discharge (to distinguish between suicide and murder)

Evaluates wound to determine type of weapon, including make of firearm

Determines time of death from measurements of body temperature, degree of muscular rigidity, extent of tissue decay

Analytical Chemistry

If arson suspected, analyzes traces of gasoline or paraffin from fumes given off by heating sample of debris. If arsenic poisoning is suspected, measures radiation emitted from samples of hair of victim

Analyzes trace elements in bullet cartridge or gunpowder, and samples of paint, glass or fibers

Ballistics

Determines range, direction and angle of discharge from position of wad (part of the bullet cartridge filling)

Confirms type of firearm used, by comparing unique pattern of grooves made by barrel on bullet with that produced from test firing suspect weapon

Anthropology

Assesses skeleton to determine age, sex, race and stature of victim

Toxicology

Analyzes fluids and tissues for presence of poisons, drugs or alcohol applying techniques of spectroscopy or gas chromatography. Procedure includes means to differentiate toxic substances from metabolites naturally produced in the body (when decomposed, samples may be taken from eye)

A distribution plot of toxins in the body can provide information about the time elapsing between ingestion or inhalation and death

► A modern forensic laboratory needs to be well equipped to handle the great variety of items sent for analysis. The scanning electron microscope, mass spectrometer, computer and other technologies all assist the forensic scientist in obtaining rapid and accurate results.

Botany

Distinguishes between death by drowning and murder before submergence (detection of diatom skeletons in kidneys, liver and bone marrow indicates heart was beating when victim entered water)

Determines time of death, by calculating how long it takes for vegetation lying beneath victim to lose chlorophyll

▲ ***The presence of diatoms in human tissue may indicate death by drowning.***

Odontology

Compares X-rays with dental records held by victim's dentist, for dental work and distinctive patterns; determines victim's age from study of calcification patterns in teeth

Analyzes bitemarks in victim and compares with pattern in suspect

Serology

Identifies blood group of victim by study of antigen/ antibody reactions in samples of fluid or dried blood, or other body fluids

Determines biochemical profile of suspect from analysis of blood, semen or hair roots found on or near the victim. Techniques include radioimmunoassays (using antibodies to tag natural identity markers in cells), electrophoresis (separating blood molecules with electric charge) or DNA "fingerprinting" (isolating and analyzing DNA from cell nuclei, the structure of which being unique to the individual)

Computer Science

Collation of records – dental, medical and missing persons

Fingerprint matching, by pattern recognition; sophisticated photo-fit techniqes; compares chemical analyses of vehicle paint and glass with those held in memory profiles

Handwriting and voiceprint analysis and recognition; assessment of serological data for probability of a suspect's implication in the crime

Psychology/Psychiatry

Extracts accurate recall from eyewitnesses; analyzes behavior pattern of criminal at large

Assists in questioning techniques; diagnoses handwriting; analyzes personality of criminal suspect

Admissibility of scientific evidence

In 1923 in the case of Frye v. United States, Justice Josiah van Orsdel rejected the use of an early lie detection technique (based on blood pressure changes) to demonstrate that a defendant was telling the truth in asserting his innocence. Noting the difficulty in drawing a firm line between established techniques and those still at an experimental stage, he ruled that a scientific method or theory's admissibility as legal testimony should rest upon whether it was "sufficiently established to have gained general acceptance in the particular field in which it belongs". During the 1970s, the Frye test was increasingly challenged because it excluded apparently useful sources of evidence when particular techniques and pieces of equipment had not yet spread throughout the entire scientific community – a new type of roadside radar, ion microprobe analysis of hair samples, and several other novel methods. By the mid-1980s however, about one in three states had scrapped the Frye ruling.

Is "scientific evidence" scrutinized?

The clash between "evidence" and the internal, rational but cautious standards of science has been highlighted by Edward Imwinkelried, professor of law at the University of California at Davis. "The lawyer who calls a scientist will want not just a critique of eyewitness testimony, but a conclusion about the credibility of a particular witness.... His testimony is reducible to a syllogism, in which the theory or technique serves as a major premise ('Failure to pass a polygraph test indicates that a subject is lying'), data about the case being tried make up the minor premise ('John Doe failed a polygraph test') and the expert's opinion is the conclusion ('John Doe lied'). Each component of the reasoning process – major premise, minor premise and conclusion – has traditionally been subject to rigorous legal restrictions. But for each of those components, the restrictions are more lax today than ever."

One result of this loosening of the rules is that witnesses often use evidence that would not be independently admissible. A forensic pathologist, for example, giving testimony about an individual's death, may rest his case on reports from toxicologists and physicians which have never been seen by the judge or made available for inspection by the jury. Furthermore, "Lawyers, judges and juries are weighing the scientific merits of theories and techniques they may find strange and confusing," according to Imwinkelried. The history of voiceprints exemplifies the problem. When first admitted into the courtrooms of the United States during the late 1960s as a means of identifying individuals from visual records of their voices, voiceprints were used to gain both convictions and acquittals. Although it soon became clear that people could disguise their real manner of speaking, voiceprints were admitted because of the general acceptance of this approach as a valid technique. Few lawyers or judges were sufficiently knowledgeable to question the technology, which many experts feel is still being misused today.

New technological developments can themselves lead to advances in science

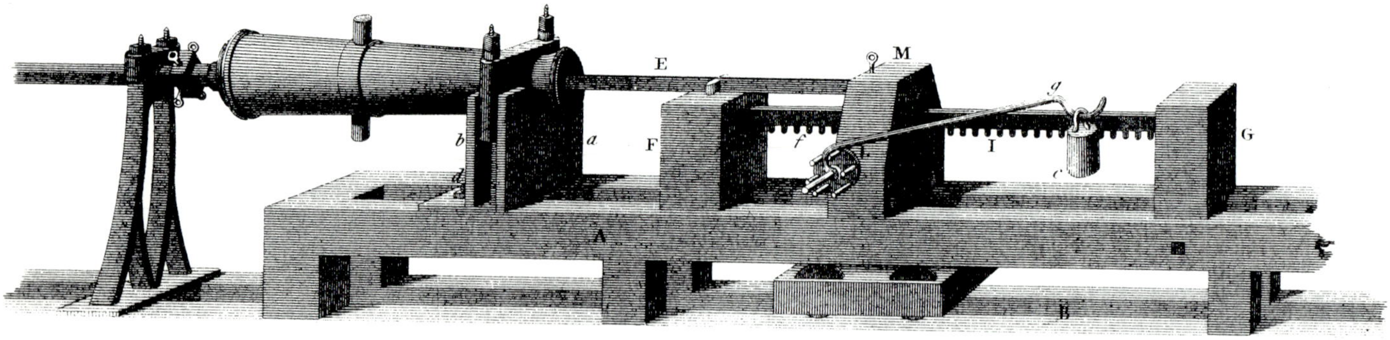

▲► The profoundly important idea that heat is not a metaphysical "thing" but is related to work stemmed from the observations of Count Rumford (1753-1814). In his "Experimental Inquiry Corncerning the Source of Heat Excited by Friction", which he sent to the Royal Society of London in 1798, he described the deductions he had made after watching the considerable quantity of heat generated during the boring of cannon. Although countless other observers had seen the same thing, Rumford carried out experiments to measure the heat in terms of the time taken to bring a specific quantity of water to the boil, and demonstrated that there was a quantitative relationship between the two. This piece of work was central to the emerging science of thermodynamics.

Gunpowder changes the course of science

In addition to the two-way intercourse between science and society, interplay between science and technology is more complex than the linear model that is sometimes proposed. According to this model, fundamental science leads to applied science, which leads to development work and eventually to new products and processes, which in turn stimulate the economic growth of companies, industries and nations. In the real world, this model breaks down completely. Technology, geared to social or commercial need, stimulates basic science almost as frequently as basic research acts as a seedbed for technology.

A key example, first highlighted by the British biologist H.D. Bernal (1901-1971), is the inception of gunpowder and cannon. Of all the inventions introduced to the West in the Middle Ages this, Bernal argued, was to have the greatest effect politically, economically – and scientifically. Whether Arabian, Byzantine Greek or Chinese in origin, there was awesome potential in the discovery that potassium nitrate, added to a combustible substance such as charcoal, could cause explosions. Combined with cannon, gunpowder brought about a revolution in warfare and placed "civilized" humans in a position of almost total superiority over supposedly uncivilized "natives". "Ultimately, however, it was the effects of gunpowder on science rather than on warfare that were to have the greatest influence in bringing about the Machine Age," wrote Bernal. "The making of gunpowder, its explosion, the expulsion of the ball from the cannon, and its subsequent flight, furnished problems the practical solution of which led to the search for causes of a new kind and the creation of a new science."

Development of chemistry

Potassium nitrate could be produced in a condition dependably generating explosions only after careful work on the separation and purification of salts. The experimenters would have learned a good deal about the phenomena of solution and crystallization. Explaining the explosion of gunpowder too stimulated conceptual speculations about how this could occur without air. Explaining the difference between this instantaneous brand of fire and other types of fire triggered the thought (essentially correct) that the nitrate contained the necessary air. In turn, these ideas became the basis for all subsequent efforts to account for combustion and indeed breathing in animals. Eventually, after four centuries of experiment and argument, the same concepts led to the discovery of oxygen by Joseph Priestley.

The steam engine and thermodynamics

Other sciences to emerge from this powerfully novel means of warfare were ballistics and dynamics – both following from efforts to understand the path taken by the cannonball through the air. But the development most closely linking technology, science and society was the making of cannon and the emergence of the steam engine. Machinery originally developed for cannon boring was later harnessed to produce cylinders to a sufficiently high standard to permit the earliest steam engines to prove their efficiency. Only by having accurately-bored cylinders could the compression of these engines be enough to make them effective workhorses.

In turn, observations made on cannon boring led the American-born Count Rumford (1753-1814) to important theoretical discoveries concerning the relationship between mechanical work and heat. As Minister of War in Bavaria during the late 18th century, Rumford noted the immense amount of heat that was generated during this process. By doing experiments in which he measured the heat in terms of the amount of time taken to bring a given quantity of water to the boil, he deduced that there was a definite relationship between the work done and the quantity of heat generated – a crucial step from the realm of metaphysics into that of exact science. Bernal also argued that the inception of gunpowder and cannon in the Middle Ages had a profound conceptual influence on the future of technology in general: "The force of the explosion itself, and the expulsion of the ball from the barrel of the cannon, was a powerful indication of the possibility of making practical use of natural forces, particularly of fire, and was the inspiration behind the development of the steam engine."

▲ Pragmatic discoveries such as that of gunpowder contributed to the gradual emergence of chemistry as a discipline concerned with studying substances and their interactions. The Englishman Joseph Priestley (1733-1804), one of the greatest chemists of all time, discovered oxygen, and numerous other gases including carbon monoxide, ammonia, sulfur dioxide and hydrogen sulfide. He made many innovations in laboratory equipment, including the pneumatic trough, shown in this commemorative medal, which is still used today.

◀ The Pershing II and other missiles, at the heart of East-West arms control discussions in recent years, might seem spectacular examples of technology – of applied science resting on foundations built up through the growth of fundamental science. But this is only part of the truth. Whether in creating missiles, particle accelerators or space probes, scientists have acquired "spin-off" knowledge that has been of direct benefit in the realm of fundamental science too. Marxist biologist J.D. Bernal first pointed out that the inception of gunpowder triggered advances in several different sciences – from chemistry (better crystallization was needed in order to produce reliable saltpeter) to ballistics (which is required to chart the movement of missiles, primitive and modern).

Television's early years owed as much to military as to civilian interest

Baird, television, and the military

In 1986, BBC Television celebrated the 50th anniversary of one of the most far-reaching applied science projects ever undertaken – the development of television and its subsequent introduction as a public service. There was a whole week of memories and reminiscences. But for people interested in the history of science and technology, there were some even more fascinating disclosures about the early history of television. These followed the release, from the Public Records Office at Kew, near London, of formerly secret papers describing events of half a century previously.

Before 1986, the debate over priority in the development of television centered solely on the rival merits of two contrasting systems. Most historians gave maximum credit to the Scottish inventor John Logie Baird (1888-1946) who, during the 1920s and 1930s, evolved a method of transmitting images by scanning a scene with a rotating disk having 30 holes around its periphery. The impulses generated in this way carried a message representing the scene cut up into 30 strips of varying intensity of light. Broadcast to a distant receiver, they were reassembled by being fed to a neon lamp, flickering behind an identical disk spinning in synchrony with the first.

The rival technique depended upon electrons, rather than equipment powered by an electric motor, to scan and reassemble the picture. Using cathode ray tubes (developed in the 19th century), engineers learned how to build cameras and receivers comparable with those still used today. So while Baird was undoubtedly the first person to transmit a simple image across empty space, electronic television was bound to triumph over his less sophisticated version.

► In March 1925, John Logie Baird adjusts one of his earliest television transmitters. It used a rotating disk to scan a scene, converting the light into a sequence of signals which could be reassembled by a receiver to create a crude image of the original scene. This was an elementary method of breaking down and recomposing images comparable with those now employed in facsimile transmission or, in a simpler form, the printing of newspaper photographs. It was eclipsed, however, by electronic scanning.

Pressure from the military

During the early 1920s, the British admiralty and air ministry had become concerned about the potential of television, and had taken a close interest in Baird's experiments. "In a letter written to the Admiralty on the start of a new phase of development, the Baird Company even offered to withhold details of the latest equipment from the public if the Admiralty so wished," wrote Jeffrey Cohen in the "Listener". "This offer demonstrates the priority the TV pioneer put on military applications of his development, and, had it been taken up, might well have delayed the introduction of TV broadcasting by the BBC."

The admiralty and air ministry seem to have encouraged the start of broadcast television, because this would heighten competition and lead to improved pictures. What happened in January 1929 was that, although BBC supremo Sir John (later Lord) Reith wanted to wait until better-quality images were obtainable, the BBC decided to begin putting out low-definition, 30-line pictures based on the mechanical system. Within a few years Baird had pushed up the speed of his motors and managed to attain 60- and then 120-line scanning.

At the same time, EMI had tried but abandoned spinning disks, and was soon attaining a definition of 240 lines electronically. Under the auspices of the

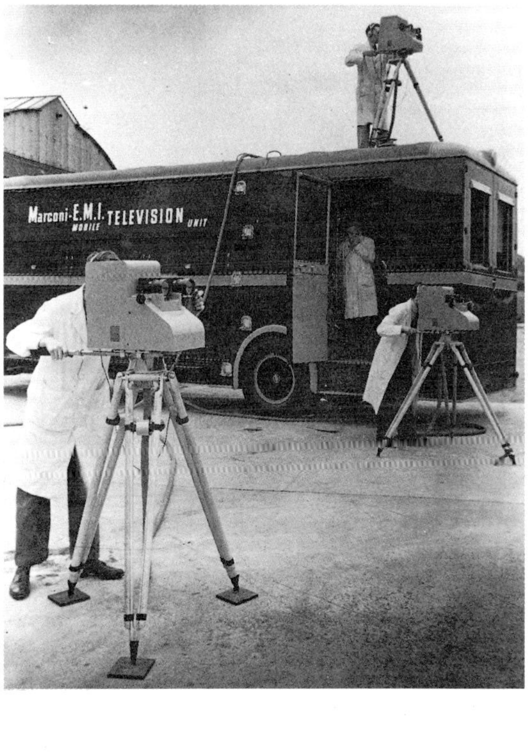

► The rival TV system was evolved a little later than Baird's by engineers working for RCA in America and EMI in Britain. It differed crucially in depending upon electrons, rather than equipment powered by an electric motor, to scan and reassemble the picture. Here Marconi-EMI cameras are being tested before use in an outside broadcast of King George VI's coronation in 1936.

◄▲ One of the earliest domestic RCA-EMI receivers used a vertically mounted cathode ray tube, with a mirror and lens arrangement to project the picture onto a horizontal screen. Alexandra Palace in north London (left) was the site for the transmission of the world's first regular TV service, which began in 1936 and was resumed following a break during the war years. Why the intrinsically inferior Baird system should ever have been tried out for public broadcasting was, until 1986, a closely-guarded secret.

British government, a comparative trial was run to resolve which of the two systems should be employed for public broadcasting, and on November 2, 1936 Baird and EMI began putting out programs on alternate weeks. By this time, EMI's equipment had evolved to the point where 405-line scanning was feasible. Baird, however, had reached his limit. Using great ingenuity, he had contrived to push up definition to 240 lines. But the writing was on the wall. After a trial lasting barely three months, the government concluded that electronic television was "immeasurably superior" to its more primitive competitor. Baird was doomed, and the modern TV age was born.

In 1986, one of John Logie Baird's surviving colleagues, Ray Herbert, no longer constrained by the pledge of secrecy he gave at the time, was able to provide a crucial missing link in the story of why the inevitably-doomed Baird system was ever tried out in competition with EMI's electrons. In order to attain 240-line scanning, the Scots inventor had needed to build a camera so complex and bulky that it could not be moved. This, together with the requirement to compete with EMI's 405 lines, led him to introduce an intermediate step into the operation. Instead of being scanned and transmitted directly, the scene to be televized was focused onto conventional ciné film. Processed remarkably quickly (in less than a minute), the developed film was then scanned and the resulting impulses transmitted. Herbert believed that this "intermediate film technique" – providing a permanent film record of a picture far more quickly than using any other technique then available – was of great interest to the military authorities. This, he suggested, explains why Baird was encouraged to persevere with mechanical scanning long after his rivals and critics believed that he was moving down a blind alley.

It has been claimed that Baird also played an important part in the development of radar, which is usually attributed to his fellow Scot, the physicist Sir Robert Watson-Watt (1892-1973). In one sense, it does seem likely that the TV pioneer made a significant contribution in this field. Even during the early days of his 30-line broadcasts, Baird noticed the type of interference on his screen, caused by passing aircraft, which became familiar to viewers when high-definition TV took off many years later. He toyed with the notion of exploiting these interference patterns to determine the range and size of aeroplanes.

"The physicists have known sin, and this is a knowledge which they cannot lose" – Robert Oppenheimer

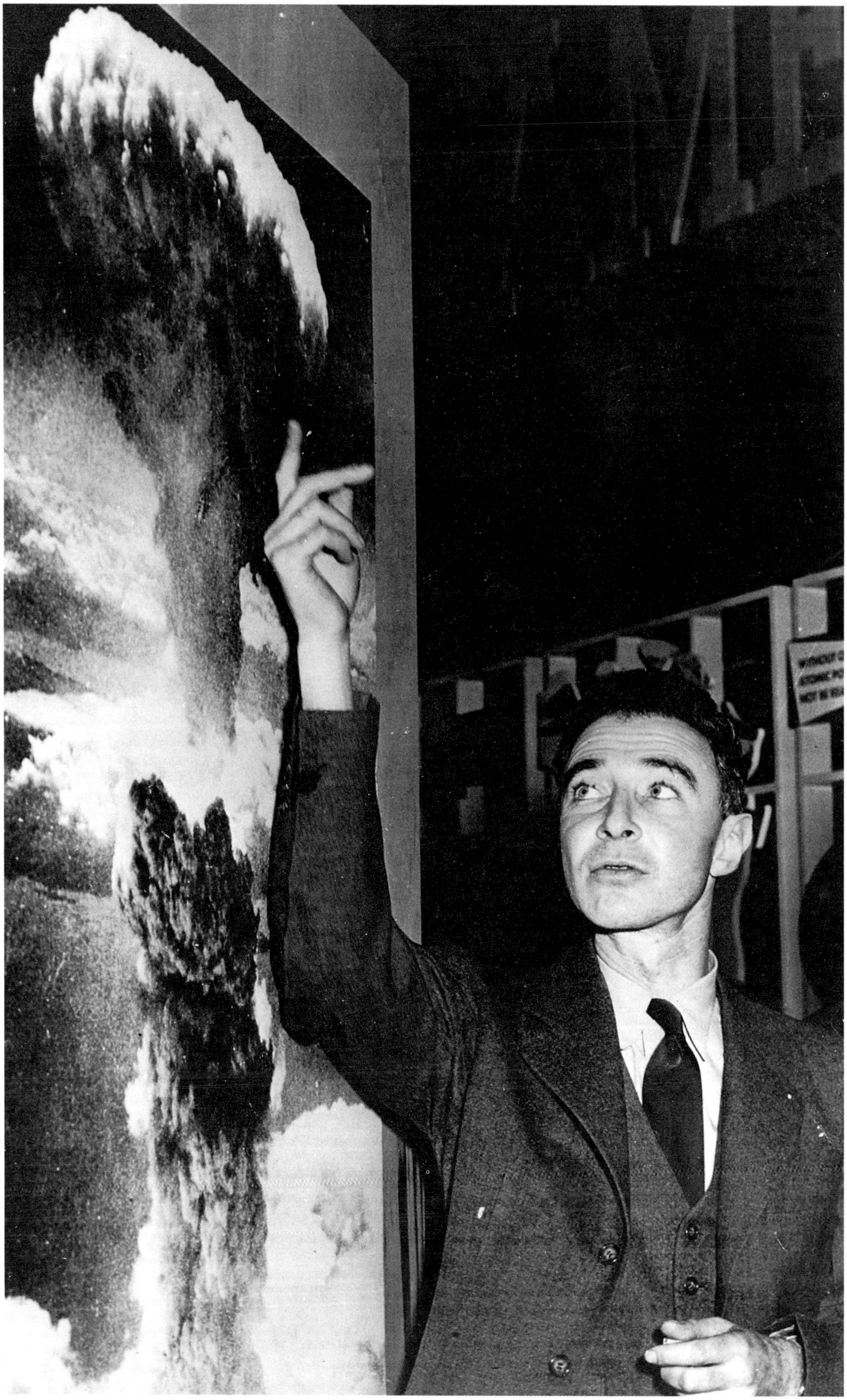

► *As chief scientific administrator of the wartime Manhattan Project, Robert Oppenheimer was central to the development of the nuclear weapons. At Los Alamos, New Mexico, he succeeded in getting the very best out of a disparate group of scientists and technicians, many of whom were initially extremely uneasy about working in a military laboratory. He was deeply conscious of his share of the consequences of introducing the atomic bomb, and in 1949 opposed on moral grounds the development of the hydrogen bomb. When this project went ahead, against the advice of the Atomic Energy Commission's Scientific Advisory Committee, which he chaired, Oppenheimer was attacked on the grounds that his principal motive was one of disloyalty to the United States. In what became a cause célèbre, he was suspended from duty and barred from access to all secret information. The government made amends in 1963, however, four years before he died, when he was given the Enrico Fermi Award, recommended by the AEC and conferred by the President.*

Scientists and the Bomb

In the mid-19th century the great German pathologist Rudolf Virchow (1821-1901) led a movement among German scientists that was designed to democratize and humanize science by making research workers ponder on wider issues and duties. Several other small groups with similar objectives sprang up later and then waned. The Cambridge Scientists' Anti-War Group appeared in England during the early 1930s, as did the Comité de Vigilance in France, to study the causes of war and the measures scientists in particular might take to preserve the peace. J.D. Bernal's "The Social Function of Science" (1939) was a major attempt to stir the consciences of scientists everywhere.

The episode that most compelled scientists to reflect on their wider responsibilities was the Manhattan Project to produce the atomic bomb. "The physicists have known sin, and this is a knowledge which they cannot lose," wrote the project head Robert Oppenheimer (1904-1967) shortly after the frenetic campaign had triumphed and the bomb's awesome power had been amply demonstrated. When the war ended, Hungarian-born Leo Szilard (1898-1964), Eugene Rabinovitch and others founded the Federation of Atomic Scientists (now called the Federation of American Scientists) which, through its magazine "The Bulletin of the Atomic Scientists", attempted to curb the proliferation of nuclear weapons and to place nuclear power development outside of military control. Today, the periodical continues to proselytize on behalf of arms limitation, but has extended its brief to cover issues such as biological and chemical warfare and the potential hazards of genetic engineering (▶ page 65).

Pugwash and "radical science" groups

With growing concern during the 1950s over nuclear weapons tests, another lobby group came into being, triggered by a manifesto drafted by British philosopher Bertrand Russell (1872 1970) and signed by American national Albert Einstein (1879-1955) which warned politicians of the unprecedented dangers of atomic weaponry. With financial assistance from industrialist Cyrus Eaton, its inaugural meeting was held at Pugwash, Nova Scotia, Canada, in July 1957 and the group became known as the Pugwash Organization. Pugwash conferences attended by scientists from both Western and Eastern blocs have continued each year to discuss disarmament, even during times of international tension. Because the organization prefers background diplomacy to publicized lobbying, its achievements are difficult to assess, but it certainly helped to bring about the partial Nuclear Test-Ban Treaty (1963) and the Nuclear Nonproliferation Treaty of 1968, as well as the Paris peace talks on Vietnam, also in 1968.

The 1960s saw the advent of several new groups concerned to promote "radical science". In the United States, Scientists and Engineers for Social and Political Action (SESPA) came into being. Focusing on issues such as defoliation in Vietnam, it worked through meetings on university campuses, protest marches and a magazine, "Science for the People".

Against ABM and "Star War" weapons

One campaign in which SESPA played a significant role was that against deployment of the antiballistic missile system in the United States. Complementing behind-the-scenes lobbying, a public campaign swung into action to orchestrate the work of politicians, independent scientists critical of and/or skeptical about the system, and bodies such as SESPA. Tactics included visits to 60 senators by SESPA activists during a meeting of the American Physical Society in Washington DC, a nationally televised anti-ABM press conference with a dozen congressmen, and a protest march to the White House by several hundreds of physicists. When the Johnson administration was supplanted by that of President Nixon, opposition grew even stronger, and the President decided to replace the proposed Sentinel ABM system by the smaller and less militarily provocative Safeguard system. Although the critics won only a token victory, therefore, they felt that they had been able to fight a battle on virtually equal terms with the President. At the final vote, the campaign to abandon entirely the ABM system failed by just a single vote to win senate approval.

There were echoes of the anti-ABM campaign during 1985-1986, when many American and European researchers began to campaign against President Ronald Reagan's proposed Strategic Defense Initiative (SDI), nicknamed "Star Wars" (▶ page 34). While many scientists and companies were happy to accept funds from this source (some of them insisting that they would be involved only in the research, rather than deployment, phase of the program) critics argued against the SDI on grounds that it threatened to destabilize international relations and that the laser and/or particle-beam weapons upon which it was to be based could not achieve what was claimed of them. Several American universities resolved to refuse Star Wars cash, and in Britain over half the physicists in 24 universities joined a boycott on work related to the SDI. Over 500 scientists, including three Nobel laureates and 25 fellows of the Royal Society repudiated the Reagan plan.

▲ Niels Bohr went to Los Alamos in 1943 and made several technical contributions to the development of the atomic bomb. He was increasingly concerned about the implications of such powerful weapons, however, and in February 1944 secured an interview with British Prime Minister Winston Churchill in which he argued for restraint in their development. In 1950, after returning to Copenhagen, Bohr wrote to the United Nations, pleading for "an open world where each nation can assert itself solely by the extent to which it can contribute to the common culture and is able to help others with experience and resources."

◀ In the summer of 1969 outside the White House, physicists protest against the US government's proposed antiballistic missile (ABM) system. They argued that this would decrease rather increase national security, and heighten the power of the military-industrial complex.

Science and Society

► *The electromagnetic spectrum classifies transmitted radiant energy by wavelength. It extends from high-energy short-wavelength gamma rays to low-energy long-wavelength radio waves. Uses of electromagnetism, via advanced technology, include therapy, lasers, and satellite communications.*

Uses of electromagnetic radiation

Gamma rays
10^{-16} meters to 10^{-11} meters
Radiation therapy
Exposing radiographs

X-rays
10^{-11} meters to 10^{-9} meters
Diagnostic imaging of the human body
Radiation therapy

Ultraviolet Radiation
10^{-9} meters to 10^{-7} meters
Fluorescent tubes
Germicidal lamps

Visible light
10^{-7} meters to 10^{-6} meters
Laser light used in telecommunications, high-precision surgery, CD players, bar code scanners

Infrared radiation
10^{-6} meters to 10^{-4} meters
Heating and cooking
Surgical heat treatment
Night-vision apparatus
Satellite photography

► *Recent revolutionary advances in molecular biology have led to major developments in plant breeding techniques. In both farming and forestry, breeders are able to grow plants with specific genetic characteristics. The appearance of disease-resistant high-yield strains will be especially beneficial to Third World countries struggling to grow sufficient crops and fuel wood.*

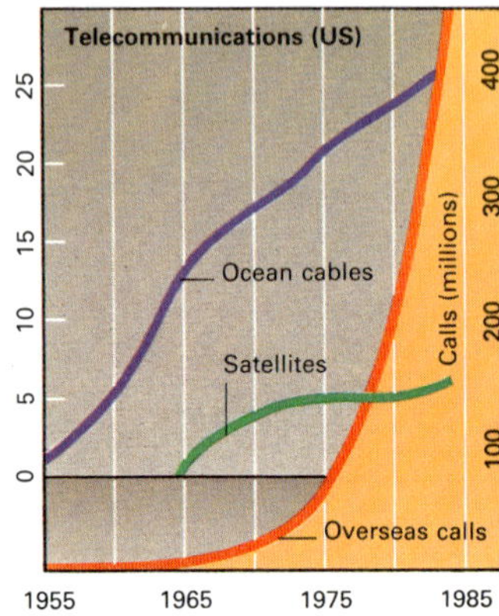

▲ *The number of overseas telephone calls made has increased dramatically since the 1950s, a result of progress in electronics and satellite technology.*

▼ *The age of commonplace long-distance air travel began with the advent of jet propulsion during World War II. The first jet airliner flew in 1949.*

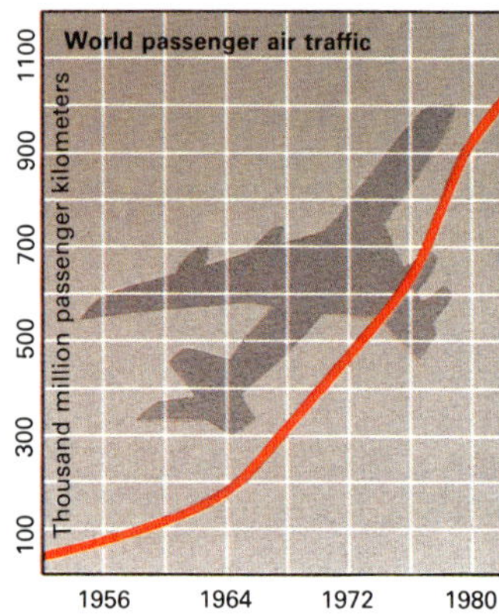

◄ *Developments in electronics and computer science have transformed the concept of "robot" from science fiction android to sophisticated engineering instrument. Since the 1970s, industrial robots have been deployed very successfully on vehicle production lines. The immediate consequence has been a sharp reduction of employment on the factory floor in car manufacturing plants.*

Microwaves
10^{-4} meters to
1 meter

Telecommunications, including satellite links
Radar
Microwave ovens

Radio waves
1 meter to
10^4 meters

Telecommunications

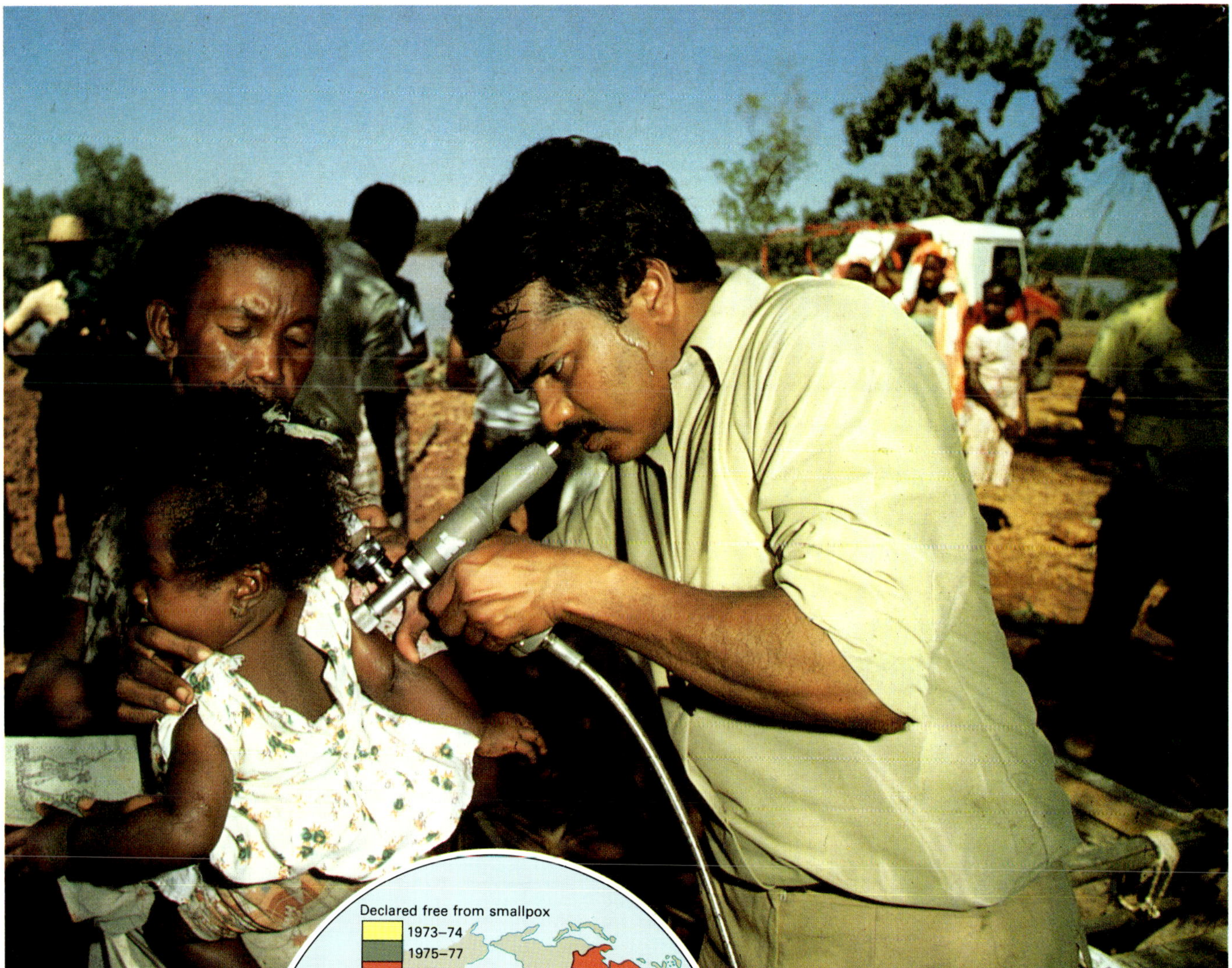

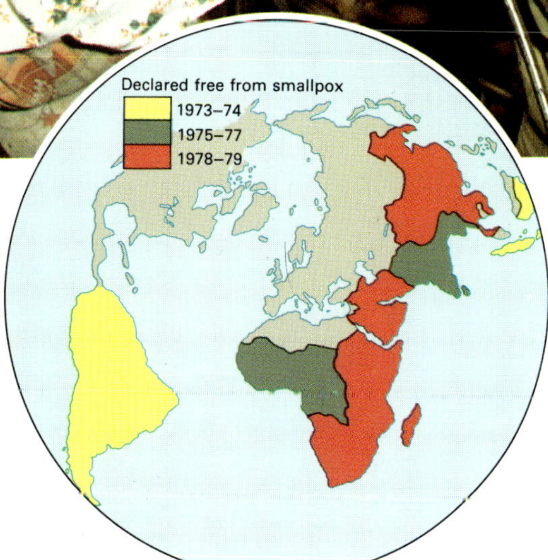

► In May 1970, the World Health Organization (WHO) declared that the world was free from smallpox. This followed a concerted attack on the virus since 1967. The technique of vaccination, which originated with the work of Jenner and Pasteur in the 18th and 19th centuries, thus proved to be of immeasurable consequence to millions of lives saved from the fatal ravages of the disease.

▲ Immunization is one of the great triumphs of science. Since the discovery that prior exposure to a pathogenic microorganism would stimulate resistance against it, inoculation has been an essential tool in the prevention of disease. A new WHO program has been launched with the aim of protecting all the world's children against measles, polio, diphtheria, whooping cough, tetanus, and tuberculosis.

See also
Paymasters 21-40
Science and Authority 41-56
Global Change 93-108

Discovery and development of a typical drug

Key
- 8,000 – 10,000 candidate substances
- Decision-making and administration
- Chemical and pharmacological development
- Biological and clinical tests
- Program

RESEARCH CONCEPT AND DISCOVERY OF ACTIVE COMPOUND 2 – 20 years

	Research target	Research program	Research project	Selection procedure	Patents
Above	• Market research • Medical needs • Literature search, research ideas	• Budget and schedule approved • Selection of candidate substances	• Extraction or synthesis of active substances • Modeling and analysis	• Proposed formulations • Stability tests	• Patent evaluation
Below	• Division policy • Financial considerations	• Chemical and pharmacological approaches selected	• Evaluation of potentially active compounds	• Analysis of active substances • Acute toxicity tests • Basic pharmacological and biochemical screening	• Patent application

PRECLINICAL TESTS 2 – 5 years

	Documentation	First detailed technical and economic appraisal		
Above	• Preparation of dossiers and summary documents of relevant data • Internal approval of proposals for clinical studies	• Development of analytical methods for active substances, degradation products and impurities • Bioavailability of formulations	• Synthesis of active substances and consideration of alternative routes • Preparation of model formulations for clinical trials and toxicological evaluation	• Synthesis of radiolabeled compounds • Stability tests of active substances and model formulations • Development of analytical methods for model dosage
Below	• Submission to licensing authority for clinical trials • Presentation of data to ethical committees	• Acute and 6-monthly toxicity studies • Detailed animal pharmacological studies (effects and side effects)	• Studies of absorption, excretion and metabolism in animals • Reproduction studies	• Tests for genetic mutation • Studies for long term toxicity and cancers begun

CLINICAL SAFETY AND EFFICACY TRIALS 3 – 7 years

	Volunteer studies	Initial controlled trials	Second detailed technical and economic appraisal	
Above	• Maximum and minimum dosages both tolerated and effective	• Assessment of effectiveness as a remedy in the patient	• Bioavailability of formulations • Scale-up of chemical synthesis • Development of formulation varieties (tablets, injection etc.) • Clarification of interaction with other medicines	• Establishment of manufacturing process • Design of chemical manufacturing plant • Confirmation of stability of product in packs
Below	• Effects and side effects		• Detailed absorption, excretion and metabolism studies • Supplementary animal pharmacological studies • Large-scale domestic and overseas clinical trials to establish optimal dosage, dosage administration, side effects and precautionary measures	• Submission of proof of effectiveness and safety • Demonstration of therapeutic advantage • Patent evaluation and application for formulation manufacture • Submission of details to medical publications

REGISTRATION, LAUNCH AND SALES 2 – 3 years

	Monitoring	Launch and sales	Preparation for launch	Registration with health authorities
Above	• Continuous monitoring and further clinical studies	• Distribution of products	• Construction and commissioning of chemical plant at full scale • Development of quality control procedures • Validation of manufacturing process	• Documentation of relevant data • Expert opinion on pharmacological data
Below		• Organization of symposia	• Marketing plan • Training of sales force • Design and preparation of packaging materials, datasheets and promotional literature	• Expert opinion on toxicological, clinical and analytical trials

▲► A lengthy and complex process, the development of a new drug neatly demonstrates the two-way relationship between science and society. The use of pharmaceuticals has, of course, had an incalculable influence on the prevention of disease and general wellbeing. On the other hand, such are the risks of unintended side-effects (as with thalidomide, which caused abnormalities in fetuses), that repeated trials and stringent tests are required before a new drug can be released.

Paymasters

2

Curiosity- and mission-oriented research...Research and military goals..."War pays"...Returns on research...R & D and the economy...The generals and science...Industry invests...Science in poor countries...PERSPECTIVE... Motives and restraints...Joint programs... Superconductors...Oil prospecting...Kondratiev cycles... Military-scientific research...SDI...Medical research in France...The TRON project...Facts and figures

Science is an intrinsically uncertain activity, in which blind alleys are common and in which honest errors, however great, should bring no discredit or shame. This makes science inherently difficult to organize and finance. The paymasters, whether industrial companies seeking to make cash profits or government institutes centered on pure or applied science, *know* that some of their expenditure will be wasted. And paradoxically, the more they try to minimize those losses by playing safe and backing relatively predictable lines of research, the more likely it is that they will neglect riskier avenues whose exploration just may spawn discoveries of the most momentous significance. The techniques of gene-splicing (➧ page 66) which underpin modern biotechnology, for example, began with disinterested investigations into how bacteria repair their DNA when it is damaged. They did not originate in work directed toward any practical end.

In this sense, applied science is a far easier activity in which to invest than pure science. "Mission-oriented" research projects such as the design of a nuclear reactor or antibiotic are usually relatively amenable to financial planning and budgetary control (although some even of these turn out costly disappointments). In contrast, "curiosity-oriented research" promises no assured economic rewards whatever.

Motives and sources for funding

The motives for which science is supported range from the cultural to the solidly practical. Before the advent of government and commercial aid for science, many of the "natural philosophers" we now call scientists were wealthy amateurs who were able to finance their own inquiries, or individuals with wealthy patrons who felt it proper to help for the same reasons that they supported artists and composers. The investigations and ruminations of natural philosophers were considered to extend our intellectual horizons and contribute to the common good, just like the endeavors of painters, poets, sculptors and musicians. But for some patrons, the expectation of practical rewards loomed large too.

Nowadays, we are much more conscious that curiosity-oriented pure science may lead to unpredictable tangible returns. Paradoxically, however, politicians have realized and scientists have been compelled to accept that the spectacular growth of science earlier this century had to come to an end. Total research and development (R & D) expenditure in the United States, for example, rose from under $600 million (6 percent of gross domestic product) in 1940 to $22·6 billion (over 30 percent of GDP) in 1966, but the economy simply could not continue to provide such burgeoning largesse. Even without some recent growth of public antipathy toward science for its alleged ill effects, the United States and other governments found that they could no longer afford such spiralling investment. This realization has triggered considerable debate concerning the amount of money going into research laboratories, as well as the machinery that determines priorities for expenditure.

►Different countries, at different times, vary in their backing for applied as compared with basic science. Japan, for example, committed itself to greater emphasis on fundamental research in the late 1980s after concentrating for decades on the exploitation of scientific "leads" that had emerged elsewhere. But in the wake of the AIDS epidemic, governments of quite diverse political complexions decided to launch programs of "targeted research" designed to combat the disease. Here AIDS studies proceed in a laboratory in Bangui in the Central African Republic.

From the "Chemists' War" (World War I) to today's "Star Wars" (SDI), the military component of scientific research funding has increased

▲ ***Vannevar Bush was the man principally responsible for harnessing US university research to the war effort as director of the Office of Scientific Research and Development. In 1945 his "Science, the Endless Frontier" called for continued generous financial backing for research work in peacetime. Bush argued that public support was likely to be repaid many times over through the social utility of scientific discoveries. The immediate outcome of such lobbying was a lavish flow of funds into "pure" science from bodies such as the US Office of Naval Research.***

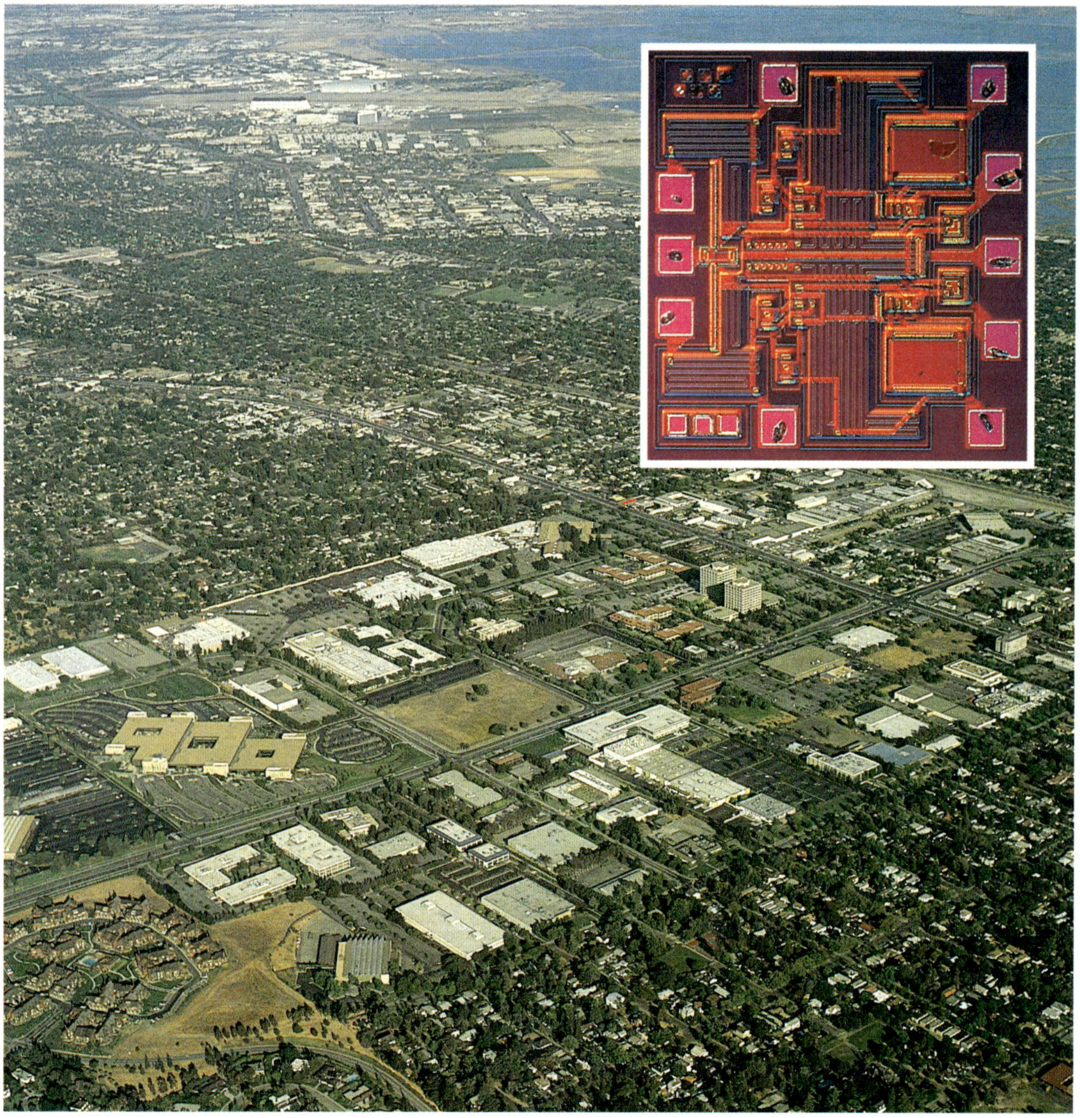

The United States experience

The mid-century explosion in science funding owed much to the fact that research, having proved its value in World War I (the "chemists' war"), spawned much of the know-how that was decisive during World War II (the "physicists' war"). The nuclear weapons evolved at Los Alamos (◆ page 16) and the radar techniques pioneered in Britain were the most spectacular products of science in 1939-1945, just as high explosives and to a lesser extent poison gases held sway during 1914-1918. But these were accompanied by a raft of other aids which, whether products of pure or applied science, contributed to victory. Freeze-dried plasma, prepared by fractionating blood, helped to reduce mortality among wounded servicemen at battle stations to less than one percent. Proximity fuzes made the high-explosive shell more powerful than ever before. Influenza vaccine, while giving far from complete protection, was used to thwart a disease that could otherwise have ravaged armies as disastrously as cholera and typhus had done in the past.

Although the atomic bomb came from the Manhattan Project – one of the most costly and tightly organized exercises ever conducted in applied science – there was growing awareness that the discoveries of *pure* science had led to many of the weapons and techniques of war.

Gradually, the Atomic Energy Commission and other military and paramilitary agencies (including the forerunner of the National Aeronautics and Space Administration) began to finance much of the physical science in the country's universities. Congress was equally enthusiastic toward the biological sciences, which received their cash support through the Public Health Service and later the National Institutes of Health. Although the National Science Foundation was established in 1950 specifically to finance pure science, some 90 percent of funds for that purpose continued for some years afterward to come from these much larger existing patrons.

"Matching the granting agencies within the government were the universities which had the strong faculties, good laboratory facilities and strong accounting and business staffs necessary to handle the unprecedented flow of money from the federal government," wrote historian A. Hunter Dupree some years later. "The research universities, some 15 or 20 in the immediate postwar years, both generated the proposals and sent to Washington their most distinguished professors to sit on the panels that judged the proposals' worth."

But by 1967, when federal finance for science levelled off, tensions had become clear between the awarding of research grants by "mission-oriented" bodies, and the disinterested pursuit of knowledge – particularly by academic scientists. By 1986, when $40 billion-worth of federal funding over the previous four decades had brought the United States to a position of world leadership, with more Nobel prizes for science per head of population than any other country in the world, those conflicts had increased further, and science was increasingly subject to political pressures. Even pure science projects became goal-oriented, and the renewal of the arms race meant that when federal funding for science did rise again during the late 1980s the extra money went largely to applied research closely geared to military objectives. The Reagan administration's science budget for the fiscal year 1988 showed an overall increase of 8 percent, from $57·7 to $62·4 billion, over 1987. But this incorporated a 15 percent rise to $42 billion for spending on defense-related activities, compared with a 3 percent cut to $20·4 billion in civilian programs.

◄ Buzz Aldrin salutes the American flag on the Moon in July 1969, at the culmination of the Apollo program. From guidance systems to life support devices, from materials science to solar power production, NASA had made an unprecedented investment which had not only produced a considerable technological triumph but had also generated spin-off techniques and insights that continue to find applications elsewhere in science.

◄ It is no accident that Silicon Valley in the United States, and clusters of microelectronics companies in other countries, tend to develop very close to the defense institutes and aerospace companies for which "chip" makers work as subcontractors. Often driven by the exacting needs of military and space projects, devices such as the central processing unit (the "brain" of a computer) have evolved to increasing levels of sophistication, and found similar uses in the nonmilitary sphere. The Strategic Defense Initiative ("Star Wars") is the latest military mega-project to spawn large amounts of work for civil institutes and private companies.

▼ Federal funding for research and development has grown 300% over 12 years. Within the total, expenditure on defense projects has increased 450%, and the proportion spent on national defense projects from 50 to 57%. The increasing numbers of US Nobel science laureates (bottom) reflect not only the financial resources for science, but also the arrival of scientists from Europe (notably refugees from Nazism) and elsewhere, and the greater frequency of shared prizes.

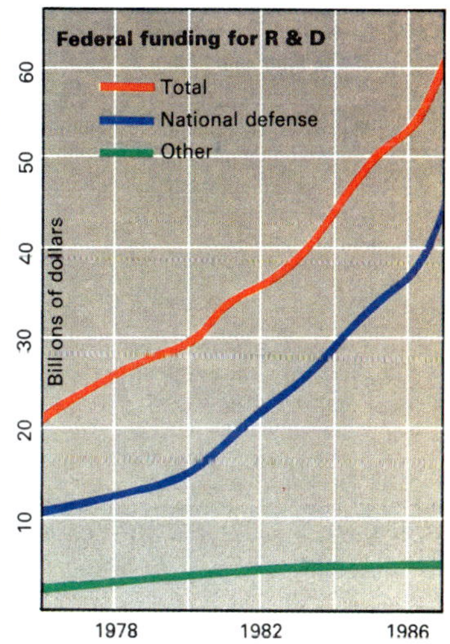

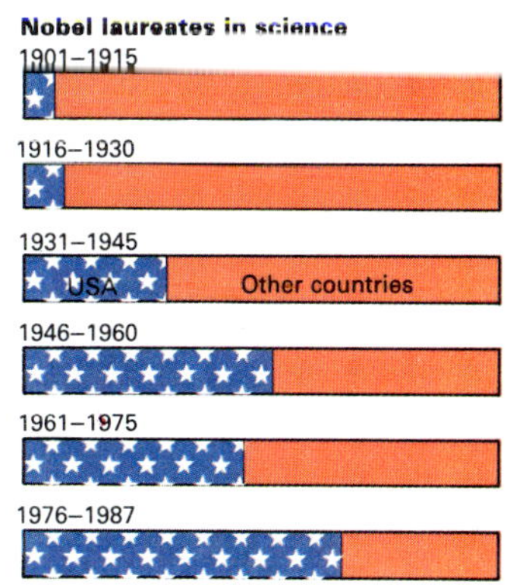

The development of funding

The pattern of events in the United States was mirrored in most other developed countries over the same period of time (for Japan, ➧ page 36). In Australia, for example, there was a period of postwar buoyancy, followed by two decades of retardation and then, during the mid-1980s, increasing emphasis on applied research and on a "user pays" principle. The intention was that all expenditure, whether on science, transportation, broadcasting, or any other sector of society, should be met directly by those deriving the benefits. This placed upon pure scientists what many of them considered to be impossible demands to identify the results of their work before its completion.

In Britain, the crunch came earlier. It was symbolized by publication in 1971 of Lord Rothschild's report, *A Framework for Government Research and Development*. Foreshadowing the Australian label, Rothschild argued that government-funded applied research should be carried out on a customer-contractor basis. This threatened the long-established Haldane principle, named for J.S. Haldane, according to which government money went to the research councils without strings attached. The "science vote" money flowed into the country's laboratories through the research councils, whose scientists themselves decided how to spend it. Lord Rothschild suggested that some of this cash ought to be channeled via the arms of government most likely to benefit. When the government endorsed the customer-contractor principle by acting on his report in July 1972, it arranged for smaller proportions of finance to be allocated on this basis than Rothschild had suggested. Nevertheless, the concepts of "relevance" and "value for money" came to dominate the whole of science funding in Britain from the late 1970s onward.

▲ ***Although much smaller than NASA, the European Space Agency has enjoyed considerable success through its Ariane rocket, which is launched from the Guiana Space Centre in Korou, French Guiana, and used for placing in orbit satellites such as Meteosat 2, for meteorological measurements. Financed by 13 nations and based in Paris, ESA has also designed an orbiting laboratory, Columbus.***

► ***European science ministers meet in Hanover, West Germany, in November 1985 to launch the Eureka program of collaborative R & D. Proposed originally by France, Eureka was catalyzed in part by the United States Strategic Defense Initiative, which provoked fears that there might be a "brain drain" of European scientists and engineers into SDI work. By October 1987, when 58 new Eureka plans were approved at a cost of $800m, a total of 165 projects – from underwater robotics to traffic control – had been launched under the scheme. Another form of collaboration designed to counterbalance the technological dominance of Japan and the USA is the European Economic Community's Framework Program. This is broken down into projects such as Brite (Basic Research for Industrial Technologies in Europe), Race (telecommunications) and Esprit (information technology).***

◄ *The Joint European Torus (JET) is another example of collaboration being promoted under the aegis of the European Economic Community. Built at Culham in Britain, it is designed to exploit the energy that is released when heavy isotopes of hydrogen fuse together. Theoretically simple, this is technically an exceedingly demanding proposition because the isotopes must be maintained as a plasma, which would vaporize the walls of the reactor if it were to touch them. Although JET has been in operation since 1983, it is essentially a research tool, providing information that may lead to the design of a fusion reactor as a safer, cleaner alternative to existing fission reactors for generating electricity.*

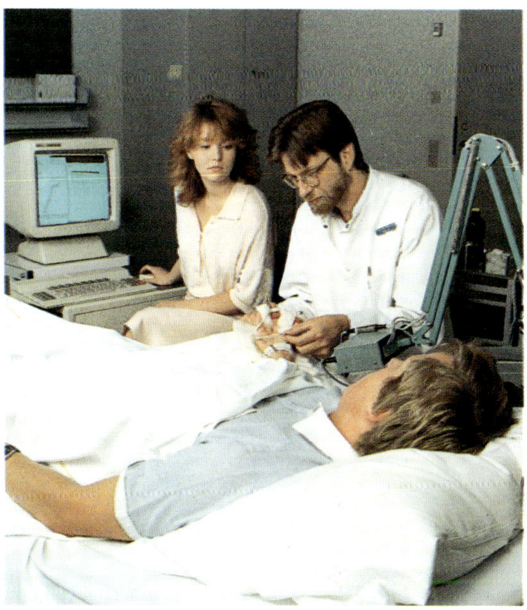

◄ *An engineer employed under the Esprit program works with a physician to measure the electrical signals generated by muscles in a patient's arm. Initiated in 1984, and funded jointly by the EEC and industry, Esprit will absorb over 40 percent of the Framework budget.*

The Framework program

European nations have moved toward collaborative research programs as a means of matching the industrial achievements of the United States and Japan. Two important funding schemes, known as Framework and Eureka have recently been announced, both involving the pooling of finance from member nations and private industry – including a revival of funding to revitalize pure academic research.

Framework, the European Economic Community's five-year program of research and development, was finally approved by European ministers in 1987, although many projects to be funded by it were already established. Framework is divided into several specific research areas: Race, for example, is a telecommunications initiative; Brite (Basic Research for Industrial Technologies in Europe) funds research intended to help rejuvenate Europe's older industries such as chemicals and shipbuilding. Other divisions cover medical research, biotechnology, and science and technology in developing countries.

Handsome returns may result from investment in research, whether "mission-oriented", or "curiosity-oriented" work in pure science

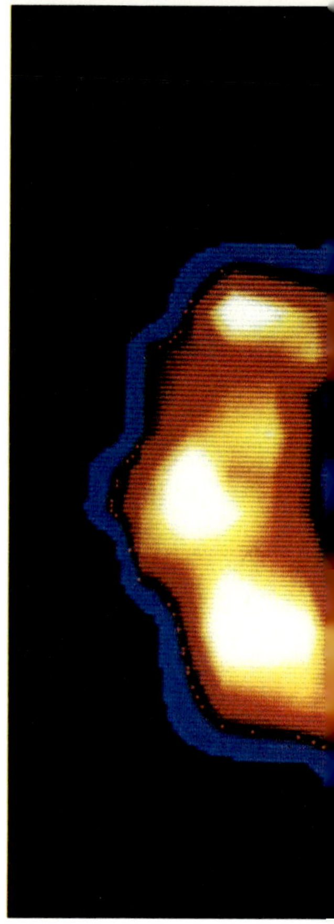

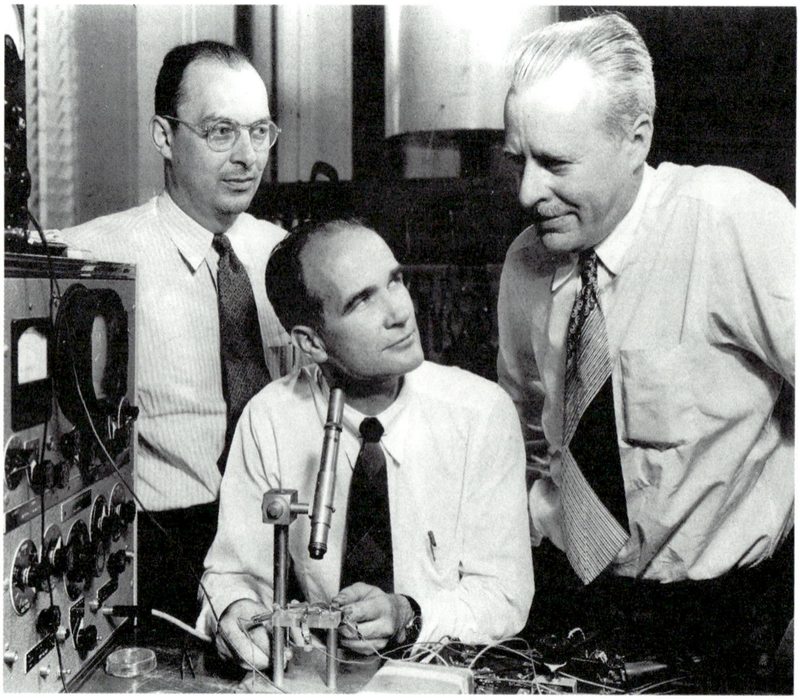

▶ *John Bardeen, William Shockley and Walter H. Brattain, seen here with their pioneering equipment at Bell Laboratories, Murray Hill, New Jersey, in 1948, the year when the company announced their invention of the transistor. Although it was eight years before the event was recognized by the award of the Nobel Prize for Physics in 1956, it was a momentous piece of work, both commercially and practically, as the centerpiece of the miniaturization of electronic equipment.*

Financial returns

At the microeconomic level, it is quite obvious that investment in science can bring handsome financial returns. Thus, in the wake of the Rothschild report (◀ page 24), a distinguished British scientist wrote to *The Times* of London to remind readers that the antibiotic cephalosporin had not only saved lives but also earned £9 million in sales. Originally discovered not by a pharmaceutical company but in laboratories of the Medical Research Council, it was cited as an example of the kind of unpredictable payoff that can result from pure science.

More consciously mission-oriented work affords countless other examples. The world list of best-selling pharmaceuticals in 1985 was headed by the ulcer drug Tagamet (cimetidine), with $940 million sales, and Zantac, with $780 million sales. Tagamet was evolved in British laboratories of the American company Smith Kline, and Zantac was introduced by the British firm Glaxo. Next came the blood pressure treatment Adalat ($570 million) from Bayer in West Germany, beta blockers Tenormin ($520 million) and Inderal ($520 million) from ICI in Britain, and the arthritis drugs Feldene ($470 million) and Naptosin ($470 million) from Pfizer and Syntex respectively in the United States.

Equally clear is the fact that the financial returns to the companies concerned are often reflected in benefits to individual countries. The British pharmaceutical industry, for example, had export figures of £1,426 million for 1985 – £200 million up on the total for the previous year. That performance was a direct result of research investment that is hard to quantify but estimated at around four times greater than the sum spent by the Medical Research Council. In the United States Upjohn spends as much as 18 percent of its sales revenue on research and development (R & D), while Squibb spends 10-12 percent. As the pharmaceutical industry itself often reminds politicians, even these conscious investments in applied science are inherently risky. Only one out of every 10,000 chemicals screened for possible use in

▲ *Billions of yen are going into Japan's TRON project, intended to abolish dependence on American computer operating systems and microprocessor chips. Based at Tokyo University, TRON (which stands for the real-time operating-system nucleus) is backed by at least 40 Japanese hardware and software companies. A major problem in developing TRON is the need for a keyboard capable of coping with the thousands of characters in Japanese script.*

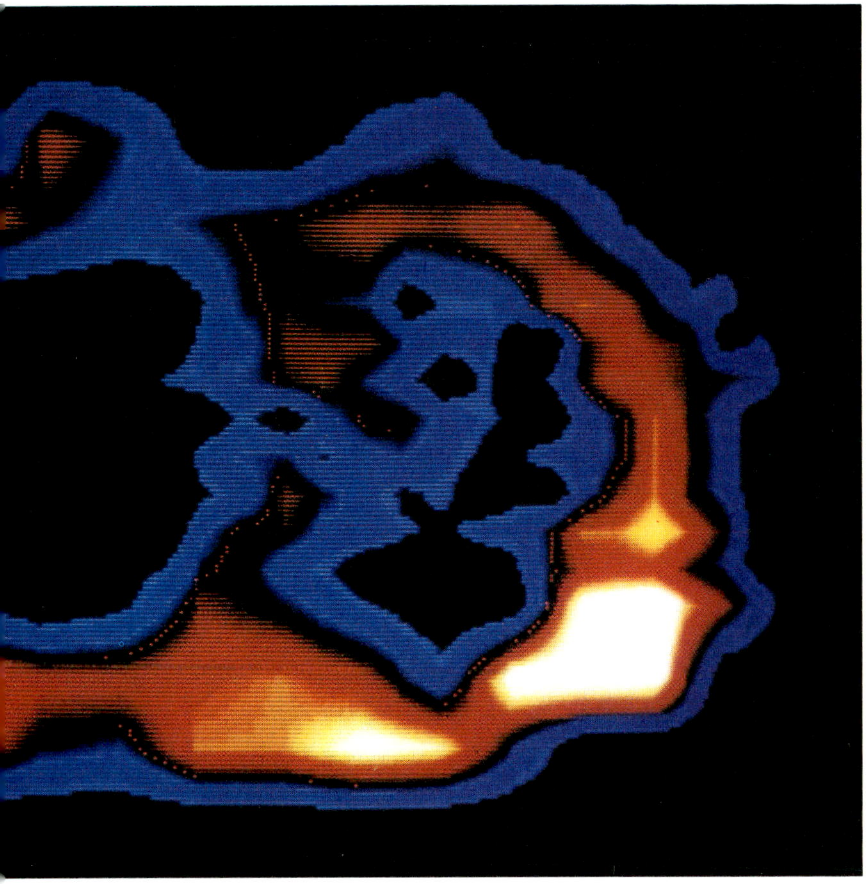

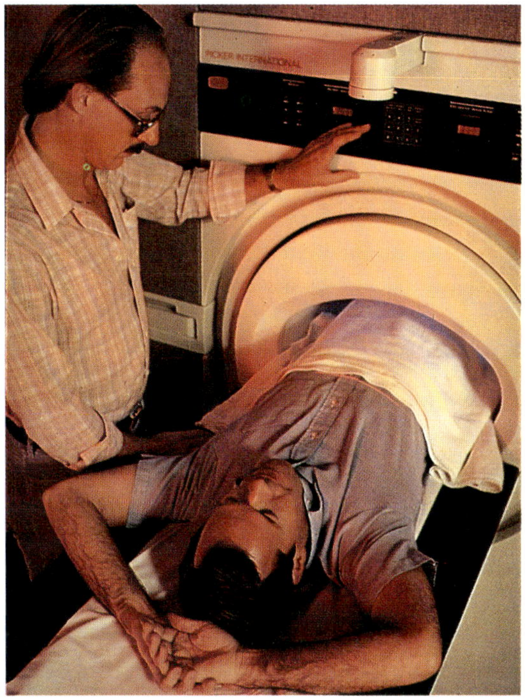

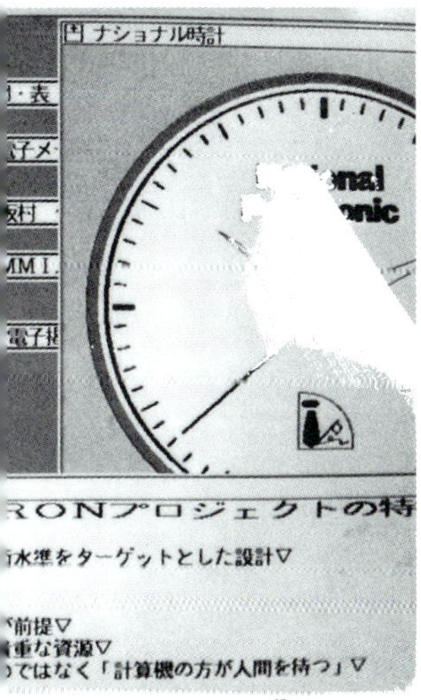

medicine survives rigorous screening tests and eventually becomes a clinical and commercial reality (◀ page 20).

Nuclear magnetic resonance (NMR) is another recent example of the economic, as well as healthcare, benefits of investment in basic science. The story began with physicists' investigations during the 1940s into the magnetism carried by atomic nuclei. They found that a spinning proton, for example, acts like a tiny magnet, so that when they applied an external magnetic field the protons aligned themselves and began spinning on the same axis. Later investigators discovered that by applying a radio signal of exactly the correct frequency, they could make the spinning protons flip, or reverse direction. And because this absorbed energy from the radio waves, they realized that they could study the structure of the atom by measuring the frequency of the absorbed energy. During the 1970s and 1980s, the technique was being harnessed as a diagnostic tool in medicine. It had many advantages over X-rays, computed axial tomography (CAT) and ultrasound imaging, and by 1985 financial analysts were predicting sales of $1-2 billion per year for NMR machines.

In recent years, scientists involved in particle physics – arguably the most esoteric brand of pure science – have begun to publicize the cash benefits flowing from their work. In 1984, for example, CERN issued a report on the economic benefits to high technology manufacturing industries having contracts with this Geneva-based organization. Based on evidence from 160 European companies which had increased their sales and/or reduced their costs as a consequence of CERN contracts, the report estimated an "economic utility" (increased turnover plus cost savings) of 3,107 million Swiss francs up to 1987. In other words, every franc spent by CERN on high technology equipment generated on average three additional francs of economic utility for the firms involved. Around the same time, it was estimated that the manufacture of one particular type of gamma ray detector which was used to study collisions inside particle accelerators had become a business with sales worth some $50 million per year.

◄▲ ***Nuclear magnetic resonance (NMR) is a vivid example of economic and healthcare benefits that can come from investment in basic science. NMR emerged from studies during the 1940s into the magnetism carried by atomic nuclei. These showed that spinning protons act like tiny magnets, which become aligned and spin on the same axis when a magnetic field is applied. A radio signal of the right frequency reverses the spin, absorbing energy. This phenomenon has since been harnessed as an imaging tool, capable of revealing carcinoma of the lung (above left), for example, when a patient is scanned using NMR.***

Research and development and the national economy

Conclusive evidence linking support for science at the national level with economic benefits is surprisingly hard to come by. Statistics in the Rothschild report (◀ page 24), for example, showed the United States heading an international league table of public money spent on research and development (R & D) per annum in developed countries. Belgium was at the bottom of the list (and Britain around the middle). But it is by no means easy to interpret comparative figures drawn from countries with widely differing populations and social needs, and at different stages of economic development. Lord Rothschild also claimed that no inferences could be made from current figures because it took at least seven years for R & D effort to have a tangible effect on a nation's welfare. He then went further than most experts in saying that it was simply not possible to be sure that an increase in the economic indicator of gross domestic product (GDP) was in part caused by a corresponding increase in a country's R & D expenditure. On the contrary, he suggested, it was conceivable that a higher research investment was a consequence of greater prosperity.

Most authorities, however, argue that the economic rewards from science, including pure science, are self-evident. "It is quite likely that the public cost of fundamental science can be justified by simply comparing it dollar for dollar with the value of the indirect benefits of science, including technological spin-off," writes Leon Lederman, commenting on the $2-3 billion of federal money that went into basic science in the United States in 1984. "The experimental work required for fundamental science traditionally leads to the invention of novel instruments and techniques that are later found to create goods and services adding to the GDP. The return to the US Treasury in the form of taxes collected on the new businesses generated is at least a substantial fraction of the cost of fundamental science." For such reasons, Alvin Weinberg of the Institute for Energy Analysis at Oak Ridge, Tennessee, and others have suggested a change in the way in which countries budget for science. Whereas the cost of applied R & D ought to be borne by its beneficiaries ("the user pays"), Weinberg argues that investment in fundamental science should be treated as an overhead for the total research and development effort.

▼ Besides its harmful environmental effects, acid rain destroys economies. Loss of timber, soil pollution, and architectural damage are among the costly consequences. These "pollution domes" are designed to explore solutions to the problem.

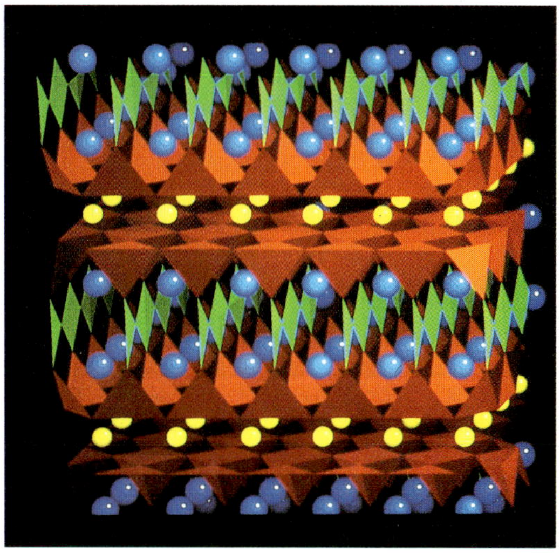

◄▼ *Enormous returns are promised by a new generation of materials with little resistance to electricity at temperatures much higher than formerly thought necessary for "superconductors" to work. The computer graphic shows the crystal structure of yttrium-barium-copper oxide, and the graph illustrates the successively higher temperatures at which superconductors operate. Alex Muller and Georg Bednorz, working at IBM's research laboratory in Zürich, Switzerland, made the first breakthrough in making these materials in 1986, an achievement for which they received a Nobel prize the following year.*

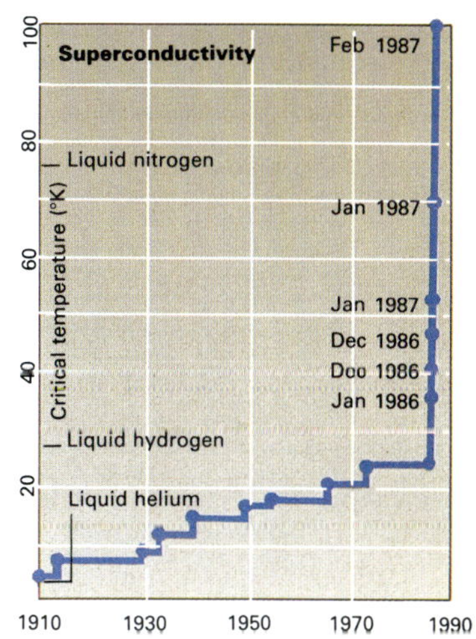

High-temperature superconductors

One sensational breakthrough which could lead to increased energy efficiency was the series of discoveries in 1986-1987 of materials which are "superconductors" at temperatures higher than once thought possible. Superconductivity was discovered in 1911, when it was found that mercury loses its resistance to electricity at 4.3K (4.3° above absolute zero, which is minus 273°C). But American physicist Dr Paul Chu and his team at the University of Houston, Texas, discovered a ceramic compound of the cheap elements barium, yttrium, copper and oxygen which superconducts at almost 100K. This means that the conducting materials can be kept cool relatively inexpensively. It also shattered previous theories of superconductivity, and offered the possibility of no-resistance materials at room temperature. In mid-1987, Chu discovered a compound with superconducting potential at 225K. The phenomenon not only raises the potential of much more efficient electricity transfer, but also of cheaper electromagnets, body scanners and computers.

Prospecting for oil

The wellbeing of any national economy depends on energy. It follows that research into means of locating and extracting fossil fuels, devising new forms of energy or discovering ways of deploying energy are likely to make important contributions to national prosperity. Funding the appropriate sciences should therefore yield high rewards.

Prospecting for oil is a clear example. Geologists' knowledge of the seabed furthers understanding of the formation of oil and the development of oilfields. Mapping and profiling can identify good prospect areas: they include organic-rich mudstones, from which kerogen, oil's parent substance, is derived, and an upper layer of sandstones or limestone to which the newly-formed oil can migrate and become trapped. Analytical chemistry helps determine whether a sedimentary rock in a particular geological environment is likely to be an oil reservoir. Even theoretical physics can be of service in unraveling complex models of fluid mechanics used to predict the movement of oil in the rocks.

◄ *A helicopter hovers over Gabon in West Africa during a seismic survey carried out by Royal Dutch Shell in July-August 1986. Although geology and related "earth sciences" are sometimes categorized as pure sciences with no immediate practical or commercial pay-off, they also provide the basic data necessary for successful exploration for oil, natural gas, minerals and other potentially highly profitable products.*

Different views about economic cycles fuel the debate about the financing of scientific research

Economic cycles and scientific expansion

At the heart of the debate about the relationship between investment in science, technological innovation and economic growth is an hypothesis based on apparent waves of economic prosperity and decline. It was first enunciated by a Russian economist who died in one of Joseph Stalin's labor camps during the 1930s after serving as head of the Institute of Economic Research in Moscow. In "The Long Waves in Economic Life" (1925) Nikolai Kondratiev (1892-c.1935) looked collectively at the world's developed nations as they successively became industrialized following the Industrial Revolution in Britain, and concluded that they had gone through successive regular cycles of growth and decline each of about 50-55 years. The first "long wave" occurred between the late 1780s and the early 1840s. The second stretched until the late 1890s, and the third ran from just before the turn of the century into the world depression of the 1930s.

Some economists and historians have questioned Kondratiev's hypothesis and suggested that those first three cycles were no more than chance. Orthodox marxists in particular opposed Kondratiev on the grounds that the only significant long-term trend is the gradual decline of capitalism. But many economists have taken his ideas increasingly seriously since it became apparent that the world's economic growth of the 1960s was being followed by a steep decline in almost all industrialized countries during the 1970s. Perhaps this downturn did indeed reflect the beginning of a fourth wave? If so, the likelihood that this reflected a natural rhythm held important lessons for the future – whether through acceptance of the cycle or through efforts to ameliorate its ill effects.

Kondratiev cycles

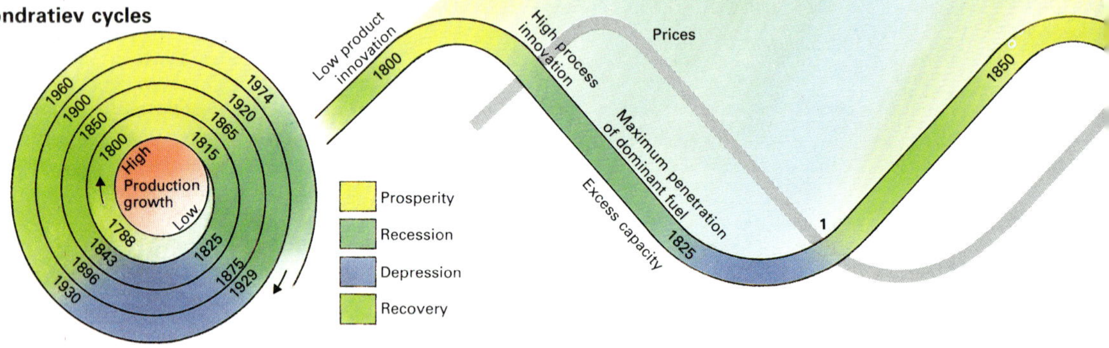

1

***►** Soviet economist Nikolai Kondratiev detected three long waves of economic activity in the major western countries between 1790 and the 1930s, each consisting of slow expansion and contraction and averaging 50 years in length. The first reflected growth from about 1790 to 1815 and contraction between then and the 1840s. The second mirrored expansion from 1850 to 1873, followed by decline in the years 1873 to 1896. And the third wave reflected economic growth from 1896 to 1920, with contraction from then into the 1930s.*

***►** Kondratiev had tried to discern broad patterns of economic development in countries as they became industrialized following the Industrial Revolution in Britain. Austrian economist Joseph Schumpeter believed that the long waves of capitalist development were powered by the successive introduction and diffusion of cotton-spinning, steam engines, electricity, and cars. Often these occurred in periods of downturn. The opening of the first railways in France in 1820 – marked (1) on the chart – was one infrastructure element required for that country's industrialization. Right: Claude Monet's "Le train dans la neige".*

◄◄ Electricity in the newly industrialized USA – (2) on chart below. Visitors to the American Institute Fair in New York watch a demonstration of Elihu Thomson's electric welding process, as shown in "Scientific American", November 26, 1887.

◄ The mass production of popular Volkswagen cars in interwar Germany – (3) on chart below. Following the industrial dislocation of World War I, the Nazi regime decided to increase greatly the manufacture of these low-priced vehicles, but the project was again interrupted by hostilities.

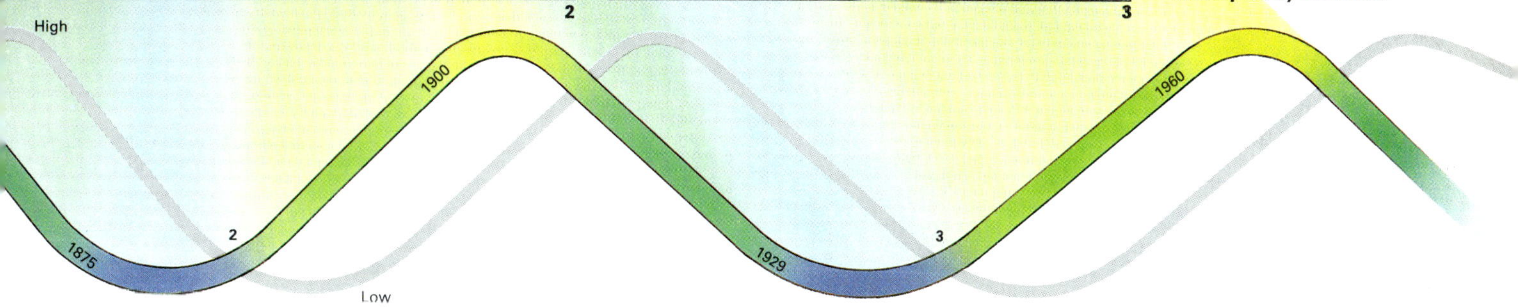

The Kondratiev theory is relevant to science and technology because, as Harvard professor Joseph Schumpeter (1883-1950) described in his "Business Cycles" (1939), each long wave has tended to coincide with the waxing and waning of innovation. The downside of each cycle seems to have been accompanied by new technological developments which in turn provided the seeds for a subsequent wave of economic expansion.

Schumpeter claimed that the first Kondratiev wave, which was almost exclusive to Britain, depended on the adoption of novel technologies by the textile industry, based in turn on the power of steam and coal. The development of railways and the mechanization of production were the key ingredients Schumpeter identified in the second wave, when Britain was joined by Germany and France. And the third wave, which also affected the United States, was founded upon the chemical industry, electrical power and the internal combustion engine.

If this interpretation is correct, it implies not only that innovation stemming from science and technology has been an input to economic growth in the past, but also that future economic recovery might be enhanced by increased government and corporate support for research and development. Schumpeter's conclusion, however, fell into unpopularity as the policies favored by John Maynard Keynes, which were apparently successful in helping the world out of the 1930s slump, were widely applied during the 1950s. It has reemerged as those policies have fallen into disfavor, and the events of the 1960s and 1970s appeared to confirm Kondratiev. Christopher Freeman of the Science Policy Research Unit at the University of Sussex, England, has done most to reintroduce the idea of long-wave economic cycles. Having observed patterns in the pharmaceutical industries, he became interested in the reason for the chronic unemployment found in Europe over recent years. Was this a temporary phenomenon, which could be overcome by Keynesian expansionism, or a "structural" one, more likely to be defeated by the injection of funds to provide a spur for technological innovation? Freeman argues that the Kondratiev hypothesis has now been authenticated by 200 years of history, and that it does support the idea of economic progress through research and development.

Thus the basic researches into molecular biology during the 1950s and 1960s could initiate the start of a fifth Kondratiev wave. Freeman believes that the difficulties now facing western countries, especially the unemployment that has resulted from the replacement of old by new technologies, are long-term problems. Their solution cannot be left to market forces. It depends rather on "massive international investment in new technology systems". Sustained government funding of pure science is essential, Freeman says, because its findings provide the only dependable seedcorn for economic expansion in future. In political circles, this analysis has been vigorously supported by the Organization for Economic Cooperation and Development (OECD). The French government has also cautiously accepted Kondratiev's ideas, and has been gathering statistical data on innovations in the hope of incorporating the information into its economic planning.

Defense research funding

The one sector of science that continued to attract the high level of financial support enjoyed by scientists generally during the 1950s and early 1960s is "defense research". Invariably protected when governments trim their research and development (R & D) budgets, science specifically geared to the needs of warfare now consumes most of the money going into laboratories worldwide. The gargantuan costs of megatechnology are obvious in the case of nuclear armaments and the laser and particle-beam weapons being developed under the Strategic Defense Initiative for use in "Star Wars". But even the most innocent-sounding projects receive military backing, as in the case of J.L. Baird's television system (◀ page 14). Today, in fact, the military authorities provide most of the support for oceanography, because of their interest in undersea communications, nuclear submarines and other seaborne weaponry.

As J.D. Bernal pointed out (◀ page 12), the generals' interest in science is far from being exclusive to modern times. Galileo was professor of military science at the University of Padua when he sold his invention of the telescope to the Venetian Signory "solely on account of its value in naval warfare". But lavish government support for defense research is a phenomenon of this century. For young scientists in particular, the blandishments afforded by this type of work can be very strong, especially in times when nonmilitary science is suffering austerity. Starting salaries and potential career earnings are invariably significantly greater in this sector. Equally (and arguably more) important is a level of equipment and technical back-up far exceeding what is available in even the most well endowed university or industrial laboratory.

▼ Deep-Star 4000, Westinghouse, a manned research submersible reaching depths of 1,220m off Cozumel Island, east of the Yucatan peninsula, Mexico. At first sight, oceanography is of very little concern to the military. In fact, defense researchers have many interests in the sea – charting the seabed for places for submarines to hide, or developing communications under the sea, where radio waves propagate differently to atmospheric radio waves.

The vastly superior facilities and finance in defense R & D give rise to the much-debated question – who is responsible for the arms race? Does the military establishment articulate its needs – such as improved night vision devices or missile guidance techniques – and then seek to persuade the politicians to finance and the scientists to develop them? Or do the sheer technological momentum and elite brainpower within financially privileged defense establishments spawn novel possibilities which the politicians and generals then feel must be developed?

► Space Shuttle Challenger being moved to the vehicle assembly building. Most of the publicity surrounding the inception of the Shuttle concentrated on uses such as placing weather and earth resources satellites in orbit, and carrying out experiments designed to investigate the possible manufacture of new pharmaceuticals and other products in space. Yet many of the early missions were carried out for the military, and much of the concern following the explosion of Challenger in January 1986 focused on consequent delays to defense research – including the assessment of laser and particle beam weapons under the Strategic Defense Initiative.

In the 1980s, Boeing's evolution of the AWACS airborne radar system illustrates a recent innovation produced in response to military need. But there is ample evidence that in the United States the reverse relationship operates too. By far the grandest mission-oriented defense program of modern times was launched in March 1983 when President Reagan announced his Strategic Defense Initiative (SDI). Founded upon the concept that nuclear weapons can be rendered obsolete by a revolutionary defense system of space-based weapons "zapping" intercontinental ballistic missiles shortly after launching, SDI has grown into a $29-billion project involving scientists not only in the United States but also in Britain and other European countries.

There are many critics of "Star Wars" who believe that the technology is impracticable, and that its deployment would seriously destabilize international relations – *and* contravene the 1962 Partial Test Ban Treaty, the 1967 treaty prohibiting the militarization of outer space, and the 1972 Anti-Ballistic Missile Treaty. Yet the SDI has acquired virtually irresistible momentum. In origin, the program exemplifies the escalation of military technology not in response to battlefield demands but as a result of "imagineering" by unusually bright researchers in a well-endowed think tank (◀ page 22).

Secondary benefits of military research funding

Many of the laboratories and scientists who have decided to take part in SDI research, whether in universities or private industry, have not done so primarily because they are deeply committed to the strategic thinking behind the project. Their motive has been to take part in a mega-project which, whatever its purpose, offers sufficient funds over a sufficient period of time to provide a considerable boost to scientific and technical innovation. They cite the American Apollo space program as a comparable exercise, with secondary and long-term benefits and spin-offs far removed from the central goal of putting humans on the Moon. Some have even expressed skepticism as to whether "Star Wars" technology will actually work. Others are content to take part in the initial research phase, while doubting whether the hardware will ever be deployed in space anyway.

Critics of the SDI

Although political lobbying for the SDI has necessarily been a highly public activity, the clandestine nature of the underlying science distinguishes defense from civil research. Defense projects are not subjected to the normal, open process of peer review. Critics who argue that the SDI is inherently implausible on technical grounds have, therefore, been handicapped by not having access to the experimental data and reports upon which its advocates have built their case.

Critics, many of them distinguished scientists, insist that the planned X-ray lasers, for example, could not pierce the Earth's atmosphere, and that the requisite computer software – the largest program ever written – would be so unreliable and uncertain that it might unleash an onslaught in space for the wrong reason. These criticisms are made without the benefit of the "O Group" (➧ page 34), but they have considerable inherent plausibility. Together with strategic and political arguments, they account for the fact that more than half of the staff at the top 20 American scientific universities have signed a pledge renouncing SDI finance. Given that quantity and quality of opposition, it is very doubtful whether such a project could have attracted $29 billion in public funding so quickly if its scientific merits and demerits had been hammered out in public. Technical objections and anti-SDI lobbies notwithstanding, the program has proved a bonanza for the laboratories of Europe, otherwise hard hit in recent years by government economies. In Britain, where 60 percent of physicists at Imperial College, London, have declined to take part, totally restricted SDI research includes a $3·3 million contract with the Atomic Energy Authority's Culham Laboratory for work on neutral particle beams, and a $9·9-million contract with the Ministry of Defence whose purpose is not known.

The SDI Story

The cradle for the Strategic Defense Initiative (SDI) was the Lawrence Livermore Laboratory, but a crucial catalytic role was played by the Hertz Foundation, a defense-oriented educational foundation that provides fellowships for outstandingly-talented students in the physical sciences. It was set up following World War II by Austrian-born John Hertz, of the Chicago Yellow Cab and Hertz car hire company.

One of the Hertz Foundation's original aims, reflecting its benefactor's own philosophy, was to "strengthen the defense" of the United States. Its original board included J. Edgar Hoover, one-time director of the FBI, who considered communism to be the principal evil of this century, and Herman Kahn, the futurologist who argued that the West could both win and survive a nuclear war. The political tenor of that original team endures in one of the conditions attached to Hertz fellowships – that recipients must commit themselves morally to making their skills available to the military in the event of a national emergency. Another survivor on the board is Dr Edward Teller (b.1908), the Hungarian émigré who helped to develop the atomic bomb and is rightly known as the "father of the hydrogen bomb". He has continued to believe that the Soviet Union is bent on world domination, and has consistently urged both politicians and the scientific community to behave accordingly.

Edward Teller provided the initial link between the Lawrence Livermore Laboratory, where he was a senior director, and the Hertz Foundation, for which he served as a talent scout and interviewer. In 1973, he appointed Dr Lowell Wood, who had been coordinator of the Foundation's fellowship program (also at Teller's instigation) as head of a new Special Studies Group which, bolstered by Lowell Wood's recruits, soon became the "O Group". "Working in a sort of scientific gulag deep inside the secret weapons laboratory, the young physicists were given complete intellectual and creative freedom to research the absurd, the not-quite-so-silly and the very serious," recalled British journalist Tom Mangold some years later. "One student worked on a Jesus Machine that actually walked on water, another worked on a starship for interplanetary travel, others on a supercomputer project that would shrink the circuitry required on to a chip the size of a thumbnail."

▼ The Strategic Defense Initiative can be traced to Nazi Germany's efforts to develop a deterrent to its own V-2 rockets, and thence to the United States' abortive Safeguard anti-ballistic missile effort of the 1970s. Its real origin, however, was Edward Teller's espousal of the hydrogen bomb, research into which provided vital information on high-energy particles. Backed technically by his Lawrence Livermore Laboratory, Teller's lobbying triumphed in March 1983 when President Reagan formally backed "Star Wars".

► Teller's original idea was that a hydrogen bomb in space would emit high-energy X-rays which could be directed at separate missiles on or near the ground. Each beam would destroy its target, and the battle station would also be annihilated. SDI embraces a variety of laser and particle-beam weapons intended to attack submarine-launched, intermediate range, and intercontinental ballistic missiles (during boost or the pre-boost stage when a "bus" ejects several re-entry vehicles). The space-based mirror system is supposed to overcome air turbulence.

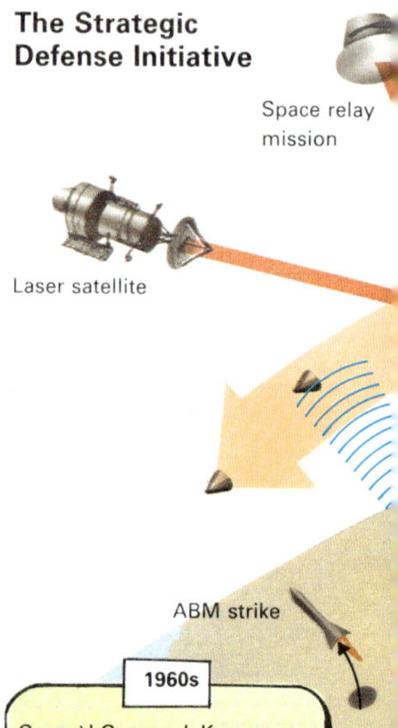

1945	Post-1945	1951-52	1954	1960s
The atom bomb, developed by J. Robert Oppenheimer, is first tested in the United States. The following month it is used to destroy Hiroshima and Nagasaki and end the war between the United States and Japan.	The Hertz Foundation is established. Drawing on the fortune amassed by benefactor John Hertz' car hire business, its aim is to provide fellowships for study in the physical sciences oriented toward the strengthening of the defenses of the United States.	The Lawrence Livermore Laboratory is set up, staffed with physicists known to be sympathetic to the development of nuclear devices and antimissile systems.	Oppenheimer is discredited during the McCarthyite hearings, the most damaging testimony against him coming from Teller. President Truman authorizes the development of the hydrogen fusion bomb. The first test is conducted on Marshall Island in the Pacific Ocean in 1952.	General George J. Keegan, head of US Air Force intelligence, compiles alleged evidence of Soviet particle beam research, which convinces the Pentagon of the need to build up a defense program in response. Keegan is one of Teller's group of defense and intelligence analysts.
The physicist Dr Edward Teller, a Hungarian immigrant to the United States, is recruited by Oppenheimer to build the atomic bomb. He advocates the development of a hydrogen fusion bomb, potentially 2000 times more destructive.	Teller is an original member of the board of trustees. Others include J. Edgar Hoover, head of the FBI, Robert Lehmann, head of a major bank, Floyd Odlum, defense industry financier and Herman Kahn, right-wing futurologist.	Edward Teller is the senior director of the Lawrence Livermore Laboratory until 1960, after which he remains a senior consultant.	The decision to fund research into the H-bomb is a personal triumph for Teller on whose scientific work its technology is based. Oppenheimer had earlier hindered Teller's work on the H-bomb.	In 1962, Teller's nuclear antimissile research program is tested in space. It is approved by the military, but meets criticism in political and scientific circles. Subsequent research is now carried out in secret.

► Decades after disputing H-bomb development with Robert Oppenheimer, Edward Teller (seen before a House committee in 1981) was lobbying as forcefully as ever. But despite Teller's advocacy, the American Physical Society and many scientists question SDI's feasibility and wisdom.

◄ The Lawrence Livermore Laboratory at Livermore, some 65km east of San Francisco, was originally established as a branch of the Lawrence Berkeley Laboratory on a site next to the University of California. Primarily a nuclear weapons laboratory, LLL now dwarfs its parent and has a staff of over 7,000 and a budget nearing $0.75bn. Its non-weapons program includes biomedical and environmental research.

What the "O Group" actually evolved, under Lowell Wood's inspired leadership, was an idea for a tiny nuclear warhead, around which are long thin metal tubes acting as conduits for massive pulses of X-rays generated when the warhead is detonated. Because the rays are "coherent" like laser light, they can travel astronomical distances. Produced from a warhead in space, they might therefore be directed earthward to track and "zap" Russian ICBMs as they begin to rise from their launch pads. The "O Group" brainchild, a prototype of which was built and allegedly worked when tested underground on November 14, 1980 in an operation codenamed Dauphin, was thus the invention that triggered serious discussion of the possibility of "Star Wars" weaponry.

Although classified, the work of Lowell Wood's team leaked to the press and was first described in "Aviation Week and Space Technology" early in 1982. Clarence Robinson, the magazine's military editor, claimed that "the X-ray lasers based on the successful Dauphin test, when mounted in a laser battle station, are so small that a single payload bay on the space shuttle could carry to orbit a number sufficient to stop a Soviet nuclear attack." The leak of this information was necessary for the "Star Wars" concept to arouse public and political interest and support. So when Dr George Keyworth, another of Teller's confidants, became presidential science adviser later in 1982, the prospect of government backing for the development moved closer. Shortly afterward Teller briefed President Reagan, who in March 1983 announced his endorsement of the project.

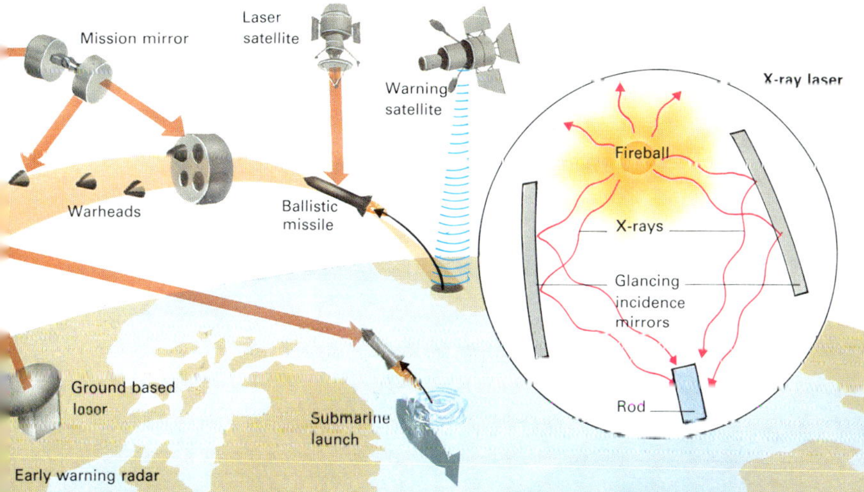

1960s

Following breakthroughs in laser engineering, research into X-ray laser weaponry applications begins, carried out by the Livermore Laboratory's "O" group headed by Dr Lowell Wood. Ronald Reagan, then governor of California, is later invited to inspect progress.

In his capacity as interviewer for Hertz, Teller appoints Lowell Wood as part of a recruitment drive for "charismatic" young physics graduates.

1979

In response to escalating Soviet antisatellite tests, President Carter sets up a program to research directed-energy weaponry at Livermore. Carter's more hawkish approach to relations with the Soviet Union leads to the resignation of Secretary of State Cyrus Vance and the appointment of right-winger Zbigniew Brzezinski.

Keegan's dossier on Soviet antimissile beam research passes via the CIA to Brzezinski. Following consultation with Teller, Brzezinski persuades Carter to step up research funding.

1980

"O" group's X-ray laser, designed originally by physicist George Chapline in 1977 under the code-name Dauphin, is successfully – and secretly – detonated on November 14.

The X-ray laser, designed by Livermore's "O" group under Teller's protégé Lowell Wood, works on principles put forward by Teller himself when developing the hydrogen fusion bomb in the 1940s.

1982

In January, the antimissile lobby group briefs President Reagan. Later that year, "O" group's work is leaked to the press; space defense enthusiast George Keyworth becomes presidential adviser.

Teller recommends George Keyworth, a close confidant, to the President. Reagan meets Teller regularly throughout the year to review the ranges of technology available.

1983

On June 14, Keyworth acknowledges existence of directed-energy weapon research. In March, President Reagan announces the inception of the Strategic Defense Initiative (SDI) project. He puts before the American people his dream of building "the means of rendering the ballistic missile threat impotent and obsolete".

Independent criticism of scientific developments may be a casualty of government cutbacks in science and the increased flow of private finance

▶ **As government money to support science has become less freely available in recent times, the role of charities, foundations and individual benefactors has grown in importance in the funding of research. When the Duchess of Windsor's jewels were put up for sale at a two-day auction at Beau Rivage Hotel, Geneva, in April 1987, they raised £31,380,197 – considerably more than the £5 million that had been expected. The proceeds went to the Pasteur Institute in Paris, a city where the Windsors lived for many years. Although the Institute had raised considerable sums of money over previous decades from the sale of vaccines and other products, this was a welcome windfall which has facilitated a considerably expanded program of research into diseases such as AIDS.**

Funding by industry

When, in Britain in the 1980s, government economies put severe strain on the scientific community, some academic researchers simply complained, seeking to persuade politicians of the long-term damage caused by cutbacks, particularly in basic science. University vice-chancellors issued a public warning that a 20 percent reduction in finance since 1980 was turning British campuses into machines for the export of talent overseas.

Other academics ruthlessly adapted their skills to the changed world, and sought support instead from industrial companies or charitable foundations. The University of Salford pulled itself around from near-bankruptcy in 1981 to entrepreneurial dynamism a few years later by greatly increasing the amount of research it carried out under contract for private firms. Warwick University, founded only in 1965, did not appear well positioned to weather the storm. Yet by 1986 Warwick's biotechnologists had attracted a higher per capita income from outside funding agencies for research and development cash than any other British university since 1983. Among many novel ideas being developed were courses for "student entrepreneurs" to encourage young scientists to consider the potential rewards from their work.

Grading campuses as a basis for allocating funds during times of austerity, Britain's University Grants Committee gave biological sciences at Warwick a star rating in 1986 as "outstanding by international comparisons". But even during the opening ceremony at Warwick, the chairman of the Advisory Board for the Research Councils, emphasized that today's practical achievements in applied biology rested on a massive corpus of pure research carried out over previous decades in molecular biology and allied disciplines. Critics of British government policies questioned what was likely to happen to such disinterested work in future if all universities were compelled to follow the same path as Salford and Warwick. Others asked where, with universities and industry coming ever closer, would society be able to find independent criticism of scientific developments.

Medical research in France

In 1987, the Necker children's hospital in Paris persuaded several European and American pharmaceutical companies to contribute 500,000 francs each toward research into new drugs and therapies. Heart surgeon Professor Alain Carpentier attracted nearly 80 percent of the money required for an experimental surgery laboratory from American firms, and signed a three-year contract with West Germany's Bayer group to support work on an artificial heart. Although private industry accounted for only about 5 percent of total funds for French medical research in 1987, this figure was thought to be growing there and in other countries.

Another change affecting biomedical science in France was the introduction of legislation bringing fiscal benefits to nonprofit foundations, such as the Fondation pour la Recherche Médicale, the Ligue Contre le Cancer, the Fondation de France and the Association pour la Recherche contre le Cancer to back new lines of investigation. This was termed "sponsorship à l'américaine", its purpose being to catalyze research involving other sources of finance, rather than to foot 100 percent of the bill.

Funding sciences in Japan

Japanese industry finances around 80 percent of all research and development in Japan, but only 0.5 percent of the total expenditure finds its way to the universities. In Japan's institutions of higher education, science has been largely removed from that country's recent history of commercial dynamism. The country's major companies have instead invested in their own laboratories, where much of the crucial applied research is carried out. Sponsorship of basic scientific research tends to be directed towards American universities.

In a new departure, however, Japanese electronics companies have turned to Tokyo University to back the Department of Information Science in its development of a new design of computer. Known as TRON (The Real-time Operating-system Nucleus), it is by far the largest collaboration between university and industry so far undertaken in Japan (♦ page 26).

▶ **Warwick University, which was only founded in 1965 and thus lacked the financial base of many other institutions, did not appear well positioned to weather the financial storms which hit UK campuses in the early 1980s. Yet by 1986 the biological sciences department was transforming itself into a new £1.3m biotechnology laboratory, with newly-forged industrial links and support from the Wolfson Foundation and the City of Coventry. Among funds drawn into the new building (whose operating budget was close to £8m) were contract fees from the American-Swiss company Biogen and from ICI and Microbial Resources in Britain.**

SOTHEBY'S
FOUNDED 1744
88
Sotheby's
3.100.000
2.066.460
1.275.712
2.400.000
3.712.560
2.627.095
SOTHEBY
FOUNDED 1744

Scientific research in developing countries

Compared with the developed nations, the resources which developing countries are able to channel into science are meager. According to a UNESCO survey in 1974, 93·9 percent of the 2,974,204 scientists then working throughout the world were based in the developed regions. Only 5·8 percent were in the developing countries and 0·3 percent in the least developed countries. The picture today is thought to show an even greater imbalance. Of the $170,000 million now going into research and development (R & D) worldwide each year, 97·4 percent is being spent in the developed countries, compared with 2·5 percent in the developing and 0·08 percent in the least developed countries. Figures for expenditure in relation to population illustrate the maldistribution even more dramatically. They show that while the United States is allocating over $200 million annually to R & D, most Asian and African nations cannot afford even $1 for this purpose.

Another problem for the Third World is that private companies tend to put virtually nothing into scientific research there. As Robin Clarke concludes in his UNESCO report *Science and Technology in World Development*: "In many developing countries there is, quite simply, no private industrial R & D at all. In other words, the state budget for R & D is always the major source of funding, and sometimes the only one. This is true even for relatively advanced developing countries such as India where, in 1979, industry funded only 14 percent of total expenditure on R & D. Under these circumstances, there is little prospect of the engine of science and technology providing added push to economic growth."

Most Third World nations now run a massive international debt, so this situation is rapidly worsening. The multinational corporations argue that countries not able to support indigenous R & D can benefit instead from "technology transfer", but the terms are invariably unfavorable to the recipients in the long term. Among the disadvantages are that multinationals restrict the fields in which transferred technology can be used; ban the acquisition of competing technologies as a condition of sale; place limits on the size of production facilities; and ensure that recipients have to purchase raw materials and other essentials at inflated prices from the multinational concerned.

▼ In contrast to the adherents of so-called "appropriate" or "soft" technologies, some experts consider that developing countries have more to gain from highly sophisticated science and technology. Here, for example, a solar panel (based on materials developed during the US space effort) powers a radio post in Rondônia, Brazil.

► High-tech science appropriate to the needs of Third World peoples may range from genetically engineered vaccines against tropical infections to educational programs beamed from space onto receiving dishes in the bush. This antenna in India accepts signals sent earthward from a satellite in space.

► "Low technology" is exemplified by this biogas installation in Yucatán province, Mexico, which not only disposes of unwanted waste material – animal feces – but also converts it into something useful – gas, to be used as a source of energy. In a process similar to one of the phases of sewage treatment, micro-organisms turn noxious materials into methane and other flammable gases. Some people believe that cheap, unsophisticated and often labor-intensive applications of this sort are more appropriate to the Third World than more advanced techniques.

An attempt to resolve the issue

*One current attempt to resolve some of the issues confronting science in the Third World is the International Institute for Genetic Engineering and Biotechnology (IIGEB) which is now beginning to function at two centers – one in Trieste, the other in New Delhi. Established in 1985 by the United Nations Industrial Development Organization with a $40·7 million budget for its first five years, the institute is aiming to harness techniques such as gene splicing (**▶ page 66**) specifically to serve the needs of the developing countries. By having the unprecedented combination of staff and facilities in both Italy (concentrating on energy, industrial microbiology and protein engineering) and India (concentrating on human and animal health), the IIGEB is hoping to exploit frontier science rapidly to meet chronic medical, agricultural and social needs throughout the deprived regions of Asia, Africa and South America. The IIGEB is scheduled to become fully operational in 1988, with 30 scientists, 20 postdoctoral fellows and 30 technicians working at each site.*

▲ *Nobel laureate Abdus Salam directs the International Centre for Theoretical Physics which harnesses frontier science to Third World needs.*

See also
Social Relations 5-20
Science and Authority 41-56
Nuclear Power and Radiation 57-64
Global Change 93-108

Government decision-making

The factors which determine the level of spending deemed appropriate by a particular government at a particular time are many and varied. They include the past achievements of that country's scientists in key fields, the government's future aspirations in important areas such as petrochemicals and biotechnology, the availability of energy and basic materials, the strategic and military significance attached to defense research, and political and social decisions taken about science-related activities such as health care and agriculture. One of the starkest contrasts in recent years has been between the cutbacks in basic science that have occurred in several European countries, and the determination of Japan – at one time considered to be solely a copier of other people's technology – to increase its investment in pure science.

▼ Investment in science mirrors the socio-economic priorities of different countries. In turn these range widely, from military and health goals to basic science in simply advancing knowledge and the need to harness natural resources or compensate for their absence.

Research and development funding

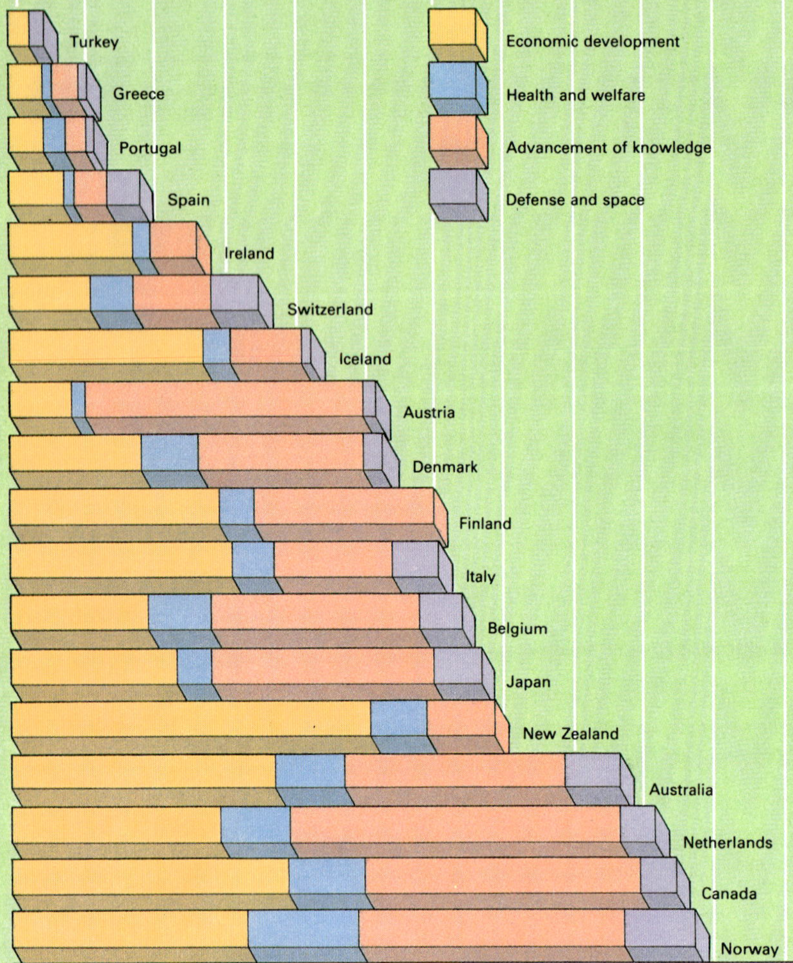

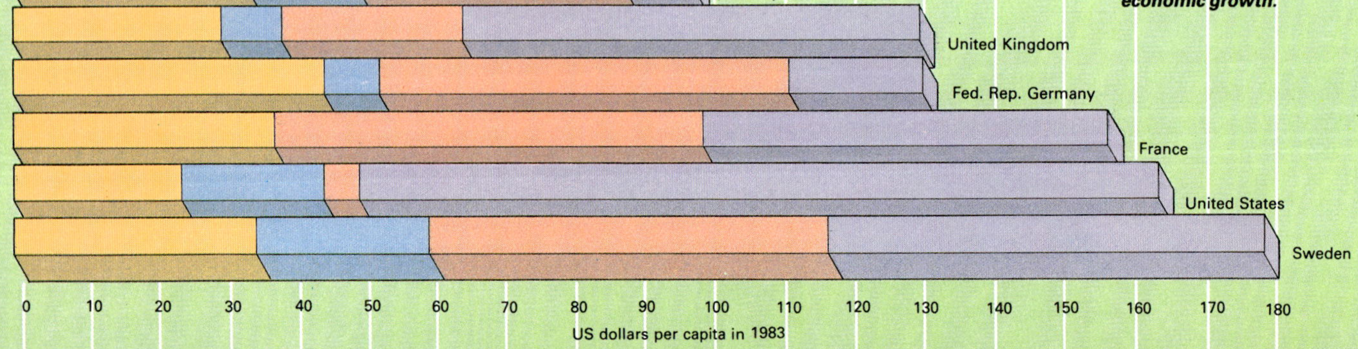

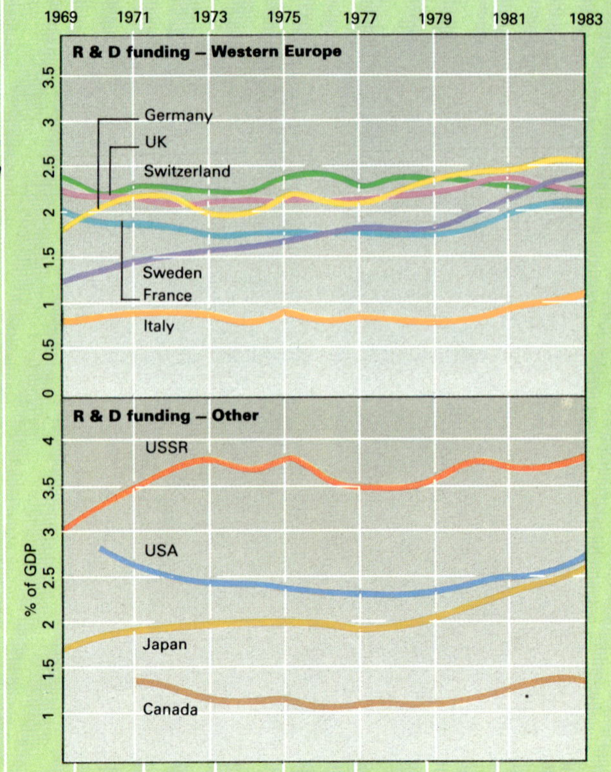

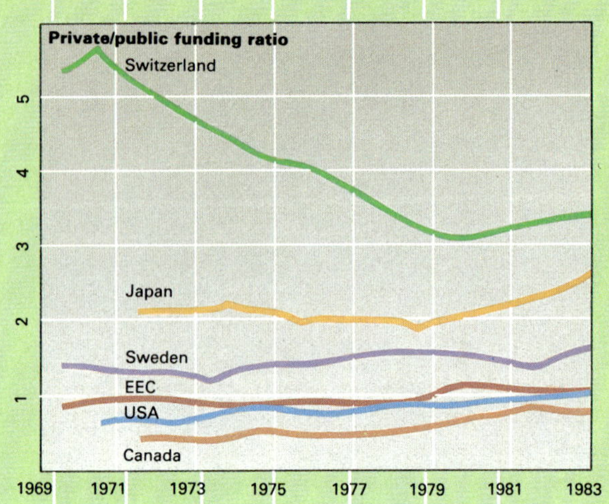

▲ While the proportion of private to public R & D expenditure fell during the 1970s in Switzerland, from 1979 it rose, and elsewhere it remained about the same. As shown by the trend in Japan, investment in R & D as a percentage of gross domestic product reflects ideas about the relationship between science and economic growth.

Science and Authority

3

A "prisoner of the Inquisition"...The evolution debate..."Marxist" versus "idealist" science...Science and Nazism...Can the state mold science?...What is accepted science?...PERSPECTIVE...Division of authority in Protestant churches...Darwin's Bulldog... Fundamentalism and science...Political ideology and scientific inquiry...Refugees from Nazism...The state of science in the USSR

Scientists are supposed – at least in their scientific work – to look at the world differently from everybody else. One of the key differences is that they are expected to question what is happening at every step in their investigations. This need to be continually questioning is usually referred to as the "organized skepticism" of scientists. "Skepticism" is obvious; but why "organized"?

More than most areas of human creativity, science is a collective activity. It builds on what has gone before in a much more fundamental way than occurs in art or literature. If Mozart, Renoir and Mark Twain had never lived, no one else would have created their works. But if Darwin had never lived, evolutionary theory would surely have developed in much the same way. Scientific knowledge only becomes acceptable after it has been absorbed and validated by the scientific community.

Perpetual skepticism is not the easiest frame of mind to cultivate. Most people for much of the time accept unquestioningly the world in which they live. Such inborn inertia was a major obstacle that had to be overcome in creating modern science. The picture of the world accepted by 16th-century Europeans had been developed over many years, mainly on the basis of Aristotle's writings. Discussions about the nature of the world were therefore phrased in terms of Aristotle's teaching. Before modern science could flourish, this teaching had to be questioned, and Aristotle's authority undermined. In the process, even those who were unhappy with the new science came to agree that authority always had to be justified.

By the 17th century, dogmatic belief in general was coming under fire. The word "dogma" is associated particularly with theology, where it means a doctrine that must be accepted regardless of any personal hesitations. But it is equally applicable in politics – for example, to the belief that matters of state must take precedence over the concerns of individuals. Religious and political dogmas may well be justified in some way – for example, by claims of divine revelation in religion. But the expectation is that, once the authority of the church or the state has been accepted, the accompanying dogmas will also be received without question. This is obviously opposed to the way that science operates. In a sense, scientists do accept authority, for they defer to the opinions of their peers on whether their work is good science or not. But they would certainly reject any suggestion that they supported dogma. The Royal Society of London long ago chose as its motto the Latin phrase "Nullius in verba". This is an abbreviation of lines from the classical poet Horace, which assert that a fellow of the Society is "Not bound to swear allegiance to any master, wherever the wind takes me I travel as a visitor". Scientists can be uncomfortable people to live with, for they constantly challenge dearly-held beliefs.

Can science be "disestablished"?

The political and ethical problems posed by state finance led Dr Jacob Bronowski to propose that science ought to become "disestablished". It should dissociate itself from the apparatus of government in general and government grants and contracts in particular. Bronowski cited growing pressures on research workers to conform politically, and the obligations of those dependent on military and quasi-military support, to back his case. Having won financial independence, in the form of a single overall grant for research, the body of scientists should "assign its own priorities on behalf of the community and with it, and divide the overall grant at its disposal accordingly." There are still echoes of this view in debates about the financing of research (♦ page 24) and the current lack of truly independent critical expertise in areas of public controversy. In biotechnology, for example, the forging of links between industry and academe has gone so far that in many countries it is virtually impossible to find experts who are free of vested interests. But most scientists now believe that the "disestablishment of science" is no longer a realistic option.

▲ The government of France tried to impose metrical weights and measures in 1799 – but 38 years later had to legislate to prohibit continued use of the old system.

▲ *Galileo was tried by the Inquisition in 1633, the year after his vigorously argumentative book "Dialogue on the Two Chief Systems of the World" appeared. He was condemned because he tried to establish an authority of science equal to that of the church. Roman Catholics were officially prohibited from reading Galileo or Copernicus until the 19th century. Yet the early Protestant reformers were no more enchanted by revolutionary ideas about the structure of the universe. Martin Luther is said to have commented of Copernicus: "This fool wishes to reverse the entire science of astronomy; but sacred scripture tells us that Joshua commanded the Earth to stand still, and not the Sun." However, Protestants were in a weaker position to argue against Copernicus than were the Roman Catholics. Theologically, they were far more sympathetic to individual interpretation of the Bible.*

The Galileo affair

The 17th-century English poet John Milton was strongly opposed to censorship. When writing in defense of the freedom of the press, he recalled his visit to the Italian scientist Galileo Galilei (1564-1642) who was then under house arrest, near Florence, "a prisoner to the Inquisition, for thinking in astronomy otherwise than the Franciscan and Dominican licensers' thought." Galileo's imprisonment is the most celebrated of all conflicts between the authority claimed by the church and that claimed by science. In historical retrospect, the outcome seems obvious and inevitable – Galileo, posthumously, proved right and the church wrong. At the time, the issues were more complicated and more influenced by personalities than this suggests.

The roots of the dispute went back to Nicolaus Copernicus (1473-1543) and the new ideas of the universe that he published in the year he died. He suggested, in particular, that the Earth moved round the Sun rather than vice versa. This was a radical innovation: the Earth had been supposed to be stationary by almost all earlier thinkers. Copernicus, a Roman Catholic cleric, was well aware that his proposal was controversial. This was a major reason why his ideas were only published at the end of his life; they were actually seen through the press by a Protestant theologian, Andreus Osiander (1498-1552). The controversy Copernicus feared came primarily not from the church, but from the ridicule of educated men. Osiander was equally aware of this possibility; so he added a preface designed to deflect criticism. He argued that an astronomer's job was to represent the way the universe worked, and it was legitimate for this purpose to introduce any hypotheses that seemed desirable without requiring that they should be interpreted literally. "These hypotheses need not be true nor even probable; if they provide a calculation consistent with the observations, that is sufficient by itself."

Copernicus's ideas were not widely accepted and led to no major controversy in the 16th century. But they became increasingly popular with the new generation of scientists growing up at the end of that

▲ *The frontispiece to the first edition of Galileo's "Dialogue", published in Florence in 1632, shows Aristotle, Ptolemy, and Copernicus, whose ideas triumph in the book. The crest is that of Cosimo, the Grand Duke of Tuscany and Galileo's patron. The word "Linceo" indicates Galileo's membership of the Academy of Lynxes.*

century. The Protestant, Johannes Kepler (1571-1630) sent a copy of his first astronomy book to the Roman Catholic Galileo. In reply, Galileo said that he had long accepted the Copernican doctrine, but had not made this public because he was "frightened by the fate of Copernicus himself, our teacher, who though he acquired immortal fame with some, is yet to an infinite multitude of others (for such is the number of fools) an object of ridicule and derision." At this stage, neither Kepler nor Galileo feared *religious* persecution.

▲ *English nonconformist poet John Milton, who wrote "Paradise Lost" after he became blind, visited Galileo while the latter was living under house arrest. A great believer in individual conscience as against authority, Milton argued for the freedom of the press in his "Areopagitica", which he wrote during the Civil War in England.*

In 1610, Galileo invented the astronomical telescope. His observations with it showed that many accepted attributes of the Earth-centered universe could not be true, and so gave a strong fillip to belief in Copernicus' Sun-centered universe. He was widely applauded for this work, even being received by the Pope in Rome. But shadows were beginning to gather. Robert Bellarmine, the leading theologian of the Roman Catholic church, saw the possible theological problems raised by Galileo's work. He had previously been involved in the trial of Giordano Bruno (1548-1600) for heretical views. Bruno, who had been burnt at the stake, also supported Copernican doctrine (though he had not been condemned for that). Controversy between Galileo and the clergy gradually increased. Their objection, as set out by Bellarmine, was to supposing that the Earth's motion was really true and not just a hypothesis. To assert that the Earth actually moves round the Sun was, he said, "a very dangerous thing, not only by irritating all the theologians and scholastic philosophers, but also by injuring our holy faith and making the sacred Scripture false." Galileo tried to counter this view. He argued that the Bible and science both give us true knowledge about the world, but they are different kinds of knowledge. Where observations seem to conflict with the Bible, it is because the scriptural passages are not meant to be taken literally.

Here the basic grounds of the forthcoming debate were set out. Galileo was saying that science provided a view of the world separate from, but of equal authority in its own sphere, to that of the Bible. For the Roman Catholic hierarchy, the Bible as interpreted by the church was the final and supreme arbiter. Initially, Galileo was simply requested to present his ideas as a convenient hypothesis, rather than truths, and for a number of years an uneasy truce reigned. But in 1632, Galileo published a new book in which he made it quite clear that he believed in the physical reality of the Earth's motion. The following year, he was arrested and brought to Rome for trial. He was forced to retract his support for the Copernican doctrine, and was condemned to confinement in his house for the rest of his life.

▲ *Giordano Bruno (1548-1600) was a Dominican monk whose new pantheistic religion outraged all parties. Bruno was burnt at the stake at Rome, not for supporting Copernicus, which he did, but as a dreadful heretic, but his case prejudiced the papacy against the whole idea of a universe with the Sun at its center.*

One result of the "Galileo affair" was that, in a Protestant country such as England, science and organized religion were not thought to be in conflict, whereas in France, where both science and Roman Catholicism were strong, scientists were frequently anticlerical. But advances in science were often seen as linking into the biblical narrative. For example, by the early 19th century, it was believed that geologists had found traces of Noah's Flood. However, possible divisions were beginning to appear. In the early 18th century, religious enthusiasm had become less commonplace, but, by the end, there was a religious revival. This led to a reaction against science, partly because it directed attention away from religion, but also in opposition to the free-thinking associated with French science. At the same time, the scientific picture became increasingly complex. For example, geologists decided on further examination that several floods must have occurred, rather than just a single great flood.

"For some years it was undoubtedly hot work" – wrote T.H. Huxley about his advocacy of evolution

Darwin, Huxley and the evolution debate

A peculiar problem faced the geologists of the 18th and 19th centuries: how to explain the existence of fossils of long-extinct animals? The basic question was whether each type of animal had been uniquely created by God, or whether it had evolved by some natural mechanism. Had Man been created as described in the Bible, or must scientific evidence lead to a different conclusion? It was Charles Darwin (1809-1882), in the mid-19th century, who posed the main challenge to orthodoxy and authority. Unlike his predecessors, he provided a scientifically acceptable description of evolution.

Darwin had originally intended to become a clergyman in the Church of England. He subsequently remarked that he "did not then in the least doubt the strict and literal truth of every word in the Bible ... Considering how fiercely I have been attacked by the orthodox, it seems ludicrous that I once intended to be a clergyman. Nor was this intention and my wish ever formally given up, but died a natural death when ... I joined the *Beagle* as a naturalist."

▲ *The French naturalist Georges Cuvier (1769-1832) founded the science of paleontology. But his view that the Creator had restocked Earth with more advanced plants and animals after successive catastrophes (an Age of Invertebrates having been followed by ages of fishes, reptiles, birds and mammals) was in flat contradiction of the "steady state" ideas of Charles Lyell (1797-1857) whose "Principles of Geology" greatly influenced Charles Darwin. While Cuvier holds a lasting place in history for his monumental work in classifying animals, his theoretical speculations have long since been superseded.*

In 1859, Darwin published *On the Origin of Species by Means of Natural Selection, or the Preservation of Favoured Races in the Struggle for Life*, Darwin claiming in his title to have found a mechanism – natural selection – which can substitute for God in the creation of new species.

Though Darwin barely mentioned Man in the *Origin of Species*, it was understood from the start that his theory was intended to apply to all living things. Religious opposition began immediately. Darwin detested controversy and rarely attended public meetings. Public defense of his ideas therefore devolved on to his friend and chief supporter, the zoologist Thomas Huxley (1825-1895). The episode that followed has gone down in history, along with the trial of Galileo (◀ page 42) as epitomizing the conflict between science and religion.

In 1860, the British Association for the Advancement of Science held its annual meeting in Oxford. One of the main events was a debate on evolution, the chief speakers for and against being Huxley and Samuel Wilberforce, bishop of Oxford (1805-1873). In the course of arguing against the case for evolution, Wilberforce joked about the possibility of Huxley having an ape as a grandparent. Huxley reported on his own reply: "'If then,' said I, 'the question is put to me would I rather have a miserable ape for a grandfather or a man highly endowed by nature and possessed of great means of influence and yet who employs those faculties and that influence for the mere purpose of introducing ridicule into a grave scientific discussion – I unhesitatingly affirm my preference for the ape.'"

Huxley's speech was widely reported and has been popularly represented as marking a turning-point in the battle for the acceptance of evolution. As with Galileo's trial, the real position was less simple. In the first place, the meeting was obviously not taken very seriously: if Huxley had failed to make a good case, it would have affected the progress of evolutionary ideas only marginally. Secondly, the authority of science was by now far greater than in Galileo's day. A significant number of clergymen recognized the danger of trying to dispute with science on grounds of its own choosing. (A few clergymen – Charles Kingsley (1819-1875) is an example – actually welcomed the idea of evolution.) Finally, the power of churches to determine what topics could be debated had waned since the 17th century. In consequence, evolution was absorbed into contemporary thought with a relative ease that staggered the main participants.

► *Within 20 years of publication of Charles Darwin's "Origin of Species" (published in 1859), much to the surprise of the main participants in the debate (Thomas Huxley and Samuel Wilberforce), evolutionary concepts had been largely absorbed and were being popularized. This print of about 1880 is surprisingly modern in outlook, depicting the fossil record as an incomplete but instructive glimpse of evolutionary history, with earlier, primitive life forms associated with older geological strata. But, curiously, the animals and plants are numbered in reverse order relative to their presumed position in the evolutionary time-scale.*

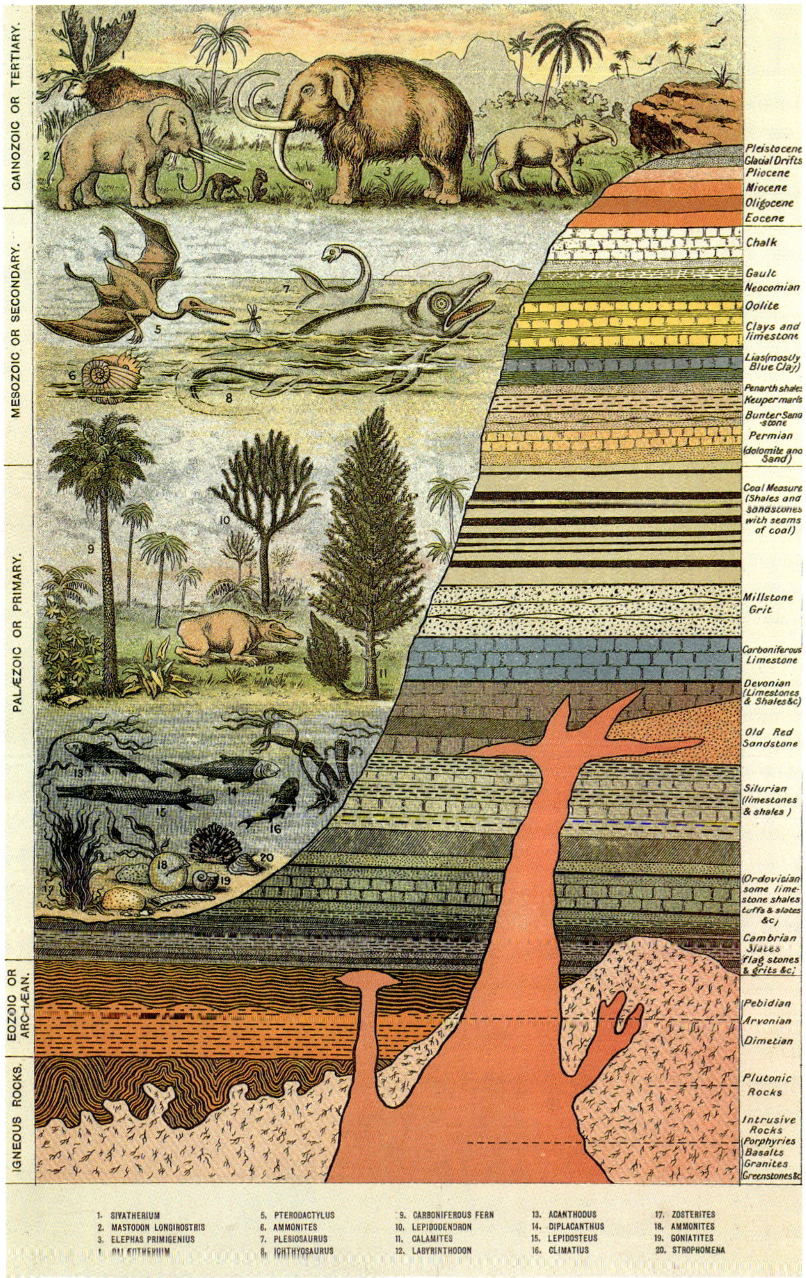

Darwin's Bulldog

The 19th-century mind associated the idea of "evolution" as much with Thomas Huxley as with Charles Darwin. Darwin not only detested controversy, he also suffered from frequent illness. Huxley therefore took up the argument on his behalf, so earning the title of "Darwin's Bulldog". There can be no doubt that he enjoyed the task. His combat with the Bishop of Oxford in 1860 was one of many disputes, both written and spoken. He also had many battles with the paleontologist Sir Richard Owen (1804-1892), the most respected comparative anatomist of the day and a vocal opponent of evolution. These were important, for here was one eminent scientist opposing another; so Huxley's overall victory in this debate carried more weight than did his arguments with nonscientists.

Huxley was not an uncritical admirer of Darwin's theory: he realized that it was weak at some points. However, the rational course, as he saw it, was "to accept 'Darwinism' as a working hypothesis and see what could be made of it. Either it would prove its capacity to elucidate the facts of organic life, or it would break under the strain." This was Darwin's belief, too, and he fully appreciated the importance of Huxley's role in making sure that evolution was evaluated on scientific, rather than religious grounds. He ended one letter to Huxley with the words, "Farewell my good and valuable agent for the promulgation of damnable heresies."

Both Darwin and Huxley doubted the truth of religion. But they did not consider themselves atheists, since they saw no way either of proving, or disproving, religious doctrines. For people with this attitude, Huxley coined the term "agnostic".

▲ The 19th-century mind linked evolution as much with Thomas Henry Huxley (1825-1895) (top) as with Charles Darwin. Darwin detested controversy, and was frequently ill. Huxley took up the argument, earning the title "Darwin's Bulldog". His combat with Samuel Wilberforce (above), the bishop of Oxford (1805-1873), in 1860 was a classic of Christian theology versus evolutionary agnosticism.

This century, United States fundamentalists and creationists have challenged the evolution theories of Darwin

▲ Co-authored by John Whitcomb from the Grace Theological Seminary, Indiana, and creationist writer Henry Morris, of the Institute for Creationist Research, California, "The Genesis Flood" is "replete with scientific data from the disciplines of hydrology, geology and archeology" and "asks the reader to reconsider the reorientation of pertinent scientific data within the framework of Biblical creationism...".

Creation science

The battle over evolution did not always run as smoothly as it did in England. The anticlericalism of some leading European scientists and the greater powers of the Roman Catholic church ensured that. But the long-term backlash has been most apparent in the United States. In 1909, a group of conservative Protestant theologians emerged there who were labeled the "fundamentalists". The term has subsequently been applied more widely to all who believe in the direct verbal inspiration and infallibility of the Bible. The outworkings of this belief have surfaced at intervals since. One of the famous episodes was the trial of a schoolteacher, John Scopes, in 1925. He was prosecuted for teaching evolutionary theory in opposition to the state laws in Tennessee where he worked. The reversal on technical grounds of his conviction was generally seen as a victory for evolutionary science over laws framed within a fundamentalist outlook.

Since World War II, a similar yet wider-ranging controversy has arisen. This dispute, which still continues, is over "creation science". The fundamentalist approach embodied in such science is now different. It is argued that evolution is, after all, only a theory. The belief that the world was created in six days and that Man was uniquely created is also a theory. Hence, fundamentalists and evolutionary views deserve to have equal exposure; in particular, school curricula should discuss "creation science" along with standard science. This argument has been regarded sympathetically by some state legislatures, and the pressure has become sufficiently intense to affect the presentation of ideas in school textbooks. The battle for the school curricula is currently being fought through the courts in the United States. But the interesting point is the complete reversal of the 17th-century position. Then the fight was to establish science as having an authority independent of biblical interpretation; now it is to place biblical interpretation on a par with science.

Disputes between religion and science are unlikely to go away. The rise of Moslem fundamentalism, for example, may influence the acceptance of science in a number of countries. Scientists are often labeled heretics in such disputes, which leads to the question – religious heretics can be fairly easily defined, but is there such a thing as a scientific heretic? At first sight, it seems impossible, since science has neither an authoritative text, such as the Bible, nor an institutional authority, such as the Pope, from which deviation can be measured. Yet science does believe in a particular way of investigating – the "scientific method" – and does distinguish between acceptable and unacceptable evidence. Hence, a person who operates under a different set of rules, such as those proposed by "creation science", might be called a scientific heretic. In practice, scientists do not see it this way. Anyone who works to a different set of rules is simply considered to be nonscientific, and their work is ignored. In many ways, this is a more effective and, for the recipient, infuriating response than any kind of heresy trial could be.

◄ ▼ Fundamentalist book-selling in 1925 in Tennessee (left), where teacher John Scopes was prosecuted for teaching the theory of evolution. Scopes is seated (below), in a light suit, in this photograph with his legal staff. Clarence Darrow, memorably played by Spencer Tracy in the 1960 movie "Inherit the Wind", is at the extreme left. Despite the battery of evidence accumulated since 1925 to support the idea of natural selection, battles over creationism have been replayed in recent years – most recently in June 1987 when the US Supreme Court struck down Louisiana's law requiring "creation science" to have equal time with evolution in the school curriculum.

◄ Fossil ammonites from the Jurassic period. Although our modern understanding of evolution is based on a rich variety of evidence, fossils continue to be the major focus of creationists' efforts to discredit the theory. Some creationists make much use of gaps in the fossil record, while others have suggested that God would have been capable of planting evidence in the strata if he so wished.

◄ On November 21, 1959, to mark the centenary of publication of the "Origin of Species", WBBM-TV staged a debate on the mechanisms of organic evolution. Taking part were (left to right) Professor Sol Tax from the University of Chicago; Sir Charles Darwin, grandson of the great man; Sir Julian Huxley, grandson of "Darwin's Bulldog" Thomas Henry Huxley; and leading US politician Adlai Stevenson.

Since the latter part of the 1960s Soviet genetics has returned to the world scene, as classical geneticists have reasserted their dominance

Marxism and evolutionary theory

The German political philosopher Karl Marx (1818-1883) and his followers believed they were putting forward a scientific explanation of the way human society must develop. After the 1917 Russian revolution, the scientific beliefs of many leading Russian scientists – among them Ivan Pavlov (1849-1936), who had won a Nobel prize in 1904 for his work on the digestive system – were criticized as anti-marxist. The leading error of such scientists was held to be "idealism" – they were insufficiently materialistic in approach, especially in their formulation of theories. Quantum mechanics proved particularly difficult for Marxist ideologs to accept. They objected strongly to the concept of an entity – such as an electron – which sometimes had to be thought of as a particle, and sometimes as a wave. Similarly, Einstein's general theory of relativity, with its complex picture of inter-related space and time, was considered unacceptable to Marxists. These suspicions lasted until after World War II, and had the effect of slowing the development of Soviet theoretical physics.

However, the sharpest dispute in the 1930s was over biology and, particularly, genetics. For a political creed like Communism, committed to the belief that Man can improve his lot by proper exertion, Darwin's was an unsatisfactory theory of evolution. Friedrich Engels (1820-1895), whose word ranked alongside that of Marx in the Soviet Union, had preferred a different approach. He argued that Man had evolved as a result of his efforts at self-improvement: such continuing efforts had affected Man's hereditary characteristics and these differences had been handed on to succeeding generations. Engels' belief was a particular aspect of a more general theory put forward years earlier by the French scientist, Jean Lamarck (1744-1829).

Marxist sympathy for a Lamarckian biology was evident soon after the Russian revolution. In 1924, Viennese biologist Paul Kammerer published a book on *The Inheritance of Acquired Characteristics* which seemed to oppose current standard views of genetics and inheritance. In 1925, he was offered a professorship at Moscow University, but his results were found to have relied in part on faked specimens, and he committed suicide before ever going to the Soviet Union. It seemed that Lamarckian ideas could finally be buried.

▼ Soviet biologist Trofim Lysenko denounced Mendelian genetics as incompatible with dialectical materialism. His views found increasing official support and in 1938 he became President of the Lenin Academy of Agricultural Sciences. Ten years later, his triumph was complete when the Academy formally repudiated Mendelism. Lysenko eventually fell from grace in 1965, after the failure of his ideas about crop breeding had become disastrously clear.

◄ Attacked with increasing ferocity by Lysenko at scientific congresses during the 1930s, Nikolai Vavilov tried to sustain the ideas of orthodox genetics but lost in his political battle with the All-Union Party. in 1940, while he was collecting plants in Bukowina, Vavilov was arrested, taken to Moscow and later placed in a concentration camp. He died in Saratov jail in 1943. Beginning in 1987, however, the authorities have been rehabilitating Nikolai Vavilov, implicitly recognizing the great harm done to Soviet biology by the Lysenko affair.

◄ *"Unite the power of science with the creative energy of the working class!" reads this 1932 poster by Alexei Kokorekin. The USSR's commitment to science attracted the enthusiasm of many western scientists during the 1920s and 1930s. J.D. Bernal, for example, wrote of the government giving science "a scope and importance out of all relation to that which it previously held...Science is to be taken no longer as a luxury but as an essential part of the social fabric. Science is in fact, in the Soviet Union, linked closely at every stage to the productive process. The prime practical object of Soviet science is the satisfaction of human needs." Ironically, even as Bernal wrote those words, the extraordinary affair of Trofim Lysenko was beginning to unfold.*

The Lysenko affair

The debate between "idealist" and "Marxist" science came to center on the work of Trofim Lysenko (1898-1976), an agricultural scientist, whose main concern was to improve crop yields. He and his supporters adopted a modified form of Lamarckism. They claimed that, by controlling the environment, they could influence future generations of plants, especially their ability to germinate and grow rapidly. This was important not only from the viewpoint of Marxist theory, but also for urgent practical ends. In the years prior to World War II, the Communist party was calling for the immediate development of new varieties of crops. Lysenko claimed that his methods could produce them within the period of a five-year plan.

Lysenko won Stalin's approval, and attacks on supporters of orthodox genetics increased. The climax came in 1940 with the arrest of the leading Russian geneticist, Nikolai Vavilov (1887-1943), who died in Saratov prison. A number of other Soviet biologists were arrested in the 1940s. After a national congress in 1948, when Lysenko received endorsement from Joseph Stalin, hundreds of biologists were arrested or demoted, and whole institutes were closed, on the grounds that they opposed the proper Marxist biology of Lysenko.

Political support for Lysenko continued into the 1960s, when it became particularly strong under Nikita Khrushchev (1894-1971). But the world of biology outside the Soviet Union was changing rapidly. News of the discovery of DNA and other advances filtered through to biologists in the Soviet Union, and strengthened the hands of those still critical of Lysenko (who had denied the existence of such genetic material). At the same time, it was apparent that the experiments of Lysenko and his supporters were not producing any major breakthrough. In 1964, Lysenko was eased out of his post as director of the Institute of Genetics, and a renewed interest in classical genetics was signalled by the attendance of a large Russian contingent at a Mendel anniversary meeting in Czechoslovakia. However, the Soviet Union has still not entirely bridged the genetics research gap that opened up during the period of Lysenkoism.

Science and Nazism

The Lysenko affair owed its celebrity to the decision by the Soviet state to endorse an ideologically acceptable version of science. Though the ideology was different, something rather similar occurred in Nazi Germany. Antisemitism became much stronger in Germany after World War I. One of the chief scientific developments was Einstein's general theory of relativity. Many physicists brought up on Newton's ideas of the world found Einstein's theory difficult to absorb and accept. For some German scientists, the fact that Einstein was a Jew suggested that he was trying to subvert their traditional modes of thinking. Most of the scientists who believed in such a Jewish conspiracy were minor figures, but two – Philipp Lenard (1862-1947) and Johannes Stark (1874-1957) – had previously won Nobel prizes for physics. During the 1920s the vast majority of German scientists, whether Jews or not, supported Einstein; but, with the advent of the Nazi party to power in 1933, the situation changed. Hitler soon appointed a Minister for Science and Education, a former schoolteacher who was mentally unstable. Almost immediately Jewish scientists, whether eminent or not, began to be dismissed from their posts. For example, Fritz Haber (1868-1934) was both a Nobel prizewinner and a leading contributor to the German application of science in World War I; yet he was dismissed from his post and forced to flee the country. Hitler was soon warned that his dismissal of the Jews was affecting the efficiency of German science. He replied that, in that case, Germany would have to do without physics and chemistry for the next hundred years.

▲ *Albert Einstein and Niels Bohr were two of the most illustrious refugees from Nazism. Einstein spent the winter of 1932 at the California Institute of Technology, but with Hitler's rise to power he decided not to return to Germany. He worked at Princeton until his death in 1955. Bohr remained at his Institute for Theoretical Physics, Copenhagen, until 1943, before escaping by fishing boat to Sweden when he was in danger of being imprisoned as a patriot.*

▲ *During Christmas, 1938, Lise Meitner, who had escaped from Berlin to Sweden, was visited by her nephew Otto Frisch (above), who had himself found temporary sanctuary in Copenhagen. Together they recognized that a prewar discovery by Otto Hahn – that uranium could undergo fission – might be exploited to release vast amounts of energy. This was the first step toward the atomic bomb used on Japan – a development greatly aided by scientific refugees from Fascism.*

Pressure now grew for alleged "Jewish science" to be eliminated from German teaching. Lenard wrote a four-volume work on *German Physics* in which he contrasted true Aryan physics with degenerate Jewish physics. He noted that most scientists considered their work to be international. "It is false," he commented, "science, like every other human product, is racial, and conditioned by blood." However, the attempt to foster a pure German science did not progress far. In view of the bizarre ideas of science that many Nazi leaders had, it is difficult to guess what its final contents would have been.

By the beginning of World War II, almost 3,000 staff had been dismissed from German universities – a quarter of their total staff complement. Many emigrated and tried to reestablish their careers in other countries. Their loss proved of incalculable significance for the future development not only of science, but of the international political balance. The most striking example concerns the atomic bomb.

Shortly before the war, the German chemist Otto Hahn (1879-1968) discovered that uranium nuclei could undergo fission (break down into two roughly equal halves). The importance of this was recognized by the Austrian physicist Lise Meitner (1878-1968), one of Hahn's former coworkers who in 1938 had been forced into exile in Sweden. She was visited there by her nephew, Otto Frisch (1904-1979), who had emigrated from Germany to England in 1933. Between them, they interpreted Hahn's experimental results and realized that fission could provide a way of releasing vast amounts of nuclear energy. This was the first step to the atomic bomb used on Japan in 1945, a development greatly aided by scientists expelled from Fascist countries.

The Nazi determination to rid Germany of Jewish scientists therefore led to their enemies producing the most important weapon of the 20th century.

Refugees from Nazism

When the wholesale dismissal of Jewish scholars from German universities started in 1933, many immediately looked for positions abroad. Clearly, there were far more refugees than could be instantly fitted into university positions elsewhere. The first response to this problem came from England. The professor of physics at Oxford, F.A. Lindemann (1886-1957), had been born in Germany and had carried out research there. He quickly realized that special finance was needed to tide the refugees over, and give them time to look for more permanent jobs. He therefore approached the Chairman of Imperial Chemical Industries, an old friend of his, and ICI agreed to provide financial assistance. Within a few months, British scholars had set up an Academic Assistance Council under Ernest Rutherford, the Nobel prizewinner and head of the Cavendish Laboratory at Cambridge. Assistance was later offered by other countries, particularly the United States.

Some of the scientists who were forced to flee from Germany were highly eminent, but at the end of their careers. Such were Fritz Haber, who died in 1934 within a year of leaving his post in Germany, and Sigmund Freud (1856-1939), who escaped Austria in 1938 and died the following year. Others – Albert Einstein is an example – were younger, but had ceased to be productive in research terms. But a high proportion were young and little-known scholars with much of their research career before them. How successful they were in adapting themselves is indicated by their subsequent activities. Of those who stayed in Britain, some 200 were scientists. Among these, 50 were elected to the Royal Society and eight were knighted.

Most of the German emigrants before World War II were Jews, who had to leave or suffer a worse fate by staying. But some were nonJewish scientists who were not prepared to work under a Nazi regime. The most eminent member of this group was Erwin Schrödinger (1887-1961), one of the founders of quantum mechanics. He eventually settled in the Republic of Ireland where he tried to encourage the growth of theoretical physics. One of the results of his stay was a slim book on the nature of life, so aiding the growth of the new science of molecular biology.

Nobel prizewinners forced to leave positions in Nazi Germany, 1933–40

	Nobel award	Year of departure	Settled in
	Physics		
Albert Einstein	1921	1933	USA
James Franck	1925	1933	USA
Gustav Hertz	1925	1935	–
Erwin Schrödinger	1933	1938	Ireland
Victor Hess	1936	1938	USA
Otto Stern	1943	1933	USA
Felix Bloch	1952	1933	USA
Max Born	1954	1933	UK
Eugene Wigner	1963	1933	USA
Hans Bethe	1967	1933	USA
Dennis Gabor	1971	1933	UK
	Chemistry		
Fritz Haber	1918	1933	(d. 1934)
Peter Debye	1936	1940	USA
George de Hevesy	1943	1934	Sweden
Gerhard Hertzberg	1971	1935	Canada
	Medicine		
Otto Meyerhof	1922	1938	France, USA
Otto Loewi	1936	1938	USA
Boris Chain	1945	1933	UK
Hans A. Krebs	1953	1933	UK
Max Delbrück	1969	1937	USA

◄ *German students joined in the action in May 1933 when the Nazis burned books written by Jews and unacceptable foreign authors in what is now part of East Berlin. The slogan reads "German students march against the un-German." This was also the moment in history when the rise of Hitler was spawning increasing hostility toward scholarship and triggering the exodus of intellectuals – including some 20 scientists who had already or later won a Nobel prize for physics, chemistry or medicine. Between 1933 and 1945, "National Socialism" was responsible for an incalculable loss of intellectual endeavor. The Nazis even failed to capitalize on the scientists that remained behind, because they wanted quick results and had little patience with the idea of speculative research.*

Fundamentalist Iran is as much concerned to use and maintain computers as any Third World country

▲ **Women science students attend a biology class in Oman. Even countries governed in accordance with holy scripture acknowledge the importance of science and technology for economic development and for agricultural and medical benefits. But there is also an increasing tendency, in countries founded upon a fundamentalist interpretation of Islam, to believe in a specifically Moslem style of science, different from that practiced elsewhere.**

What kind of science?

Ever since it became apparent that science can have a strategic importance for the economy, states have been concerned with planning science policy. Such questions as scientific manpower and funding support for scientific research are frequently discussed, and determined, by politicians. The state is certainly able to decide how much science, and what kind of science, a country "needs". What states rarely try to determine are the methods that shall be used in carrying out scientific research. Scientific method and the results it brings are typically regarded as operating universally with no regard to national boundaries – in much the same way as the Sun shines equally on the just and the unjust. Occasional attempts have been made to impose an approach to science which fits in better with the ideology of a ruling section of society (◀ pages 48, 50).

The question remains whether the state can influence the way science is done at a less fundamental, and less potentially damaging, level than was attempted in the Soviet Union and Nazi Germany. Here China provides an interesting example. At the time of the Communist takeover after World War II, the amount of scientific research in China was small. Under Communism, some branches of science, such as those involved in the development of an atomic bomb, expanded rapidly, but there was also some growth in most other areas of science. This was greatly affected by the Cultural Revolution of the late 1960s. One major aim of this revolution was to eliminate any bias in favor of mental over manual work. Universities and research institutes were closed, or had their activities considerably modified, and academic staff were forced out into the countryside. Research ceased to appear, though strategic research seems to have been protected. The consequences were predictable. The adverse impact of the Cultural Revolution on education and the economy has led in recent years to the reopening of the universities, the reappointment of their staff and the initiation of a desperate effort to catch up the ground that has been lost.

During the Cultural Revolution, as part of the attack on "elitist science", attempts were made to encourage a "people's science". An example that has been frequently cited is the prediction of earthquakes. People were encouraged to look for "everyday" indicators of a forthcoming earthquake – changes in the water level of wells, unease amongst domestic animals, and so on. Initially, results seemed at least to equal those produced by "traditional" (western) scientific methods, but longer trials indicate that they are seen better as supplementing these methods than as replacing them.

Another activity stimulated by the Cultural Revolution was the exploration and use of folk medicine, including acupuncture. Again, some useful results have been obtained, but they supplement traditional medical research, rather than replace it. In both these cases, the new approaches tended more to extend the scope of science, by taking account of observational material that had previously been ignored, than to reconstruct its basis.

State control of the application of science does seem a livelier possibility than altering the nature of science itself. Even so, there are limits to how far a country dare go in this direction before it becomes vulnerable to external pressures. For example, fundamentalist Moslem religion is antipathetical to much scientific thinking; yet even the strictest Moslem states have to reach some accommodation with their scientific needs if they are to survive.

► **During China's Cultural Revolution of 1967-1969, there was renewed emphasis on traditional medicine. Here citizens return from the fields carrying bundles of herbs gathered for medicinal purposes, and a woman receives acupuncture for a knee ailment. Rediscovery of neglected therapies was, however, coupled with damaging disparagement of modern, science-based medicine.**

▲ **Combine harvesters at work on State Farm No. 853 in the People's Republic of China. The centralized control of farming meant that socialist economies such as China did not suffer the problems experienced in some free-enterprise systems during the "Green Revolution" of the 1960s and 1970s, when wealthy farmers became wealthier, and peasants poorer, with the advent of high-yielding varieties of cereals.**

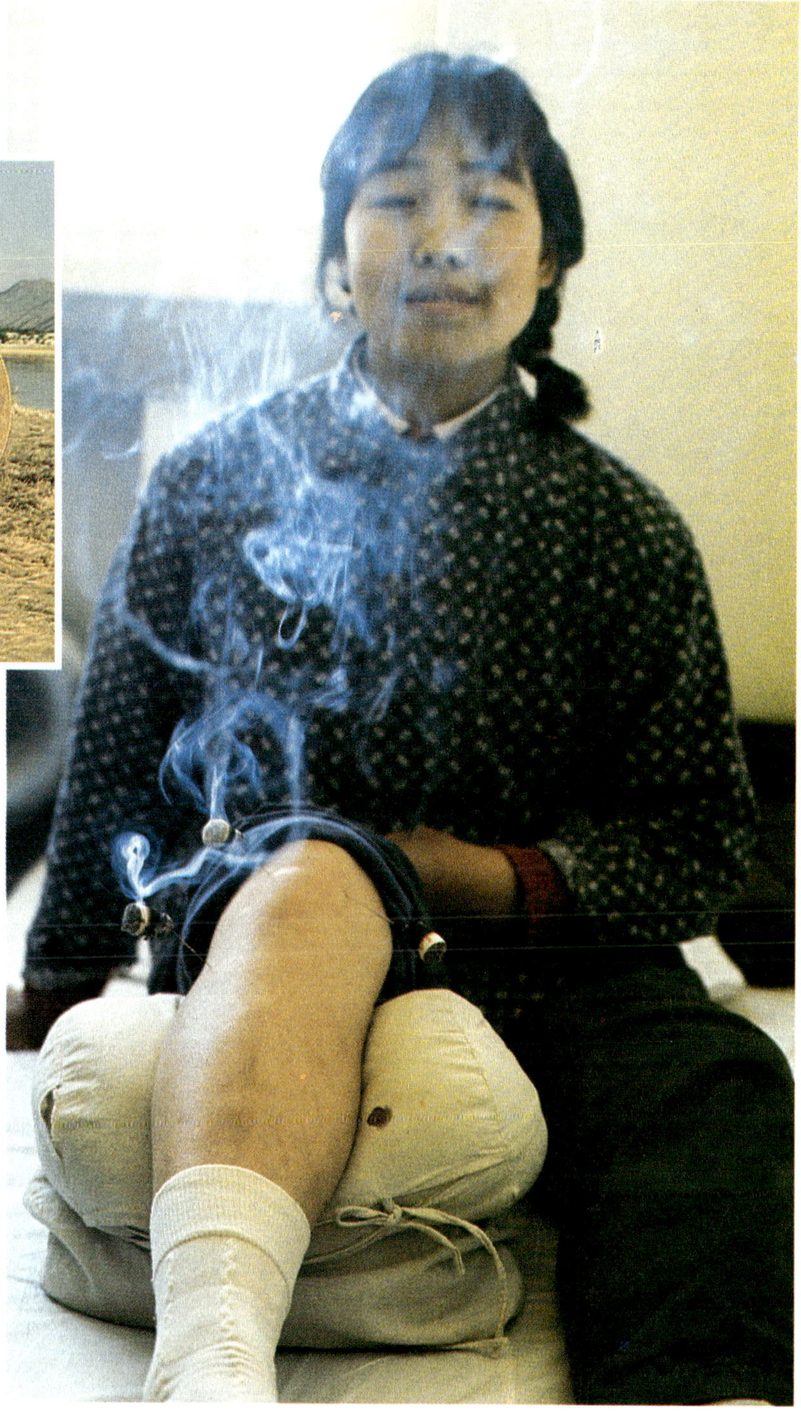

The Green Revolution

A desire by states to adapt scientific research to local conditions is far from unusual either in the past, or today. The authority of the state can certainly have an impact on the application of scientific knowledge to indigenous problems. Perhaps the most obvious example is the "Green Revolution". From the 1940s onward, scientists in developed countries began to produce high-yielding varieties of grain. By the 1960s, revolutionary new varieties, especially of wheat and rice, were being adapted for use in developing countries. Within a few years, crop yields had doubled in a number of countries. However, it was apparent by the 1980s that all was not well with the revolution. Though developing countries had moved toward a more self-sufficient agriculture, not all their people had benefited. The wealthier farmers became relatively even richer as the result of introducing new crops. When, in the 1970s, crop yields reached a plateau, the wealthier farmers survived while others became unemployed.

The societies which suffered least from this problem were those where the Green Revolution was subject to strict state control. In China, for example, the long history of intensive agriculture, allied to strong centralized state control, ensured that farming communities survived the advent of the new crops. In consequence, the Green Revolution has helped to reduce malnutrition in China to a much lower level than before. That this achievement depends on the history of the economy, as well as on central control, is illustrated by the different results obtained in other Communist-controlled countries. For example, success in Cuba has been less marked than in China, partly due to a lack of experience in intensive multicrop farming.

Science in the Soviet Union

Soviet science today is in the difficult and painful process of *perestroika* (restructuring) while under official and public criticism. The Soviet leadership, which was always proud to declare that Soviet science has the largest complement of research personnel in the world (1·5 million research scientists), now faces the negative consequences of political interference in academic and intellectual spheres, isolationism, bureaucracy and deliberate planning of self-sufficiency in nearly all areas of science and technology.

The Soviet planned economy, in which every branch (industrial, agricultural, medical, etc.) represents a state monopoly, was considered in theory to be particularly responsive to innovation, which should be imposed by the planning organs. However, this kind of indirect cooperation between research and practice could support the development only of some highly visible giant priority projects, while many thousands of small research projects were neglected.

The organizational structure of Soviet science, in which many research networks are very poorly coordinated and do not interact freely, has proved to be inefficient. There are too many academies, which have developed independent research networks for purely political, rather than scientific reasons. The existence of academic and other educational networks in every national republic (such as the Ukrainian, Armenian, Uzbek, and Estonian Academies), in which

▼ The world's first assembly-line operating theater was installed at the Moscow Institute of Eye Microsurgery. Each surgeon carries out one part of the complex operation. The system, which is only used for routine operations, has made it possible to perform several hundred operations daily. The institute is directed by Professor S.N. Fyodorov, and has pioneered use of laser technology in microsurgery and made significant advances in curing myopia and removing cataracts. Branches of the Moscow Institute have recently been opened in other Soviet cities. More recent "assembly lines" are being set up in the form of a circle.

► Soviet civil engineers lay a new oil pipeline. Along with space and nuclear energy programs, and the aircraft and defense industries, gas and oil supply is one technology that has received national priority and high visibility in the USSR – in contrast to the financial and political neglect of many other sectors of science and technology. Oil production in the Soviet Union increased at the rate of 20-30 million tonnes a year during the 1950s and 1960s, but has since slowed considerably as recovery has become more difficult. Soviet geologists are now prospecting for oil in the Arctic shelf.

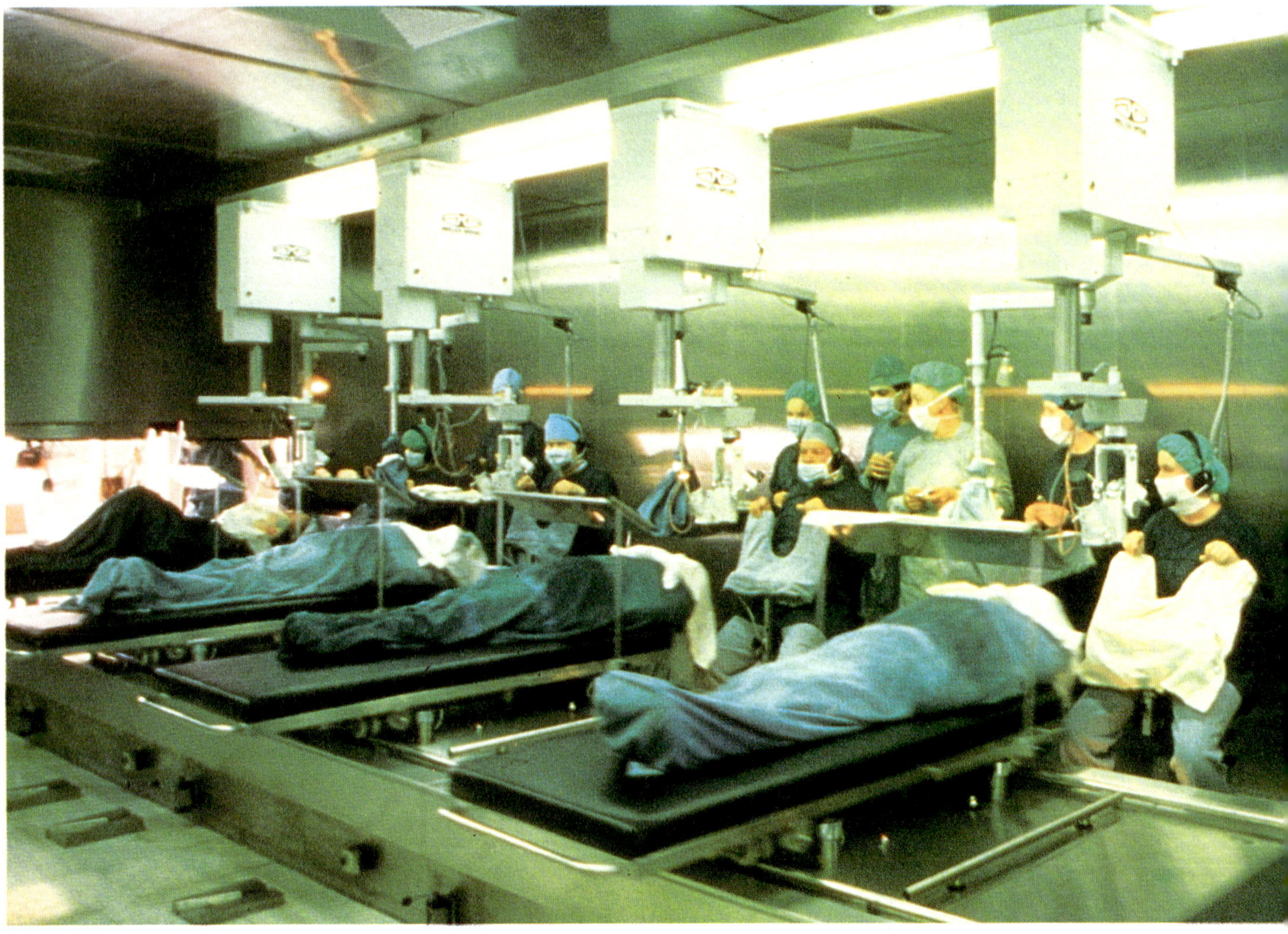

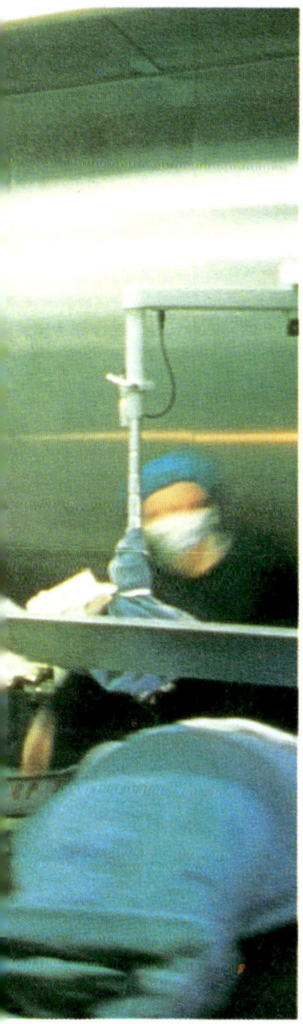

the national language is also accepted as that of research communication, has proved a very costly development. It has served to isolate many such networks from the rest of the world and from each other – indeed, there is more cooperation between the Soviet Academy and the Royal Society in London than between national academies.

Rigid control of applied sciences through bureaucratic systems has also prevented spontaneous and flexible forms of cooperation between the sciences. The requirement that Communist Party leaders confirm every senior research appointment, every assistant and full professorship, and the award of every senior academic degree, together with a significant erosion of incomes in research, education and medical spheres during the last 20-30 years, have significantly reduced the recruitment, and particularly the promotion, of independent and talented individuals. Attempts to accelerate economic development without serious alteration of the whole system of research, which the government pressed hard in 1985 and which were incorporated into the decisions of the 27th Party Congress in February 1986, produced very poor results, including a rise in industrial accidents. One of these, the Chernobyl nuclear plant accident in April 1986, was a turning point in relations between the political system and science.

In 1986 and 1987 at least ten separate decrees of the Communist Party Central Committee and the Council of Ministers tried to reform the system of higher education, science and technology. There was a modest increase in the incomes of graduate students and junior scientists. The government has introduced more differentials into research positions, relaxed requirements for academic degrees in senior academic appointments, introduced a compulsory retirement age in academies, and tried to provide economic and other incentives for innovations. The arrangements for travel within the Comecon block (Hungary, Poland, Bulgaria and other Eastern European countries) were simplified. Several hundred "problem commissions" and "science-technical complexes" were created to overcome the restrictions of separate networks and unite scientists from specialized and national academies, universities, ministerial networks, etc. Dozens of "non-productive" research institutes were closed down.

However, the new measures are clearly intended to integrate Soviet science only with East European allies and a few "friendly" developing countries such as Vietnam and India. All scientific and personal contacts with the Western industrial countries and Japan are still restricted. The Soviet government does not allow Soviet students any form of graduation or postdoctoral work abroad. Foreign academic degrees are not recognized as valid inside Soviet scientific establishments and there are no positions in Soviet research or educational establishments for temporary or long-term appointments for foreign scientists or lecturers. All social sciences must still conform to strict ideological principles of Marxism-Leninism and all works of science are still subject to censorship. Salaries of research scientists of junior rank (even with PhD or MD degrees) are still below the level of pay for qualified industrial workers.

In general the Soviet Union can claim a lead in two contrasting areas, those which do not need any sophisticated equipment, such as pure mathematics and mathematical physics, and those that need large-scale and expensive installations which most smaller countries cannot afford (space projects, high-energy physics, astronomy). But it is lagging well behind the West and Japan in consumer-oriented technologies and the relevant research and development.

▼ The world's largest optical telescope is the USSR Academy of Sciences' 6m reflector, sited at some 2,000m in the north Caucasus mountains near the village of Zelenchukskaya. Construction and test-assembly of the 850-tonne instrument took place at Leningrad, where a special furnace was needed to melt the glass, which took two years to cool. The telescope, which has a tube some 25m in length, is used to study such faint objects as nebulae and galaxies. Astronomy receives generous support from the Soviet government because it plays an important role in the USSR's prestigious space research program.

See also
Paymasters 21-40
Global Change 93-108

Do scientists accept dogma?

The church that puts forth dogma may claim divine revelation. State authority and patronage may be used to guide expression of scientific thinking (and certainly its application) along acceptable pathways. At certain times when scientific ideas are being questioned, the motives of defenders of the old ideas may be frankly religious or political. For example, perhaps the most vehement opponents of Einstein's general theory of relativity were German scientists who believed that this was part of a wider Jewish conspiracy to subvert accepted ideas. They defended a scientific orthodoxy that was fast losing its attraction among scientists and public alike, by reference to a superior "German" science. But the essence of scientific method is precisely to question and test scientific ideas. Scientists can be uncomfortable people to live with, for they constantly challenge dearly-held beliefs. The picture of the skeptical scientist is accepted in many descriptions of how science works – for example, that developed in detail by Sir Karl Popper. In his view, the progress of science depends on the constant questioning of received knowledge, whether it is new or old.

However, a quite different picture of how science operates was drawn by T.S. Kuhn a quarter of a century ago. He believed that science develops by a repetition of two successive stages – normal science and revolutionary science. Normal science, as its name implies, is the way scientists work for most of the time. They accept a particular view of the world – called a "paradigm" by Kuhn – and use it to decide what questions they are prepared to ask, and what sort of answers they will accept. Then, for various reasons (for example, new and unexpected observations), the old paradigm may come to be questioned, and science enters a period of revolutionary change. This ends when a new paradigm receives general assent, and the scientific community settles down again to a new phase of normal science.

The great difference between Popper and Kuhn lies in the latter's concept of normal science, in which the basic framework of science is accepted without much questioning. In fact, Kuhn has referred to working within a paradigm as equivalent to accepting a scientific dogma.

Few, if any, scientists would go so far, though most would agree that their work is not always intended to challenge basic scientific beliefs. Still, they would see scientific knowledge as differing from other types of knowledge, not least in the level of agreement that can be reached within the scientific community. Scientific beliefs, they would say, cannot legitimately be called dogmas, since scientists can, and usually do, change their views in the light of new knowledge. Yet it is true that scientists who have worked for much of their life within a particular paradigm need a good deal of convincing before they will change to a new one.

▼ In "A Philosopher Giving a Lecture on the Orrery", painted in 1766, the English artist Joseph Wright of Derby not only helped to pioneer new ground in exploiting artificial light, but also used it to emphasize the excitement of the age when Ptolemaic thought was being superseded by Copernican ideas. In Kuhnian terms, "normal" science was giving way to revolution.

Nuclear Power and Radiation

4

A "Faustian bargain"...Safety and the public right to know...The future of irradiation of foods...The energy-efficient use of resources...PERSPECTIVE...The perception of risk...The Chernobyl accident curtails nuclear power programs

Together with genetic manipulation (➧ page 65), nuclear power is the major technological issue that is now thrashed out in the public arena. At the heart of this debate is what Dr Alvin Weinberg, when director of Oak Ridge National Laboratory, Tennessee, described as a "Faustian bargain". In exchange for the promise of the luxury of cheap electricity today, we accept the eternal risks associated with potentially highly dangerous ionizing radiation created by atomic reactors. In return for energy from nuclear plants to provide warmth, food and other bodily needs, developed societies generate and accumulate radioactive waste. Because there is a close link between civil and military nuclear programs, both in their inception and today in the provision of plutonium for reprocessing and use in nuclear weapons, many critics add a further comment – that for the sake of our videos, microwave ovens and compact disk players, we are content to live with the threat of nuclear annihilation.

Qualitative risk assessment

A proposal to build a new nuclear power station arouses more public outrage but (the nuclear industry argues) poses considerably smaller hazard to life than does smoking. People's perception of risk may diverge substantially from the risks as measured. In one US survey, respondents overestimated by three times the likelihood of dying by suicide, while underestimating by a factor of 20 the incidence of strokes.

Previous statistical evidence may be available for making precise forecasts, but sometimes only informed guesswork is possible. Thus comparisons of large groups of people, carefully matched for age and other factors, indicate that the average smoker runs 25 times the risk of contracting lung cancer and double the risk of coronorary heart disease, as compared with a nonsmoker. On the other hand, predictions about the chances of being killed in an airplane hijack vary widely: the element of randomness makes it impossible to make reliable actuarial calculations. An important distinction must be made between voluntary and involuntary risks. The chances of a person being killed by driving a car or rock climbing during any one 10-year period in Britain can be computed at one in 600 and one in 700 respectively. Such data allow people to decide whether or not to engage in these activities. But the same individuals also face risks of one in 500 of being killed by influenza and one in a million of being destroyed by lightning.

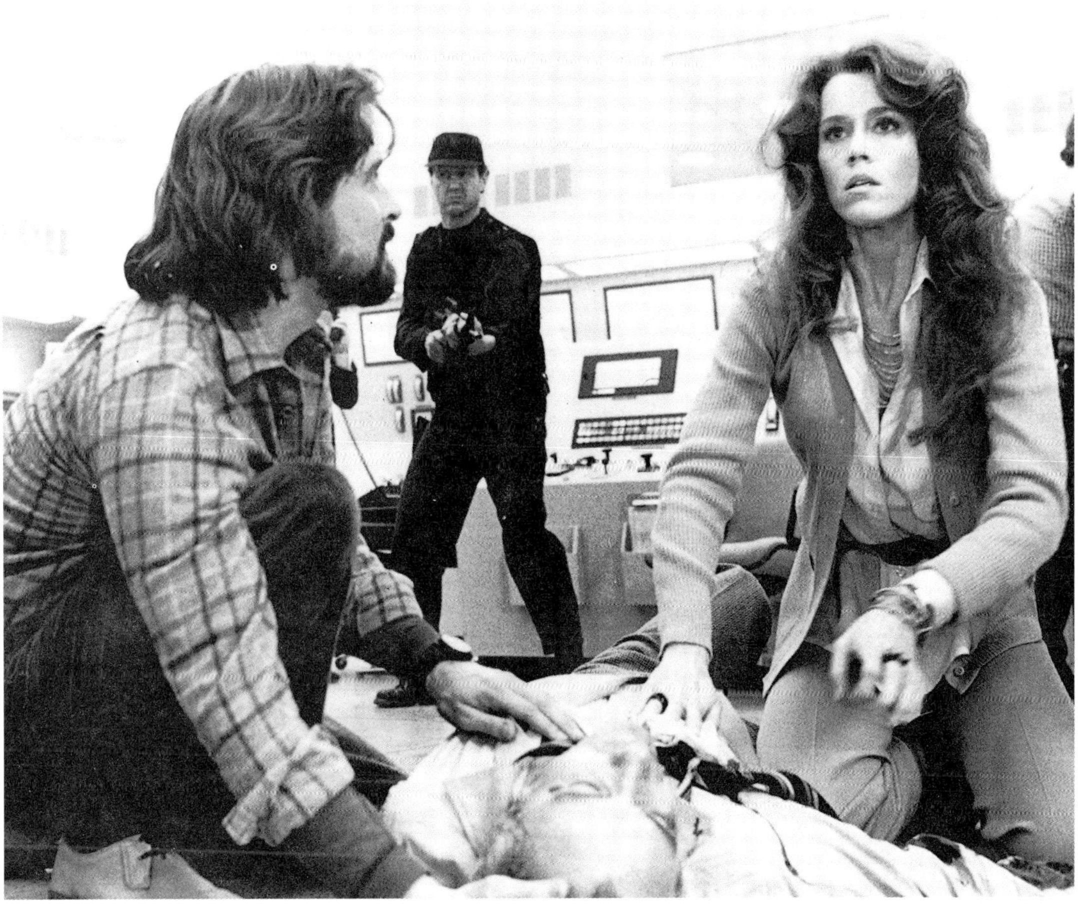

◄ Reporter and cameraman kneel by the body of the power station manager in "China Syndrome", shot because he "blew the whistle". Dramatization of nuclear energy in this movie, and other media, has added an extra dimension – and the grave risk of factual misunderstanding – to an already contentious technology with considerable vested interests.

The fortunes of the nuclear power industry vary greatly from country to country

► Campaigners block the road outside a proposed disposal site for nuclear waste at Elstow, England. Despite assurances that "low level" wastes to be dumped at such locations pose no hazard, many people are unconvinced. An even greater problem is posed by the much more radioactive material from nuclear power stations.

▼ 1979 was a catastrophic year for the nuclear industry's image, especially in the United States. Within two months, the discovery of pipework cracks had led to a shut-down of the country's boiling water reactors, and the movie "The China Syndrome" had portrayed an attempted cover-up of a design flaw jeopardizing the safety of a nuclear power station. Then, at 4.00am on March 28, several water pumps failed in Metropolitan Edison's new nuclear plant at Three Mile Island, near Harrisburg, Pennsylvania, precipitating an incident that saw the core fuel rods and grid spacing (inset) melted down by temperatures up to 2,775K.

The nuclear power debate

While there is no variation across the entire globe in the facts of nuclear fission – the process which nuclear reactors are constructed to exploit – different countries have responded in very different ways to those facts and the associated benefits and drawbacks. Even within one country, attitudes toward nuclear power, as reflected in the press, have altered remarkably quickly. The American media, for example, swung around violently during the early 1960s after a decade during which nuclear power had been invariably portrayed in glowing terms as a clean, limitless alternative to the filth of burning fossil fuels. Reporters who formerly had passed on enthusiastically to their readers every piece of information they received from the Atomic Energy Commission suddenly began to distrust everything they were told and to describe nuclear power in the most alarming and odious terms imaginable.

Contrasts between countries are illustrated by some comments made by Alvin Weinberg during a Ciba Foundation symposium in London in 1971. Discussing one of the possible outcomes when a technical issue such as nuclear reactor design is thrashed out in public, he said: "There develops an escalation of contingency: each unlikely event connected with a reactor, once it becomes a matter of public discussion, seems to acquire a plausibility that goes much beyond what was originally intended. In consequence, reactors now, at least in the United States, are loaded down with safety system after safety system – the safety and emergency systems dominate the whole technology."

But Weinberg – despite being on the receiving end of much anti-nuclear propaganda, as a consequence of his senior position in his country's nuclear establishment, did not complain about what had happened. He went out of his way to contrast the American situation with that in the Soviet Union where, "reactors, until recently, had no containment shells, no emergency core cooling systems, no pressure suppression systems. The Soviet engineers insist that the primary systems are built so ruggedly that a catastrophic accident of the sort American designs are intended to deal with is entirely incredible. There was here a sharp divergence between the American and Soviet view of how safe is safe enough. One cannot attribute these differences simply to the existence of the very influential Advisory Committee on Reactor Safety in the United States, since review mechanisms exist in the Soviet Union. I would rather attribute the contrast to the difference in the degree of access of the public to technological debate."

Later in his talk Weinberg emphasized that, "in a democratic society, the public's right of access to the debate is as great as the public demands it to be." Public opinion is, of course, also affected by the vigor and skill with which governments pursue their technological obejctives.

Leading the way in its determination to exploit civil nuclear power to the full is France, which generates about 70 percent of its electricity from over 40 reactors and has another 17 under construction. One opinion poll indicated a slight increase in public apprehension following the Chernobyl nuclear accident in 1986 (➧ page 60). But although that accident claimed 31 dead and sent a radioactive cloud across much of western Europe, it did not significantly dent the confidence of either the French government or the French public toward nuclear energy.

▲ "An enriched uranium fuel rod contains as much power as 78 tonnes of coal", runs the text accompanying this image in a recent publicity leaflet from the United Kingdom Atomic Energy Authority (UKAEA). Many countries have made the decision to curtail or discontinue their programs of nuclear power station construction, while in Britain the nuclear power debate is a lively one, with the industry spending increasing amounts to woo the public. In France, however, the aftermath of Chernobyl barely dented the public's confidence in nuclear power, in a country where over 70 percent of electricity comes from nuclear power plants.

Chernobyl – The Political Fallout

In the United States, against a background of considerable opposition to nuclear power mobilized by lobby groups such as Friends of the Earth, the nuclear program has been severely retarded in recent years, in marked contrast with the situation in France (♦ page 58). The most conspicuous causes, which have profoundly influenced the public and the politicians, are the Three Mile Island accident which occurred early in 1979 together with the premiere of the movie "The China Syndrome" shortly afterward, and the more recent and much more serious Chernobyl tragedy.

Between the two extremes of France and the United States, debate about the future of energy supplies in most other countries had been deeply influenced by what happened at Chernobyl, just north of Kiev in the Ukraine on April 26, 1986, when a severe explosion occurred in one of the four reactors. In West Germany, where opposition to nuclear power had been substantial and growing for several years, that accident put question marks against the nine plants which were at the planning stage in 1986 and due to join the 20 already operating and five under construction. Shortly after the Chernobyl accident, the opposition Social Democratic Party approved a plan to phase out nuclear power over ten years.

In Britain too, the Labour opposition committed itself to phasing out this source of energy. The lobby group Greenpeace argued that this was inadequate and that this goal could and should be achieved within four years of a Labour government being returned to power.

The Swiss government announced a "de facto moratorium" on three proposed new plants, and the country's second largest party, the Social Democrats, came out in favor of the gradual elimination of nuclear power. Austria's sole nuclear power station, which had never been operated because of an antinuclear referendum in 1978, seemed likely to be dismantled. The Dutch government scrapped plans for two new reactors, while Finland shelved plans for its fifth reactor, probably permanently. In Sweden, a national referendum in 1980 voted to eliminate nuclear power by the year 2010. This move had been increasingly questioned as impracticable, but events at Chernobyl catalyzed a renewed commitment to see it through.

There is another consequence, which provides a further illustration of the delicate interplay between science and technology. Several countries have now begun to look again at the concept of an "inherently safe" reactor – one which simply could not malfunction. Such a design does seem feasible, but its perfection will depend to a large extent upon the work of physicists – scientists – rather than the engineers whose efforts have formerly been so important in the creation of emergency safety systems.

►* *The Chernobyl plant, showing structural damage, photographed from a helicopter on April 30, 1986, four days after the worst incident ever to occur at a nuclear power plant. Although the immediate local effects and more distant repercussions of the released radiation have been well documented, it will be several years before scientists can provide a comprehensive view of the effects on the biosphere.

▼► A radioactivity check at a market garden in France, and the dumping of fresh vegetables in Milan during a two-week ban on consumption, were just two immediate reactions to the 1986 Chernobyl nuclear accident.

Radioactive fallout from Chernobyl

► In the days following the explosion on April 26, 1986, a radioactive cloud wafted across Europe. An accurate pattern of the contamination it produced has been obtained from a computer model drawing upon detailed meteorological data, including pressure and precipitation. This map gives the changing distribution of iodine-131 deposition over the period. "Wet deposition" of this and other fission products occurred wherever it rained.

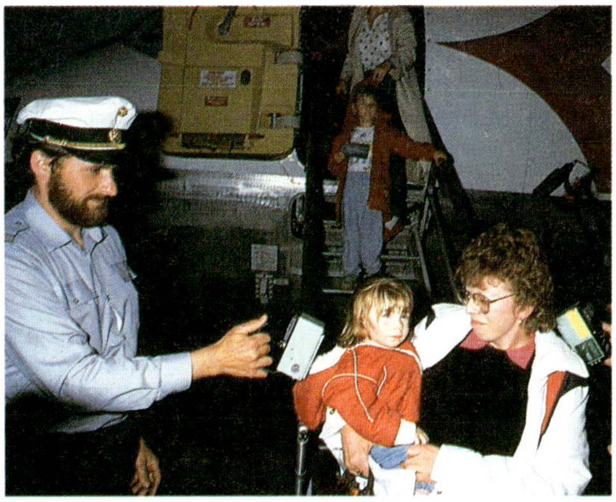

◄ *Monitoring passengers from the Soviet Union for radioactivity as they arrive in Austria a few days after the Chernobyl incident in April 1986.*

◄ *A massive clean-up and evacuation operation, involving police, military and civil authorities was instituted in the wake of the explosion. Although the Soviet government was heavily criticized at first, for a lethargic reaction to the incident and for failing to give adequate information to other countries, the USSR later provided comprehensive data and facilities for inspection by overseas scientists.*

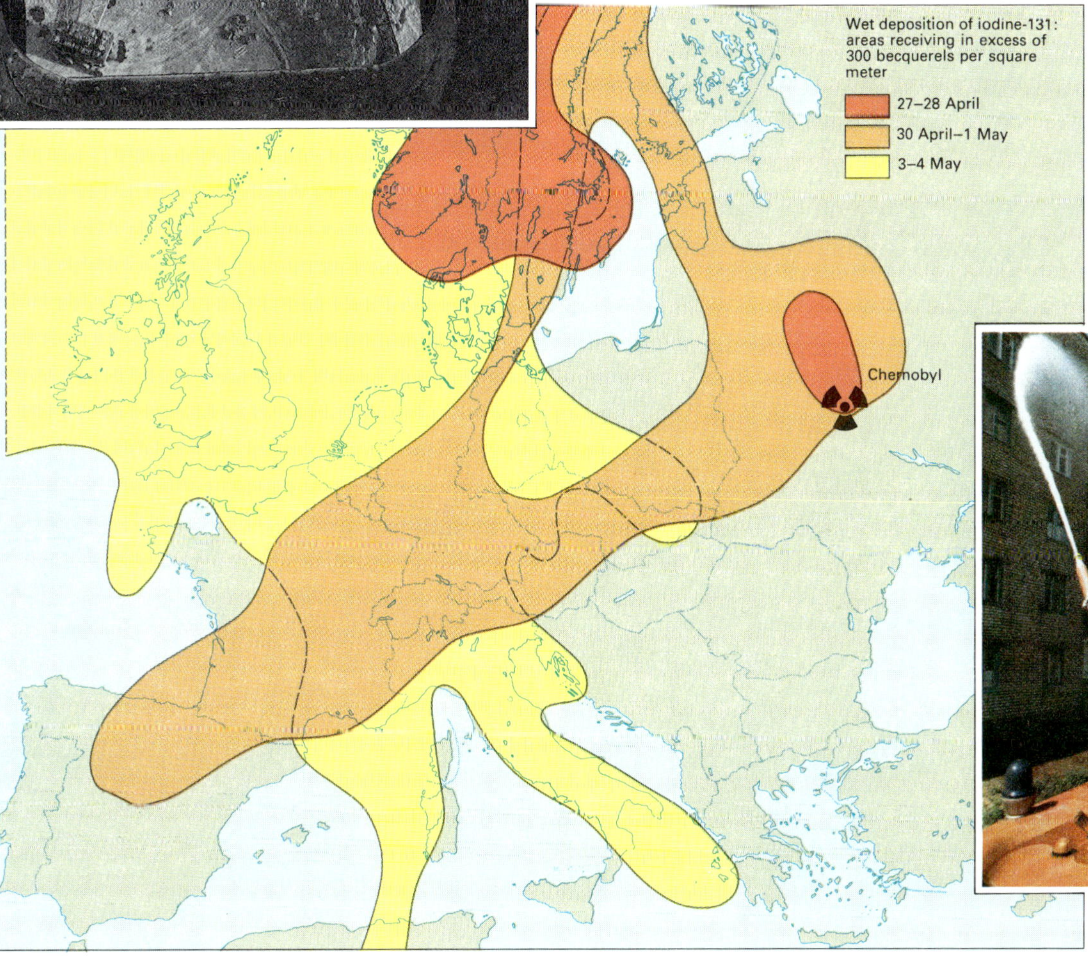

▼ *Washing down apartments near Chernobyl, to remove radioactive dust which was released by the explosion and which posed a threat not only to humans who were to return home but to all animal and plant life.*

Irradiated foods

Sometimes, different pressing public concerns about the applications of science and technology themselves conflict with each other. For example, outright demands for an overnight ban on the use of animals to screen new pharmaceuticals for side-effects contradict the simultaneous demand that all such drugs should be totally safe. A rather more subtle clash of interests came to light in May, 1986, when microbiologists gathered in Berlin to attend the 2nd World Congress on Foodborne Infections and Intoxications. A major theme of that event was the apparently inexorable rise that was occurring in most European countries in food poisoning caused by various species of *Salmonella* and other bacteria. Despite moves such as the compulsory pasteurization of milk, and improved hygiene training for catering personnel, the amount of foodborne gastroenteritis was growing more formidable each year. Evidence from the Central Public Health Laboratory in London indicated that two particular developments required urgent attention. One was a growth in the number of sporadic, individual infections caused at home by crosscontamination of foods from chickens and other uncooked meats. The second was an increase in the number of cases per outbreak that was apparent in mass catering – in restaurants, canteens, hotels and hospitals.

One solution to the frustrating problem of foodborne infection is to sterilize chickens and similar high-risk items by exposing them to ionizing radiation. Much older techniques are already widely practiced – from refrigeration to curb the multiplication of microbes to various sorts of sterilization that obliterate them completely from canned meats and other foods. But the organizers of the Berlin congress had chosen to focus on the unusually convenient and inexpensive technique of irradition. They hoped to encourage countries then undecided about the new technology to embrace it and thereby combat more effectively the rising tide of bacterial food poisoning.

Among many groups scheduled to discuss food irradiation was a team from the Soreq Nuclear Research Center in Yavane, Israel. "From the public health point of view, pasteurization of chickens by irradiation offers a unique method of disinfecting them of pathogens and extending their shelf life, without significantly impairing eating quality," wrote Dr E. Eisenberg and his colleagues, in a paper composed several months before the congress opened. "The effect is achievable at low dose levels, well within the already rigorous safety limits. It is this particular aspect which will no doubt result in the wider use of irradiation." Other participants complemented Dr Eisenberg's sentiments. A contributor from Agriculture Canada in Ontario wrote with pride about his country's world lead in nuclear technology and about plans to promote the "excellent promise" of food irradiation. He was echoed by another bacteriologist, from the Communicable Diseases Unit at the Ruchill Hospital in Glasgow, who extolled the advantages of irradiation in ridding chicken carcases of the contamination inevitable even in the most punctilious intensive units. "Hopefully," he wrote, "legislation to permit such treatment of food will be introduced in the United Kingdom in the near future, and will provide a safeguard for poultry meat."

But all of those words were composed *before* April 26, 1986, date of the world's worst nuclear accident. By the time participants gathered in Berlin a few weeks later, it had become clear that attitudes toward nuclear power, radiation and radioactivity – even among formerly uncommitted members of the public – had been drastically affected.

▼ A Soviet cosmonaut enjoys his irradiated food. During the late 1950s, the USSR pioneered the preservation of food by gamma radiation. Initially used to prevent tubers from sprouting, it later proved to be a cheap and efficient method of destroying microbes responsible for food poisoning and those that cause spoilage too.

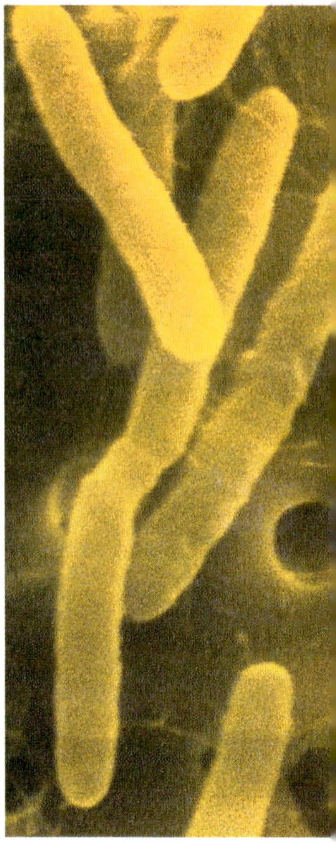

▲ Salmonella food poisoning, caused when the bacteria are consumed in contaminated food or water, has been increasing in most countries in recent years for reasons ranging from poor hygiene in mass catering establishments to meat contamination by feces in abattoirs. There are many different species of Salmonella, like the one seen here in a false-color scanning electron micrograph. Several of them, such as Salmonella typhimurium, are transmissible between humans and other animals, but all are vulnerable to radiation.

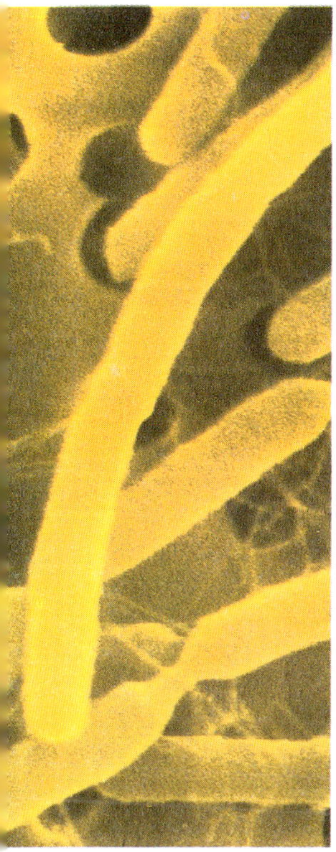

As a result, several congress speakers set aside their printed papers and argued instead that food irradiation was no longer a serious option to be considering at all in the immediate future. The public and regulatory authorities simply would not accept the implied dangers of food irradiation, despite its potential advantages. One speaker even suggested that the technique would never again be on the agenda for discussion as a viable possibility.

Some participants dismissed these sentiments as overreactions. They pointed out that there was no meaningful connection between the Chernobyl reactor tragedy and the exposure of foodstuffs to ionizing radiation – that the technique was already being employed with great benefit and total safety in several countries around the world. They insisted too that the blame for western public disquiet after the incident should be placed squarely on the Soviet authorities for their delays in providing information about what had happened until several days afterward.

Even before the Chernobyl accident, however, food irradiation had been a highly sensitive issue, because words such as "radiation", "nuclear" and "radioactivity" have wholly harmful connotations for many people. *After* Chernobyl, even people whose doubts had been just marginal felt that their apprehensions had been vindicated. And organized opposition, in the form of lobby groups against nuclear power in any form whatever, had also grown immeasurably stronger (◀ page 60).

▼ A technician at the Lawrence Livermore National Laboratory, California, maneuvers a cylinder of strawberries into a pool containing a 2 million electron volt accelerator, which will irradiate the fruit with X-rays. The water acts as a barrier to insulate the operator from exposure to radiation. Strawberries which have been irradiated (compared here with non-irradiated fruit of the same age) are protected from the growth of molds and other organisms that cause spoilage and deterioration.

See also
Social relations 5-20
Paymasters 21-40
Global Change 93-108
Futurology 109-124

After nuclear power?

The Chernobyl disaster, which led many European governments to think again about the desirability of nuclear power, came at a time when the nuclear power industry was already running down. Since the mid-1970s, orders for new commercial reactors, apart from in France, have almost ceased. The emphasis has instead been on energy efficiency, itself one of the cheapest and most reliable "sources" of new energy. Many nations improved energy efficiency steadily, to such an extent that despite economic growth, the industrialized world consumed about one percent less energy in 1985 than in 1980. More efficient new heaters, irrigation systems and other energy-using devices consume one-third to one-half the energy of earlier devices, while new thermally-tight buildings designed in Sweden and the United States use 90 percent less heat than traditional buildings.

Efficient energy is thus a priority for mission-oriented scientific research. Current advances in superconductor science (♦ page 28) promise to come up with materials that conduct electricity with minimal resistance at room temperature. Other efforts concentrate on ways of limiting the wastefulness of power stations themselves. Studies have been made of different forms of large-scale generation, whether coal-, oil- or nuclear-powered, which avoid the turbine altogether. In a procedure known as magnetohydrodynamic generation (MHD) an electric current is created by passing high temperature ionized gas through a magnetic field. The basics of the technique were understood as early as the end of last century, but it took rocket technology to provide containers for gases heated to as high as 3,500K and flowing at about the speed of sound. The improvements in superconducting materials and the better magnets they offer are expected to give MHD another boost. When the hot gases of an MHD system, powered perhaps by natural gas, are hooked up to a conventional steam turbine and generator, then the overall efficiency of converting heat into electricity is raised from 35 to about 50 percent and the cost of generating electricity reduced by 10 percent. Furthermore, MHD systems almost completely eliminate sulfur emissions and cut the nitric oxides and carbon dioxide in exhaust gases by 20 to 30 percent. The Soviet Union expected to commission a 270 megawatt MHD system connected to a 312 megawatt conventional steam turbine generator by the end of the 1980s, and Israeli scientists are working on lower temperature MHD systems which use liquid metals as the fluid conductor.

▲ "Clean" energy, safely produced, for the future? The Southern California Edison Company's Cool Water Demonstration Plant converts coal into a clean-burning gas whose combustion products power a gas-turbine generator. A steam-turbine generator is also driven by the steam produced from the otherwise wasted heat in the exhaust from the gas turbine. Such non-nuclear processes could become increasingly important.

Nuclear reactors – commercial orders

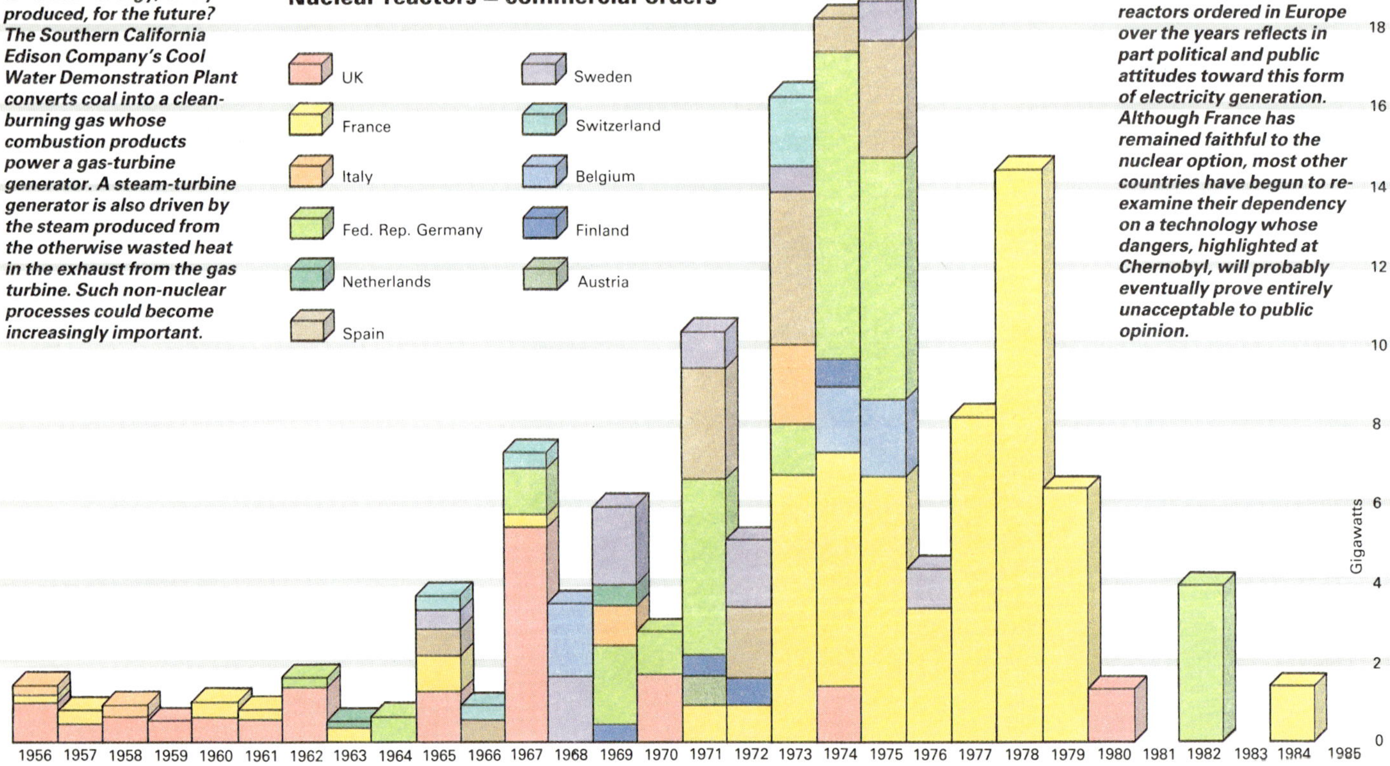

◄▼ The number of nuclear reactors ordered in Europe over the years reflects in part political and public attitudes toward this form of electricity generation. Although France has remained faithful to the nuclear option, most other countries have begun to re-examine their dependency on a technology whose dangers, highlighted at Chernobyl, will probably eventually prove entirely unacceptable to public opinion.

Genetic Engineering

5

Artificial microbes and plants...Gene splicing and the anxieties it arouses....Releasing engineered organisms ...The history of species manipulation...How might transferred genes behave? Testing and monitoring... PERSPECTIVE...Recent developments in plant engineering...The Philadelphia conference...The history of a food plant...The regulation of products of genetic engineering

However fierce the disputations, internal and external, of science in the past, the last two decades have witnessed altogether new trends in public concern about science and technology. Much of this furore has centered upon hazards allegedly created by technical developments. Among the questions asked have been, how can we realistically estimate those risks, and how can society best respond? Partly in response to these concerns, quantitative "risk assessment" (◀ page 57) has now become central to exercises as disparate as the design and siting of a new power station, the launch of a pharmaceutical product, and the introduction of a novel technique for controlling agricultural pests.

One of the most sensitive issues of this sort is the question of whether artificially contrived microbes and plants, produced by genetic engineering, should be released into the environment. The issue began to gather political momentum in the United States during the mid 1980s, centered upon suggestions that feckless scientists wished to create organisms capable of doing irreversible damage to crops, animals and the planet's delicate ecology. A fierce public debate ensued, with, at the opposite pole of opinion, those researchers who represented what they saw as ill-informed obstruction to advances which had far-reaching practical (and financial) potential.

Breakthrough in genetic engineering of plants

Conventional crop-breeding involves first seeking out a gene wanted for, say, disease resistance in a wild variety of crop plant and then crossing this wild variety with the cultivated plant. Many generations of the hybrid then have to be grown to breed out all the unwanted characteristics of the wild variety absorbed along with the one wanted gene. Genetic engineering, by contrast, allows breeders to take a wanted gene from any living organism – plant, bacterium, animal or even human – and to insert this directly into a crop plant.

It has proved more difficult to transfer genes into crop plants than into bacteria. In particular, it has proved very difficult to find a way to introduce foreign genes into the Class of plants known as monocotyledons, to which almost all important crops, such as rice, wheat and corn belong. In 1986-1987, however, the crucial advances to make this possible were achieved. Researchers in West Germany injected solutions of genes into young buds growing on corn plants, the buds which later form flowers. Then, when the flowers formed, plants which had been treated in this way were cross-fertilized by each other. The hope was that, in some of the plants at least, the injected DNA would find its way into the reproductive cells, the pollen and the ova (egg cells) of the flowers, and thus into future generations. In just one or two of more than 3,000 plants treated in this way, this proved to have happened. Clearly the success rate needs to be improved, but the technology needed to introduce new genes into corn, and so by implication into rice, wheat or barley, now exists.

Reporting their findings in 1987, Belgian scientists have shown that crop plants can be made resistant to insect pests by implanting new genes.

◀ Activists representing the "People's Business Commission" protest against commercial sponsorships of genetic engineering work during a recombinant DNA forum held in Washington DC in 1977 by the US National Academy of Sciences. Such demonstrations were common following the advent of gene splicing in the early 1970s, but waned when many fears voiced at the time proved groundless. There were renewed protests during the mid 1980s, when scientists began to argue the benefits of releasing genetically engineered organisms into the environment, and particularly following the April 1987 decision in the United States that animals can now be patented.

The undreamed-of possibilities suggested by genetic engineering range from life-saving treatments to biological weaponry

Early controversy over genetic engineering

Controversy over the release of genetically engineered organisms began in the 1970s, when scientists first discovered the technique of "gene splicing" (➧ page 72). This is a method of taking a piece of DNA from one living organism and inserting it, and thus the capacity for the characteristics coded by the DNA, into another organism. Gene splicing suggested hitherto unimagined possibilities, such as the transfer of the human insulin gene into bacteria, which could then be grown in bulk to make a hormone better suited to long-term use by diabetics than the pig insulin that was used previously. Such a product has since been developed and is available commercially. Among numerous other substances now being made in this way are tumor necrosis factor and interferon for cancer therapy, and human growth hormone for treating children of unusually short stature.

However, because the new science of genetic engineering seemed to break natural barriers, facilitating hybridizations that would never occur in nature, some scientists considered it potentially risky. Postulated hazards ranged from the accidental creation of cancer-causing bacteria, to the deliberate production of particularly virulent weapons of bacteriological warfare. It was decided

▲ In 1974 Stanford University biologist Paul Berg and colleagues proposed a temporary moratorium on certain types of gene-splicing experiment until the possible hazards posed by "recombinant" organisms had been fully assessed.

► Preparing chemicals for use in a diagnostic capacity in recombinant DNA research. By the 1980s, greater reassurance about the safety of genetic engineering meant that professional and public disquiet had died down. Controversy now centered elsewhere, for example on the long-term project of American Nobel chemistry laureate Walter Gilbert and his private Boston-based corporation, to decode the human genome – every one of our genes – and then copyright the findings.

◄ *After growing inadequately for the first nine years of her life, Tracy Moreno of Burson, California, was given injections of human growth hormone. During the following year she put on 13cm in height – a spurt in growth attributed to the hormone, which had been produced by E. coli bacteria carrying the appropriate gene. This is far safer than using hormone extracted from cadavers.*

▼ *In a cold room at Bethesda Research Laboratories, Maryland, a technician prepares vials of restriction endonucleases. These enzymes act as "biological scissors" to snip out desired genes from long DNA sequences for splicing into the DNA of other organisms. Now used in biotechnology, the enzymes were unknown before discovery of the ability of bacteria to repair their own DNA.*

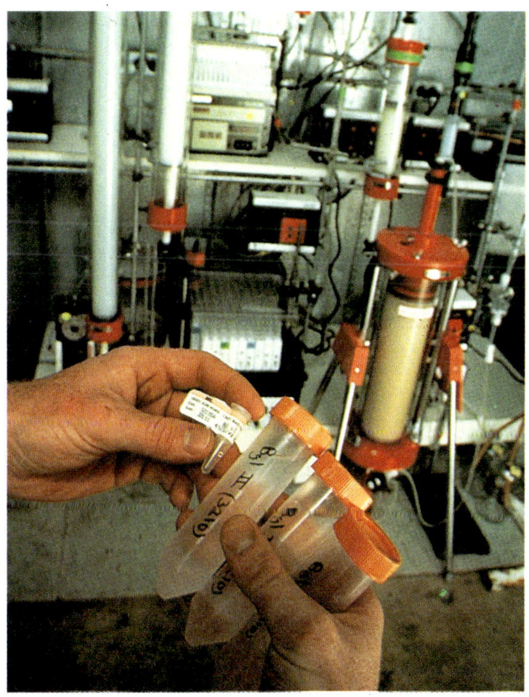

to draw international attention to the possibility that microbes carrying so-called recombinant DNA might prove dangerous to humans or other living things. The first steps were taken by two scientists who spoke at a Gordon Conference in New Hampshire in June 1973 and wrote afterward to the journal "Science" and to the president of the United States National Academy of Sciences, to ventilate their anxieties. The latter approach led to the publication of a further letter by Stanford University biologist Paul Berg and colleagues suggesting a temporary moratorium on certain types of experiment until their possibly adverse consequences could be assessed.

In February 1975, there was a major international meeting at the Asilomar Conference Center, Pacific Grove, California, at which further restraints were debated vigorously but agreed. The outcome of these deliberations was the establishment of formal guidelines for recombinant DNA work by bodies such as the United States National Institutes of Health and what is now the Advisory Committee on Genetic Manipulation in Britain.

These regulations governed the containment of organisms and experiments inside facilities, graded according to the supposed degree of risk, from which the organisms could not escape. The NIH rules were followed in many other parts of the world. Some countries, however, took a more leisurely view of the supposed dangers. Several of those in Europe never got around to drawing up their own regulations.

Furthermore, in practice, none of the postulated dangers materialized. This allowed the NIH and other committees to successfully relax their guidelines. By the early 1980s, growing reassurance about the safety of genetic engineering meant that the initial professional disquiet, and its consequent political and public clamor, had died down too.

Releasing engineered organisms: uses and dangers

The proposal to release engineered organisms outside the laboratory provoked considerable furore. Much of this focused initially on work by scientists at the University of California, Berkeley. Researchers there wanted to know why plant tissues sometimes, but not always, fail to freeze when chilled well below their nominal freezing point. They found that the key factor was the presence or absence on leaf surfaces of a bacterium, cells of which provide "nucleation cells" for the formation of ice crystals. If that particular bacterium is present, ice forms: if not, the temperature can fall past the nominal freezing point without this happening. This suggested a stratagem for preventing at least some of the vast amount of frost damage caused to crops every year. The researchers therefore set out to identify the particular substance in the bacterium, *Pseudomonas syringae*, that triggers ice nucleation. They then located the gene responsible for this substance and deleted it by genetic manipulation. Finally, they sprayed the altered bacteria onto plants in the hope that they would compete with and replace the natural varieties. It worked. "Ice-minus" bacteria prevented frost damage in greenhouse tests, and the researchers then wished to proceed with larger scale trials in the open air. But a sequence of legal actions by activist Jeremy Rifkin (◆ page 65) and his Foundation on Economic Trends prevented them from doing so.

▲ ***One potentially highly rewarding application of genetic engineering, developed by Steve Lindow at the University of California, Berkeley, is in preventing frost damage to crops. It is based on the discovery that bacteria act as nucleation centers for ice crystals to form on the surface of plant leaves, and that the gene responsible for this effect can be deleted to yield "ice-minus" strains. Here Dr Lindow shows green corn plants which wilted when they thawed after being frozen, beside undamaged plants protected by being sprayed with "ice-minus" bacteria.***

► ***In May 1987 Jeremy Rifkin, pictured here at the Royal Society of Arts in London, toured Europe in an attempt to catalyze political efforts to thwart applications of genetic engineering such as the environmental release of modified microbes and plants. In the United States, his Foundation on Economic Trends had been successful in securing successive legal injunctions over three years to delay experiments such as the spraying of potato plants with "ice-minus" bacteria – a project that finally went ahead in April 1987 in Oakland, California.***

Another candidate for release into the environment was a novel pesticide developed by researchers at Monsanto Agricultural Products. Their starting point was *Bacillus thuringiensis*, a bacterium which attacks gypsy moth and many other caterpillars that destroy important agricultural crops. Farmers have been using commercial preparations of the bacillus for over 20 years to protect plants such as cabbage, cotton, beans and potatoes. Much safer than chemical control, this form of biological control has no effect on animals and plants other than the target insect species at which it is directed. Furthermore, the organism does not persist in the environment. But this advantage is coupled with the disadvantage that crops must be sprayed repeatedly.

► ***The pine beauty moth caterpillar is responsible for considerable damage every year in pine plantations. Like the gypsy moth and other pests, the pine beauty moth is vulnerable to attack by the bacterium Bacillus thuringiensis, which has been used for over 20 years to protect plants as diverse as cabbage, cotton, beans and potatoes. The safety of this "biological insecticide" and its failure to produce harmful environmental effects, encourage biologists to believe that genetically altered microbes will prove to be harmless too when used in the environment.***

What the Monsanto workers set out to achieve was to transfer the gene responsible for the organisms' toxicity into *Pseudomonas fluorescens*, a harmless bacterium which tends to colonize plant roots. Applied to seeds or soil at the time of planting, the engineered organism could thus provide long-term protection against soil-borne pests. But again, having demonstrated that the engineered organism was an effective pesticide in the laboratory, the company's researchers ran into opposition. Protests and legal actions delayed further work with the bacterium in the open air. Some scientists too have been cautious about the potential safety of releasing engineered organisms in the environment. It is unrealistic to expect to be able to "recall" them in their entirety should anything go awry. Even with plants, destroyable by fire if they were confined in a plot or a field, one could not be certain that pollen, seeds, or other tissues (and thus the genes they carry) had not been broadcast far from the site of the experiment.

How, then, can we assess the potential dangers in releasing such organisms? At the center of public and professional debate have been four principal answers: by studying previous experience of alien species introduced into new environments, and of organisms produced by conventional breeding techniques; by *a priori* arguments about how particular organisms behave; by preliminary testing in "microcosms" designed to simulate nature; and by monitoring the behavior and movement of organisms *after* release.

The Philadelphia Conference

The hazards of releasing engineered organisms were reviewed at a meeting called by the American Society for Microbiology in Philadelphia in the summer of 1985, attended not only by scientists from different disciplines but also by politicians, press and public interest representatives. Many participants were persuaded that the likely consequences following the release of alien organisms should be analyzed ecologically. A decision whether or not to release "ice-minus" Pseudomonas syringae, for example, ought to be based on wider considerations than its likely effects on particular crops. Entomologists pointed out that the same bacterium may be carried by insects too, making them more or less susceptible to freezing (according to the strain). If the new bacterium were to affect adversely a beneficial insect such as the honeybee the outcome could be devastating.

◄ The US Environmental Protection Agency reprimanded Gary Strobel (left) in August 1987 for inoculating genetically altered bacteria into elm trees without having received the EPA's approval beforehand. The Professor of Plant Pathology at Montana State University, Strobel's aim was to test a modified version of the bacterium Pseudomonas syringae for its ability to combat the fungus Ceratocystis ulni, which causes Dutch elm disease. In a letter to the EPA, Strobel stated that he had carried out similar experiments five years earlier, and had released strains of Rhizobium in 1983, before the issuing of regulations covering experiments of this sort. Given the state of public concern over such work, Strobel was quickly condemned by many of his own colleagues for "jumping the gun".

Millenia of corn breeding have produced no plants capable of causing environmental damage

▸ Although not products of gene splicing, prickly pears illustrate the possible repercussions when alien species are released without careful thought as to how they are likely to behave. Introduced into Australia from Texas and Florida, two species of prickly pear spread widely and rendered millions of hectares of land useless for cattle and sheep. They were eventually controlled by introducing a South American moth that parasitizes the plants.

Species manipulation in the past

Although genetic engineering is new, mankind has a long record of interfering with nature and in particular of introducing foreign species into new environments – long before public debate or disquiet became facts of life for working scientists. The most relevant examples concern pest control. From the very beginning of crop cultivation, humans pulled weeds, picked insects off crops, and encouraged birds and insects that preyed on pests. More recently, as with *Bacillus thuringiensis* (◂ page 68), organisms have been cultivated and consciously released to combat other forms of life which are destructive to crops. Agriculturalists have controlled about 108 different pests by introducing and establishing natural enemies of the nuisance species.

But there have been failures too, and many cases of adverse consequences after particular organisms have been released in new terrain either accidentally or purposely but without adequate thought. When two species of prickly pear were introduced into Australia from Texas and Florida, they spread widely and rendered millions of hectares of land useless for cattle and sheep production. Attempts at biological control using pests from the two original American states failed. Only when agriculturalists imported a particular South American moth were they able to defeat the alien pears.

Some scientists cited other case histories as providing reassuring evidence *against* the possibility of harmful consequences following the release of organisms created by gene splicing. One concerns strains of *Rhizobium*, a bacterium which forms nodules on the roots of leguminous plants and "fixes" nitrogen from the atmosphere into a form in which the legumes can use it. Around the beginning of this century, microbiologists realized that they could encourage nodulation, and thus boost plants' nitrogen supplies, by inoculating seeds with these naturally-occurring microbes. Ever since then, an industry has existed to supply preparations to farmers, although such efforts have been only modestly successful, because in many cases the percentage of nodules formed by introduced rhizobia has been small compared with those produced by existing, often inferior strains. The ecological lesson here is that an organism introduced into a new environment will persist only if it finds a suitable "niche" – a set of favorable environmental conditions to which it is particularly well adapted.

▴ Variety of color and color-pattern in corn cobs hanging up, ready for next year's sowing, in the house of an Andean farmer. Responding to attacks by activists such as Jeremy Rifkin, some researchers cite corn as an example of an invaluable, manmade plant which belies the idea that artificially-contrived organisms are likely to reproduce uncontrollably. Their opponents argue that the structural changes that had made corn dependent upon humans are relatively unusual, and that no overall principles should be based on this experience.

The first crop plant

The history of corn (maize) goes back some 10,000 years. Quite different from its nearest wild relatives, teosinte and tripsacum, corn seems to have been our earliest and most important feat of plant breeding. Whereas teosinte and tripsacum are grasses which produce seed in the tassel at the top of the plant, corn produces its seed on bulky ears growing out of the stalk halfway up. Because it appeared in an evolutionary instant, corn is almost certainly a product of human intervention, based initially on the simple selection of seed for propagation and the intercrossing of odd-looking plants, before the advent of more sophisticated breeding techniques. Corn cannot grow as a weed, and does not occur in the wild, because the kernels are so firmly attached to the ears that they do not fall off. It has no natural dispersal mechanism, therefore, and is entirely dependent on human beings for survival. Even if an ear is left in a field and becomes buried in the soil, the plants are so crowded together when the kernels germinate they generally do not thrive.

There is general agreement that centuries of corn breeding, carried out with gradually increasing understanding, have not yielded plants capable of causing environmental damage. Those keen to proceed with genetic manipulation add that even today conventional plant breeding entails gene transfer far more indiscriminate and uncertain than the precise splicing now possible through recombinant DNA techniques. This gives them further confidence that such maneuvers are unlikely to throw up unpredictably hazardous products.

◄ The nitrogen-fixing bacterium Rhizobium forms nodules on the roots of legumes, here French beans. Rhizobia have long been sold to promote soil fertility, providing evidence against the possibility that released microbes may be dangerous.

▼ Myxomatosis virus was introduced into France in June 1952 to attack an agricultural pest – the rabbit, populations of which were rapidly decimated there and in other European countries. Within a decade, however, resistant strains were emerging.

Gene transfers: studying their behavior

The greater exactitude of recombinant DNA manipulations compared with natural gene transfers is becoming one of the most crucial *a priori* arguments in the public and political debate about the release of engineered organisms into the environment. Enthusiasts claim that the ability to insert desired genes with exquisite precision makes it possible to determine with much more certainty how the organism will behave afterwards. Thus "weediness" in plants – the capacity to outgrow other species, and a significant hypothetical hazard of genetic engineering – is the consequence of several genes working together. It is therefore very unlikely to result from recombinant DNA manipulations. Decades of experience with plants and microbes *before* the advent of gene splicing has also provided a corpus of knowledge upon which to predict how novel combinations of genes are likely to behave, and how an engineered organism will compare with its parents.

A closely related argument centers on the novelty of making recombinant DNA. We now know that genes move "horizontally" in nature – between organisms – as well as being passed vertically from one generation to the next. This makes it impossible to draw a hard-and-fast dividing line, as was done at the time of the Gordon and Asimolar conferences during the early 1970s, between those transfers and allegedly "unnatural" laboratory manipulations. Moreover, at least some recombinant DNA manipulations yield organisms indistinguishable from those that have acquired their new genes in nature. The transfer of antibiotic resistance among bacteria is one example. To this extent, there is nothing unnatural about the new techniques.

Scientists continue to haggle over another possible conclusion – that, given the richness of natural gene flows, and the eons of time which have elapsed since life originated on Earth, evolution has already generated all possible combinations of genes anyway. On this theory, those constellations that have endured are represented by the

▼ Although it appears unchanged, this tobacco plant has been genetically altered by Agrobacterium tumefaciens. The bacterium, carrying additional genetic material (DNA), was added to a disk of leaf from the parent plant, and the new plant was then grown from the transformed tissue. The bag covering the plant ensures self-pollination. The crucial part of A. tumefaciens for genetic engineers is the Ti plasmid – a self-replicating piece of the microbe's DNA, into which a foreign gene can be spliced to give a "recombinant" plasmid. The foreign gene may be expressed when a plant is regenerated following the genetic manipulation.

Gene transfer using a vector

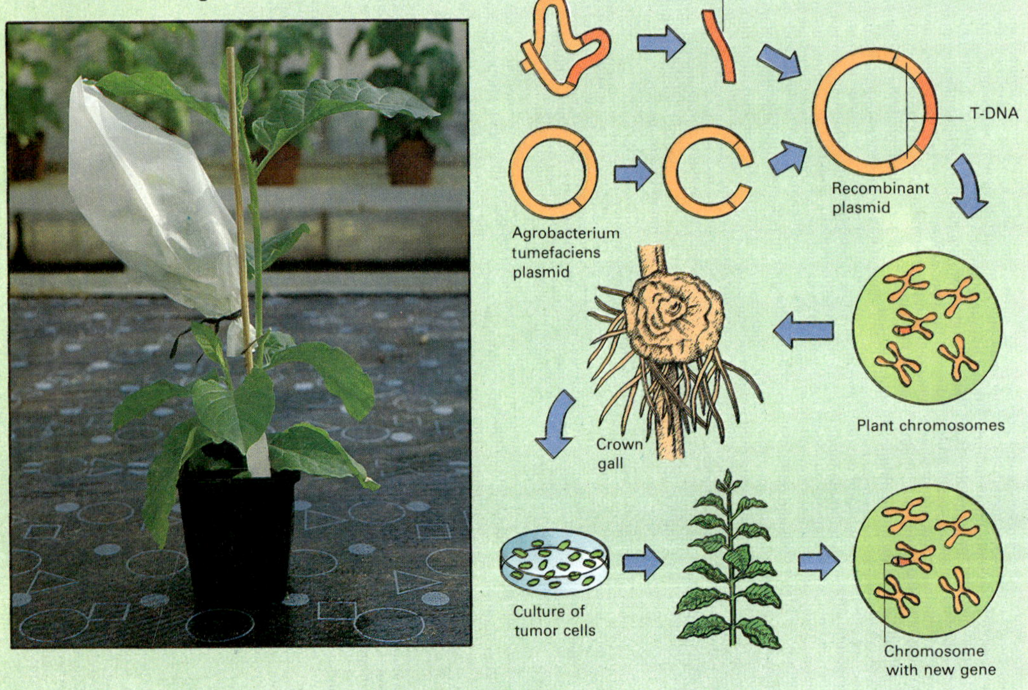

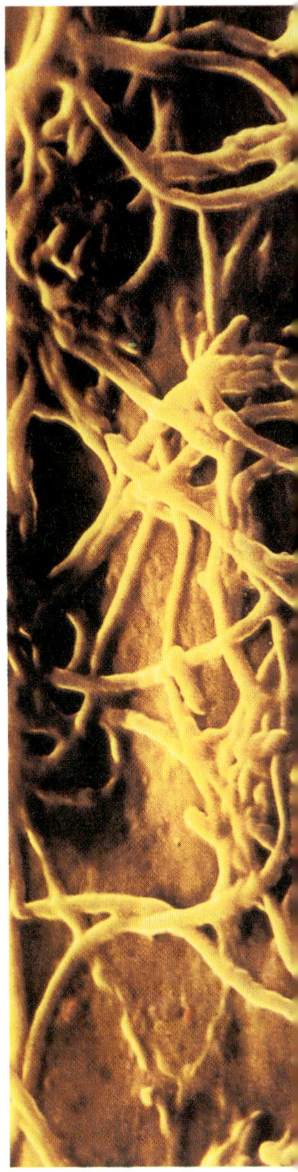

► *An air-filtering device sold at the height of the 1918-1919 influenza pandemic which killed 15-20 million people. Major influenza pandemics follow sudden genetic changes in the structure of the causative virus – as happened in the "Asian flu" and "Hong Kong flu" outbreaks of 1957 and 1968-1969. These rapid changes probably take place because the virus can hybridize with flu strains in other animals. Today, protection against flu is being sought through vaccines of weakened viruses, or genetically engineered ones based on human and bird strains. The difficulty is to ensure that the genetic engineering keeps up with the naturally-occurring genetic changes.*

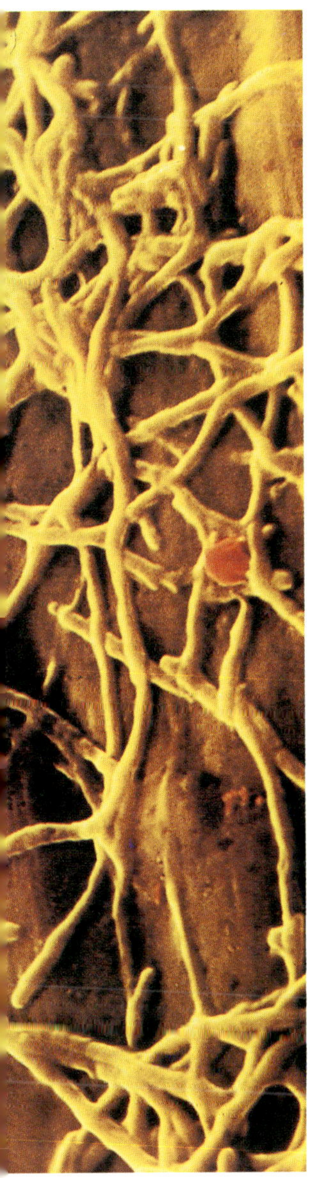

◄ *Legionella pneumophila, seen here in a false-color scanning electron micrograph, was identified as the cause of a form of pneumonia later known as Legionnaire's disease which affected people attending an American Legion convention in Philadelphia in 1976. The organism has since been found in many streams and lakes and is now called an "opportunistic pathogen" because it causes diseases only under certain unusual conditions – when it is inhaled into the lungs in a fine mist. One of the essential properties of genetically altered organisms for release into the environment is that they must not be capable of acting as opportunistic pathogens. Biologists believe that this can be predicted from a knowledge of their biological properties and behavior.*

plants, animals and microbes forming our biosphere today – the vast majority having been eliminated by natural selection.

Perhaps the most valuable *a priori* approach to the problem is to forecast the behavior of an organism by studying its biology. Many species of tropical insects, for example, will become established if introduced into the northern temperate region. A parasite from a humid environment will probably not colonize a highly arid habitat. Bacteria dependent upon particular food substances are certain to fail in an environment lacking those substances. Likewise, careful assessment of an organism's nutritional and other needs will permit confident predictions about those habitats which it *is* likely to colonize.

Ecologists also stress the importance of assessing what may happen to a released organism's genes, as well as to the organism itself. Genes are transferred using "vectors" such as plasmids. Is such a plasmid, carrying a spliced gene, likely to travel farther, entering other strains or species of microbe? Is an introduced plant gene likely to find its way, through pollen, into other plants with which the alien one is sexually compatible? One practical example is a strain of *Agrobacterium radiobacter*, which has been employed with great success in recent years to control crown gall caused by *Agrobacterium tumefaciens*. It works by producing an antibiotic called agrocin. If a plasmid containing the gene responsible for this antibiotic were to be transferred to *A. tumefaciens*, the crown gall bacterium would become immune to the antibiotic and thus be incapable of being controlled as before. Although this has not yet been reported in the field, it does occur in the test tube and is a source of concern to plant pathologists.

So too with an organism such as Monsanto's pesticidal *Pseudomonas fluorescens*. The researchers developing this agent have compiled a comprehensive list of its essential characteristics. The organism must not cause disease in plants or animals, and must (in order to do its job effectively) have a high affinity for plant roots. It should have a strictly limited capacity for genetic exchange, and possibly contain *no* indigenous plasmids. It should be capable of persisting for only a limited period in the environment, and be sensitive to antibiotics – just in case it proves capable of causing an infection. Such criteria do not satisfy Mr Rifkin and other critics, however, because they are opposed *in principle* to the release of engineered organisms of any sort.

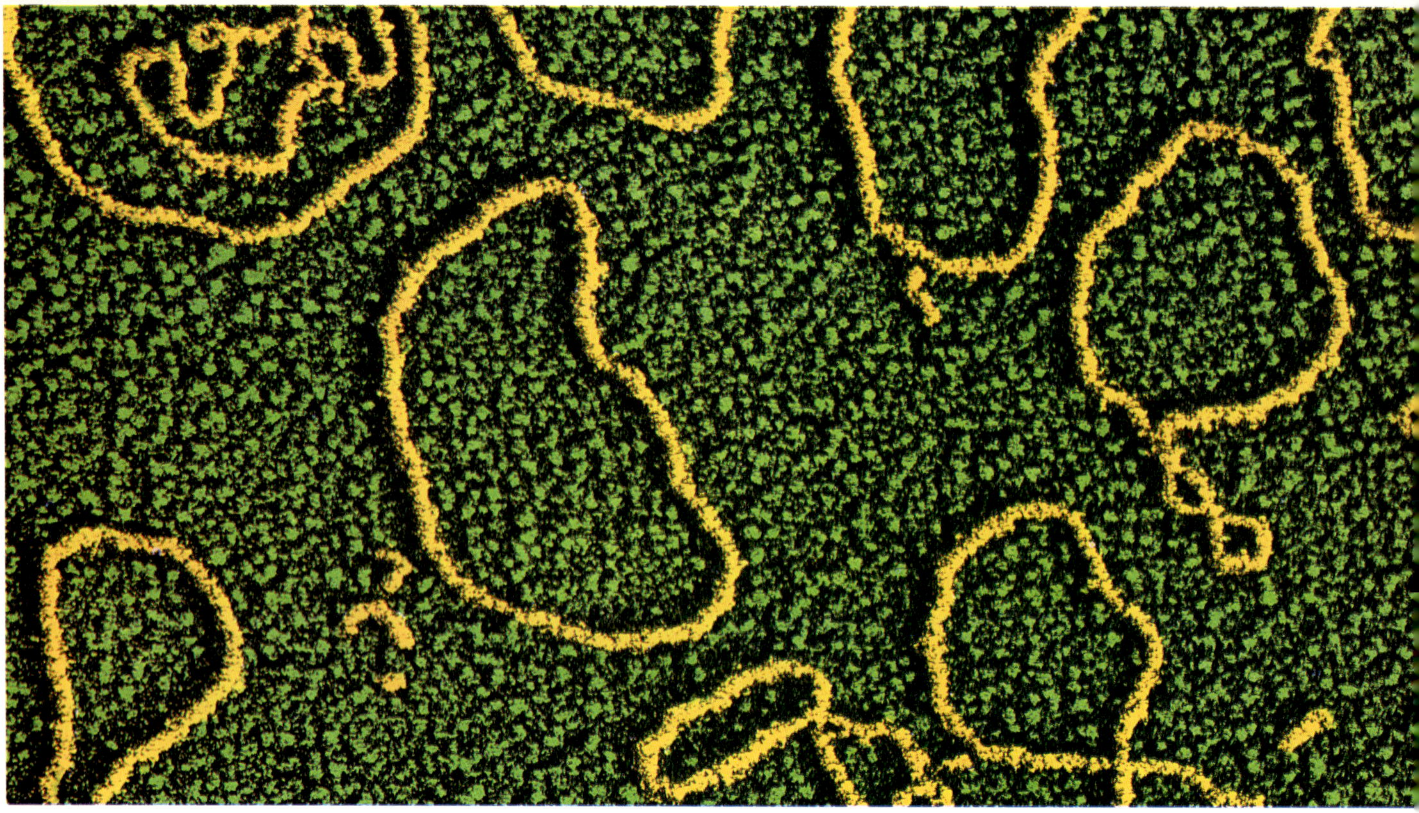

▲ *A plasmid – a circular piece of DNA that replicates separately from the cell nucleus – is the "vector" most commonly used for genetic engineering in the bacterium Escherichia coli. Plasmids carry genes for characteristics such as drug resistance, but additional "foreign" ones can be incorporated by the process known as gene splicing. When such a plasmid, carrying recombinant DNA, is reinserted into a bacterial cell, it replicates as generations of cells divide – the process known as gene cloning. This is now the basis for much of modern biotechnology.*

Testing and monitoring engineered organisms

The consensus of the Philadelphia conference (◆ page 69) was that the efficacy and hazards of releasing engineered organisms should be evaluated via a graded sequence of tests similar to those employed in assessing novel pharmaceuticals (◆ page 20). But the gulf between experiments conducted in this fashion and the major experiment of introducing an engineered organism into the rich fabric of the Earth's biosphere remains enormous. In nature, a recombinant organism will encounter a vast panoply of species, as well as having to contend with the weather and other hazards. Some authorities argue for the testing of engineered agents in "microcosms" or climate chambers – enclosed environments containing mixtures of living creatures similar to those they will meet in the world outside. But given that there are several millions of species of life on Earth, many of the scientists attending the 1985 ASM meeting argued that it would be impossible to set up microcosms coming anywhere near the same complexity.

Time scale is another problem. Particularly with engineered plants, which require at least one growing season before their performance can be assessed, microcosm experiments would have to be conducted over a period of years. Long-term greenhouse trials are not only feasible but well established as a means of studying plants produced by conventional breeding. They are useful in indicating, for example, whether a newly-created species may have robust, weedy characteristics, making it a potential nuisance. But (as with new drugs screened in the laboratory) such limited trials can give atypical results. Even closely supervised microplots in remote areas, are to some degree artificial. The only true test comes when a novel plant is introduced into the field, where it must interact with other species of life.

All researchers agree that because recombinant organisms are living creatures, rather than lifeless chemicals, it will be even more important to monitor their behavior and survival after release, than is the case with new drugs. This will be particularly difficult in the case of microbes, which will probably form the majority of candidates for release, certainly over the next few years. Do they disappear quickly, because they are unable to compete with the natural flora? Or do

they proliferate and become temporarily or permanently established in the area where they have been released? Are they transported far away from the initial site?

Many of the participants at the Philadelphia conference pointedly dismissed the theoretical danger inherent in the impossibility of such surveillance being comprehensive, by recourse to examples such as lengthy commercial experience with *B. thuringiensis* as a living insecticide (◀ page 68). Although this bacterium possesses the machinery for transferring its own toxin gene, no adverse environmental effects have been noted during more than 20 years of worldwide use. Other speakers suggested an alternative strategy – for organisms to be engineered in such a way that there is low possibility, or none, that an introduced gene will be transmitted farther.

The only way in which a plant or microbe could be altered genetically to ensure that its performance in nature was totally predictable would be by making it incapable of survival. Without that certainty of early demise, it will not be possible to predict precisely the environmental fate and effects of any released organism. The alternative, on which agreement is now emerging, is to carry out "environmental impact analysis", based on *a priori* consideration of all possible realistic hazards – and perhaps microcosm tests where these seem realistic.

Some biologists argue that an engineered organism will meet severe challenges if it is even to survive in the outside world, amid competition from the countless other species it will meet, with the physical and chemical threats to the environment. But there is an important counterargument: such an organism will have been specifically manipulated to help it to become established in a particular habitat, and will be introduced in considerable numbers. Initially at least, it will be given a massive "leg-up" in its struggle to survive. Moreover, some of today's environments are not in their natural balanced state, but have been disturbed by human activities. They may therefore be more vulnerable to invasion by a newcomer of this sort.

▼ Large-scale cultures of microbes are prepared in a "fermenter". Also called a "bioreactor", the heart of the equipment is a vessel within which the chosen organism multiplies under carefully regulated conditions of temperature, nutrient supply and acidity or alkalinity. Genetically-modified microbes, or their chemical products, can be extracted continuously or in a batch.

▼ Tissue culture is another technique that is transforming the practice of agriculture and horticulture. Single cells, taken from almost any part of an adult plant, are grown in nutrient medium. Among applications already in use are the propagation of "elite" oil palms and the eradication of viruses from plants previously bedeviled by disease. A major breakthrough came in 1987 when researchers learned to regenerate rice plants from protoplasts (naked cells, lacking their thick protective walls) after foreign genes had been injected into them.

See also
Social Relations 5-20
Global Change 93-108
Futurology 109-24

▼► At the Plant Breeding Institute at Cambridge, England (below), Professor Martin Wolfe employs conventional plant breeding techniques to introduce into local barley genes from strains grown in Israel that are resistant to mildew fungus. In terms of which new organisms need to be regulated, there is nothing intrinsically different between plants or microbes that have received new genes through conventional or recombinant DNA techniques. Right: turnip plants treated with mutagenizing agent and selected over generations may flower in just three weeks under glass; normally the plant needs to overwinter in the ground before it can flower.

Requirements for impact analysis

The task now beginning to face regulatory bodies throughout the world is to decide the type of requirements they should lay down for the environmental impact analysis of engineered organisms. Given the complexity of the biosphere with its milllions of species of life, it would be possible for someone opposed to controlled release on principle to impose a never-ending series of requirements before such work would be permitted to go ahead. At the most absurd level, an unyielding opponent could request conclusive evidence that a nitrogen-fixing bacterium destined for use in Third World countries would have no effect whatever on the salmon in Scottish rivers – and insist on a five-year trial to confirm that this was the case. Countless other demands could be formulated along similar lines, each being capable of being expressed in plausible terms but each being both unrealistic and unnecessary.

Although they speak with different perspectives, gene splicers and ecologists are mostly agreed on two central points. Firstly, regulations ought to be applied to the products – the organisms intended for controlled release rather than the process through which they were fabricated. There seems to be nothing intrinsically different between a microbe or plant which has received a new gene through conventional breeding techniques and one which has received it through recombinant DNA procedures. Secondly, the two sorts of specialist believe that, in the early stages at least, regulatory authorities ought to proceed on a case-by-case basis in deciding whether to permit particular experiments. Although general principles will probably emerge in due course, experience should be gathered through a gradual approach. Given the enormous promise which engineered organisms hold for agricultural and other purposes, the key question is whether professional and public debate will make it possible to blend confidence with appropriate prudence to realize these possibilities.

Popularization

6

Popular regard and ignorance of science...Science in public opinion...Science and education...In print and on TV...In the movies...Science education on the screen ...Science fiction movies...PERSPECTIVE...Alternative medicine...Popularizers

In whatever country they are carried out, investigations into public attitudes toward, and general knowledge of, science and technology tend to reveal paradoxes. First, there is considerable regard for the practical achievements of scientists and technologists in the past, but this is usually coupled with distrust and apprehension over specific present-day and planned developments (such as nuclear power and genetic manipulation). Second, there is widespread interest in the world of science, accompanied by areas of great ignorance; these can often be traced to the inadequacy of school science education. A third mismatch is that public debate and fear concerning scientific "progress" often ranges far ahead of public comprehension of underlying facts and ideas. All of these attitudes are shaped in schools, and by the books, magazines and educational programs on television and radio that are the work of the popularizers of science. Opinions of science are probably molded no less by movies and science fiction writers.

◀ ***Jogging on Brooklyn Bridge, New York City. Wider awareness of the relationship between coronary heart disease and risk factors such as lack of exercise and consumption of a diet rich in animal fat has prompted many people to change their lifestyles. This in turn has almost certainly been responsible for the improvement in coronary mortality figures in recent years. Similarly – and despite frequent assertions that greater knowledge does not lead people to reject unhealthy practices – there is evidence that more educated individuals have been more influenced by the statistics linking smoking with lung cancer and have been more likely to cut the habit.***

The need to understand science

A study published by the Royal Society in Britain in 1985 gave several reasons why more widespread understanding of science is desirable.

"There are few, if any, public issues, including unemployment, that do not have a scientific or technical component," the report said. "Conversely, issues that appear to be largely scientific or technical in nature mostly have major social and political implications. Obvious examples of such issues include disposal of radioactive waste, pollution of the environment, fluoridation of water supply, whooping cough vaccine, prescribable drugs and seat belt regulations. There are also many examples of technologically-based areas where the political and social areas may be dominant, such as "in vitro" fertilization, the introduction of technologies in manufacturing or service industries, defense procurement, overseas aid, land use and fishing quotas."

Because science and technology should be major considerations in public policy, both the public and the policy-makers needed to be technically literate.

The report also claimed a strong prima facie case for the existence of a link between public comprehension of science and national prosperity. For example, "hostility, or even indifference, to science and technology, whether by shopfloor workers, or by middle or senior management or by investors, weakens a nation's industry." Further, "an understanding of science is also important for the individual in his or her private life. Personal decisions, for example about diet, smoking, vaccination, screening programmes or safety at home, should all be helped by some understanding of the underlying science. Greater familiarity with the nature and findings of science will also help the individual to resist pseudo-scientific information." Finally, "the major findings of science, about cosmology, for example, or about evolution, profoundly influence the way we think about ourselves. They are themselves an important part of our culture."

A survey of over 1,000 people showed that three-quarters believed astrology to be scientific, while a bare majority thought this was true of ecology

Scientific knowledge: the MORI survey June 1986

Question 1

I'm going to read out a list of substances, some of which are mixtures and some of which are chemical compounds. Please tell me whether each one is a mixture or chemical compound.

	Mixture	*Compound*	*Don't know*
a) Salt	1	2	3
b) Concrete	1	2	3
c) Water	1	2	3
d) Pastry	1	2	3
e) Nylon	1	2	3
f) Paper	1	2	3
g) Carbon dioxide	1	2	3

Question 2

Here is a list of pairs of foods. Which pair do you think are *both* high in protein?

Cabbage and cheese 1
Beef and cheese 2
Beef and potatoes 3
Cabbage and potatoes 4
Don't know 5

Question 3

From the list which I'm going to read out, which of these gases do you think is the main cause of the pollution of the atmosphere known as acid rain?

Carbon dioxide 1
Nitrogen 2
Hydrogen 3
Sulphur dioxide 4
None of these 5
Don't know 6

Question 4

When a thunderstorm is some distance away, the lightning is seen before the thunder is heard. Which of these explanations do you think is the right one?

Air offers greater resistance to sound waves than to light waves 1
Sound waves travel at a slower speed than light waves 2
The human eye responds more rapidly than the ear 3
The lightning actually occurs two or three seconds before the thunder 4
None of these 5
Don't know 6

Question 5

When we look at plants or animals we find many similarities between parents and offspring. What is it in animal and plant cells that ensure that offspring have many similarities with their parents?

Genes 1
Chromosomes 2
RNA/DNA 3
Other 4
Don't know/no opinion 5

Question 6

Which of these do you think provide most of the energy needs for the human body? Do you think it is ...?

Minerals 1
Proteins 2
Vitamins 3
Carbohydrates 4
None of these 5
Don't know 6

Question 7

I'm going to read out a list of statements. For each one tell me whether you think it is true or false or if you don't really know?

	True	*False*	*Don't know*
a) Smoking 4 or 5 cigarettes a day does no harm to your health	1	2	3
b) Cat fleas cannot live on humans	1	2	3
c) The sex of a baby is determined by the male sperm, not the female egg	1	2	3
d) High and low tides of the oceans are caused by the gravitational pull of the moon	1	2	3
e) Heroin and marijuana are equally addictive	1	2	3
f) Freezing meat kills harmful bacteria	1	2	3
g) Plants release oxygen from their leaves during the day	1	2	3
h) Aids is a disease which can be caught by *any* contact with a carrier	1	2	3
i) If a solution has a low pH value it is acidic rather than alkaline	1	2	3

Question 8

Do you think oxygen is transported to the cells of the human body by ...?

White blood cells 1
Hormones 2
Enzymes 3
Red blood cells 4
None of these 5
Don't know 6

Question 9

Which type of organism is attacked by penicillin. Is it ...?

Viruses 1
Bacteria 2
Fungi 3
Protozoa 4
None of these 5
Don't know 6

Question 10

How long do you think it takes before nuclear waste is no longer radio-active?

Less than 10 years 1
Between 10 and 100 years 2
Between 100 and 1000 years 3
Over 1000 years 4
Never 5
Depends on the type of waste 6
Don't know/no opinion 7

RESPONSES
(percentages)
Correct answers in ***bold***

Question 1
Salt *13* / ***78*** / *9*
Concrete ***85*** / *9* / *6*
Water *24* / ***64*** / *12*
Pastry ***89*** / *5* / *6*
Nylon *50* / ***39*** / *11*
Paper ***64*** / *28* / *8*
Carbon dioxide *30* / ***57*** / *13*

Question 2
1 *17*, 2 ***60***, 3 *12*, 4 *10*, 5 *2*

Question 3
1 *20*, 2 *6*, 3 *3*, 4 ***59***, 5<*1*, 6 *12*

Question 4
1 *6*, 2 ***49***, 3 *4*, 4 *33*, 5 *1*, 6 *6*

Question 5 *
1 ***52***, 2 *7*, 3 ***4***, 4 *4*, 5 *34*

Question 6
1 *4*, 2 *37*, 3 *19*, 4 ***36***, 5<*1*, 6 *4*

Question 7
Smoking *19* / ***79*** / *2*
Cat fleas ***46*** / *38* / *16*
The sex ***55*** / *22* / *24*
Tides ***72*** / *10* / *18*
Heroin *63* / ***28*** / *9*
Meat *37* / ***52*** / *11*
Plants ***74*** / *16* / *10*
AIDS *24* / ***69*** / *9*
pH value ***31*** / *21* / *48*

Question 8
1 *16*, 2 *2*, 3 *4*, 4 ***62***, 5<*1*, 6 *17*

Question 9
1 *33*, 2 ***53***, 3 *4*, 4 *1*, 5<*1*, 6 *9*

Question 10 *
1 *7*, 2 *21*, 3 *23*, 4 *19*, 5 *8*, 6 ***14***, 7 *18*

* "Unprompted answers" – response categories not offered to interviewees, used only to code responses.
"Correct" = "most appropriate" answer.

What people think of science

In 1977 the Commission of the European Communities (CEC), concerned about opposition toward industrial innovation, carried out its first survey of "Science and European Public Opinion" by questioning a sample of about 1,000 adults in each of eight countries within the EEC. This revealed strong support for the idea that science is an important factor in the improvement of daily life, and recognition of its possible dangers. Medical science and food production received especially enthusiastic support, and the CEC concluded that, in principle, there was no crisis of confidence in Europe with regard to science. A similar study two years later confirmed this picture, and revealed a keen public appetite for a better grasp of the details of technical developments. A clear distinction emerged between science (which people considered good in itself) and applications (which were sometimes thought to be harnessed without adequate thought).

Two more recent CEC surveys have highlighted particular topics. One on energy (1982) revealed strong backing for increased research into renewable energy sources, followed by successively less enthusiasm for increased exploitation of existing sources, energy-saving schemes, and nuclear power. Many interviewees were unimpressed by the information they had received from the press, radio, television and educational bodies, and tended to blame the media for their own ignorance. A survey on the environment (1983) showed that Europeans placed a high priority on pollution control and nature conservation, although they were much more concerned about global and national environments than about their own localities.

Results of a 1985 Gallup survey of a representative quota of adults in the United Kingdom mirrored the 1977 CEC survey, and showed that 89 percent of the sample thought everyone should study science up to the age of 16, and that 84 percent believed scientists ought to pay more attention to the implications of their work. But 36 percent could not think of one major postwar scientific achievement, and 47 percent were unable to name three major scientists. The sample also ranked science below medicine and even the armed services and the law as a social institution whose leaders were to be trusted.

Public support for science dwindled in the United States during the 1970s, compared with the buoyancy revealed by opinion polls in the 1950s and 1960s. But this change paralleled a loss of confidence in the community's institutions generally, with science losing less ground than others. In contrast to the situation in the United Kingdom, science rose from fourth to second place (below medicine) in the list of the most trusted institutions. According to the biennial *Science Indicators* report published by the National Science Board in 1986, nearly 60 percent of United States citizens believed that the beneficial consequences of research had outweighed the harmful consequences.

The largest-ever survey of attitudes toward science in one country also took place in 1986, when 5,000 French teenage readers of the magazine *Okapi* replied to questionnaires. The results indicated considerable optimism about science, again coupled with a degree of anxiety. Nearly 90 percent expected scientists to have found a cure for cancer within 20 years. Over 40 percent believed that scientific research would eliminate world hunger during that time and 61 percent expected it to make life easier – but 13 percent feared that scientists were likely to "blow up the world". While a large number of respondents said they were "fascinated", "enthusiastic" or "confident" about science, nearly as many also confessed to feeling "afraid".

◄ As scientific issues have come into greater political and public prominence during recent years, increasing attempts have been made to measure scientific literacy and public attitudes toward scientific developments. With the aid of Market & Opinion Research International, Professor Arthur Lucas of London University carried out one such study in 1986. He sampled the knowledge and ideas of over 1,000 people at 80 locations throughout the United Kingdom. Among his findings were that three-quarters of the respondents believed that astrology was scientific – whereas only a bare majority felt that this was true of ecology (which is now a firmly established science). But the public's understanding of even the most elementary scientific ideas, as revealed by the survey, was surprisingly poor – even in areas, such as nutrition and pollution, which are matters of considerable controversy and topical interest.

Science in the classroom

Although the media (► page 84) are all-pervasive in their influence, the classroom at school is the main formal channel through which nonscientists learn about the worlds of science and technology. All countries have long since acknowledged their central importance in modern society by ensuring that science, divided in later years into constituent disciplines such as biology, physics and chemistry, appears alongside history, geography and other subjects in school curricula. But the inadequacy of much elementary science education has also been highlighted by a sequence of critical reports in recent years in the United States, Europe and other parts of the world. Reflected in the findings of the Bassey and Lucas reports (◄ page 78), these have suggested that existing syllabuses do not provide the familiarity with science that is necessary for future citizens to understand the many public and personal issues that now involve scientific information and ideas.

Certain innovations in curricula have sought to make good this deficiency. For example, under the Nuffield scheme, which was introduced in schools in Britain in the late 1960s and early 1970s, syllabuses have been reshaped around an open-ended rather than traditional, closed approach to knowledge. Thus pupils performing experiments in the laboratory are encouraged to adopt an exploratory, "problem-solving" attitude, rather than being instructed in inflexible, rigid routines each of which has one (and one only) correct answer. But such courses have been criticized, in part because they work well only with the brightest students (and put heavy intellectual demands on teachers), and because they still often fail to instill the principles as opposed to facts of science and to place science in its full setting. Similarly, while initiatives such as the launch of SISCON (Science in a Social Context) courses in Britain have helped to integrate science education with the rest of life, these isolated efforts have not led to a corresponding broadening of science teaching in general.

An international consensus has emerged among educationalists in recent years about what needs doing to match classroom science with the real needs of today's citizens – though there has been only slow progress toward the implementation of these reforms. A balanced education in science is considered essential for all children up to the age of 16. The ideas of science, together with the nature and limitations of scientific method, should be emphasized as much as raw facts. Teaching ought to cover the practical applications and social implications of science. And because the notion of risk is of increasing public importance in relation to issues ranging from nuclear power to coronary heart disease (◄ page 57), there should be adequate grounding in ideas of statistics and probability. Better material resources are also required in the classroom, as well as improved in-service training to acquaint teachers with rapidly changing scientific ideas.

A problem peculiar to certain countries of the world is the narrowness of education after 16, at which age pupils can and usually do concentrate solely on either arts or science subjects. The 1985 Royal Society report (◄ page 77) called for an end to this specialization, so that pupils can take a wider range of subjects. "Only in this way can we hope to achieve the broadening of our educational system that will ensure at least some scientific literacy among all our leaders in central and local government, the Civil Service, industry, commerce and elsewhere in society."

◄ Children play with the Plasma Globe light sculpture at the Exploratory, a hands-on center in Bristol, England. The glass sphere contains rare gases at low pressure and has a radio transmitter at its heart. Writhing snakes of glowing plasma are produced by moving hands around the surface. Directed by Professor Richard Gregory, the Exploratory has won high regard for teaching science not by static displays but by encouraging active exploration of phenomena.

Unsound therapies – the need for scientific "literacy"

Medical science is one field in which there probably has been a discernible growth in public understanding during recent years. At least to the extent that more people in the United States and other countries are now interested in diet, exercise and other factors relevant to their health, public literacy has increased. There is today a wider understanding of the principles of nutrition and even of technicalities of "aerobic" exercise. The beneficial effects of this greater concern seem amply demonstrated by the decline that has occurred in recent years in the so-called "modern plague" of coronary heart disease in the United States.

At the same time, many people have fallen foul of particular "health foods" and "alternative therapies" that have become popular in part as a result of significant public ignorance of elementary physiology. Physicians are now having to deal with a wave of patients who have become unwell as a result of heavily promoted but essentially unsound therapies. With more widespread scientific literacy in the population, such remedies would not have found favor anything like so widely.

The scale of the current craze for alternative explanations and supposedly more natural remedies is illustrated in a recent paper in the *Journal of the American Medical Association* by Dr Gregory Curt and colleagues. They reported that Americans now spend $10 billion a year on unproven treatments – more than twice the total research budget of the country's National Institutes of Health. Ironically, the accompanying human costs have become apparent at just the time when conventional medicine is suffering financial hardship. Physicians and scientists believe that the positions would be reversed if there were greater public understanding of the facts and ideas of science.

▲ *An aerobics class in progress. There is now abundant evidence that at least 15-20 minutes of exercise daily to the point of breathlessness reduces the likelihood of a person contracting coronary heart disease, and is greatly preferable to the weekly squash game interspersed with six days of sitting. Although sometimes combined with highly unscientific habits such as the consumption of huge doses of vitamins and trace elements, more prudent exercising and dieting is founded upon sound knowledge of principle.*

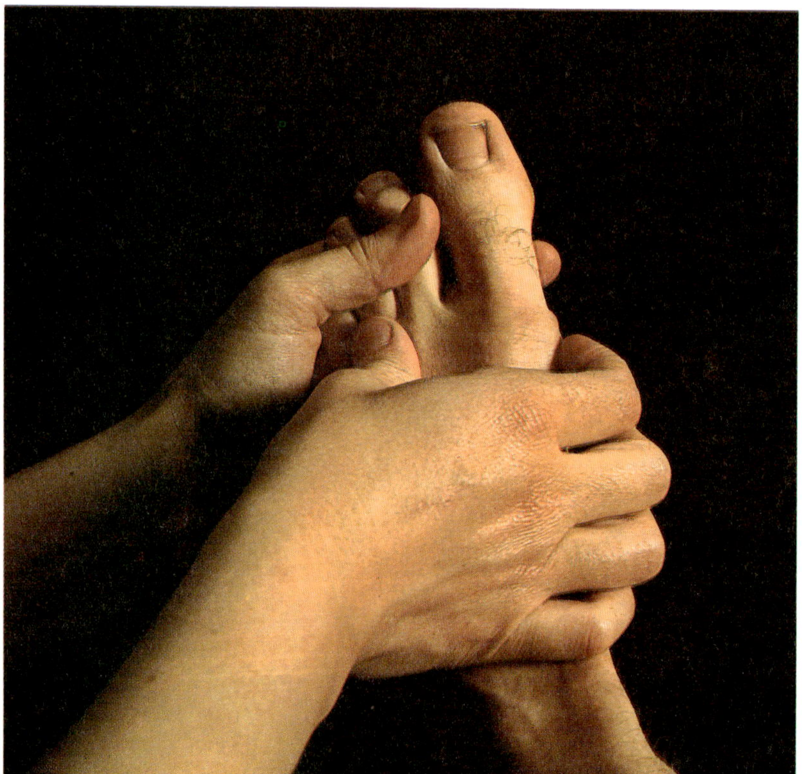

► *A "reflexologist" massages a patient's foot under the guise of "reflexology", according to which the body is divided into ten meridians. Running from head to toe, these are said to pass through various organs and terminate in the feet. Discomfort in a particular part of the foot is supposedly related to a malfunctioning organ, which can thus be helped by foot massage. Reflexology is one of many popular "alternative" therapies that have not been vindicated to scientific standards.*

▲ ***A medical hypnotist at work with a patient. Sometimes unjustly dismissed or relegated together with other "fringe" therapies as a practice of dubious merit, hypnotism is in fact now used by doctors and dentists to help relieve or cure a substantial range of illnesses, as well as personality problems and psychological conditions. Well-attested applications include the easing of pain during childbirth and assistance in abstention from smoking. One limitation, however, is that the subject must be willing to be hypnotized.***

A high-risk diet

Particularly disquieting are the adverse repercussions that have followed the appearance of best-selling books concerned with crank diets and bizarre recipes for healthy living. When Judy Mazel's "The Beverley Hills Diet" first appeared in 1981, it was followed a few months later by a highly critical paper by Drs G.B. Mirkin and R.N. Shore in the "Journal of the American Medical Association". This highlighted the book's many factual errors, which were so blatant that they would have been recognized by anyone with the most basic understanding of nutrition and digestion. Ms Mazel claimed, for example, that "as long as food is fully digested, fully processed through the body, you will not gain weight", and that "it's only undigested food, food that is 'stuck' in your body, for whatever reason, that accumulates and becomes fat". These statements (upon which the diet is built) are, quite simply, nonsense. Yet the book carrying them remained at the top of the "New York Times" bestseller list for over seven months.

The two physicians also drew attention to some potentially serious consequences of following Ms Mazel's advice. "The diet can cause severe diarrhea, which can result in hypovolemic shock, potassium deficiency, and arrhythmia. It is also a low-protein diet, at least in its first six weeks. It is possible to become deficient enough in protein during this time to suffer hair loss." Drs Mirkin and Shore wrote. "Recently we have seen three patients in whom severe diarrhea, muscle weakness and dizziness developed while in their first week on the Beverley Hills diet. We believe the muscle weakness and dizziness were due to hypovolemia caused by the diet itself."

"Natural" medicines

Also causing apprehension among US doctors is the current fad for homeopathic medicines, which are sold through health food stores and are said to be more "natural" than their orthodox equivalents. A few doctors look benignly on these preparations. They consider ill-effects to be highly unlikely because the supposedly active ingredients are diluted to vanishingly tiny concentrations. Most medicos, however, fear that homeopathic nostrums will be selected in preference to those that actually work.

Another anxiety is that some of these preparations are themselves harmful. Writing in the "New England Journal of Medicine" in 1986, Drs Harry Kerr and Garland Yarborough reported one case in which a 34-year-old man developed pancreatitis as a result of taking homeopathic "BHI Regeneration Tablets" for a pain in his neck. Among the ingredients were nitric acid, phosphorus and blister agents. Kerr and Yarborough have called for stricter legislation to control hazardous preparations of this kind.

Science in print and on TV

Aside from formal science education, the main public sources of information and ideas about science are the media – newspapers, magazines, television and radio, books and films. Each of these channels has seen significant expansion over recent years. Many daily newspapers, for example, have introduced substantial regular sections providing research news. They include the *New York Times* in the United States, the *Frankfurter Allgemeine Zeitung* in West Germany and the *Guardian* in Britain. *Time* and *Newsweek* have found they can lift their sales by featuring scientific topics on the cover, while the *Economist* has launched a highly successful science and technology section. Around 1980 four new magazines arrived on the US market to join *Scientific American* which was already there. They were soon selling over half a million copies each. *Science 80* came from the American Association for the Advancement of Science. *Science Digest* (a much larger and glossier version of an existing title) from Hearst. *Discover* from Time-Life, and *Omni* (which also contains science fiction and fantasy) from Penthouse International. Although the first two disappeared in 1986, they failed not through lack of adequate readership but because there was insufficient advertising revenue to support such extensive printing and production.

Elsewhere too, many popular magazines, including *Natuur & Techniek* in the Netherlands, *Mada* in Israel and *Sciences & Avenir* in France, reached record circulations, and were joined by newcomers such as *Tiede* in Finland. There were similar vigorous developments in broadcast science. Carl Sagan's *Cosmos* and other spectacular series centered on science, medicine and allied topics were screened worldwide. Audience figures burgeoned for regular TV and radio programs, and the Australian Broadcasting Corporation launched a weekly radio show, *Science Bookshelf*, devoted solely to reviews of popular science books.

Some scientists are very ready to complain about sensationalism, trivialization and inaccuracy in print journalism and broadcasting. On occasions, this is justified. Yet the most able science reporters bring considerable skill to the task of interpreting highly complex technical issues, often against the pressure of urgent deadlines (➧ page 92).

▼ The American astronomer Carl Sagan (b.1934) is one of very few scientists who have combined high-level research with continuous involvement in the popularization of science – as in his highly praised "Cosmos" television programs. Screened throughout the world, "Cosmos" typifies several spectacular ventures that have taken the formerly somewhat earnest genre of televisual science to new heights of excitement and clarity. Carl Sagan's conspicuousness as a popularizer of science has helped him in his political activities, such as his public lobbying on the subject of the "nuclear winter", upon which he and his colleagues have carried out much of the background research.

▲ The public appetite for popular science is reflected in the success of magazines interpreting research in relatively nonspecialized terms – although many of them tend to be read not only by nonscientists but also by scientists keen to follow developments outside of their own field. Three new periodicals of this sort were launched in the USA during the early 1980s, and although two later ceased publication this was a result not of lack of readership interest but of insufficient advertising revenue. All three magazines achieved circulations of around two-thirds of a million copies monthly. "Scientific American" has spawned several overseas editions – even in the People's Republic of China.

While it is simply not possible to reflect in a popular account all of the caveats and qualifications that are necessary when writing a paper for a scholarly periodical, the best science journalism is that which provides accessibly and accurately the key elements of a story and sets them, and any divergences of professional opinion, in appropriate context.

As well as surveying factual information, newspapers, broadcasting and periodicals affect their customers' beliefs about science and technology. In Britain, for example, the *Financial Times* has given a relatively favorable picture of nuclear power for many years now, whereas the *Guardian* has adopted a more critical stance, giving more space to its alleged dangers. Sometimes newspaper campaigns trigger official actions (◆ page 57). However, many of the most profound effects on public opinion can be traced not to daily journalism, but to books and their associated publicity.

A publishing house about to release a work which it believes particularly important (or likely to generate a large profit) makes energetic efforts to ensure widespread exposure. Public relations officers see that the author is interviewed on as many radio and television programs as possible. There are also offers of specially-written articles, or extracts from the book for serialization in periodicals and newspapers. In these and other ways, an "amplifier" guarantees that the public is not only offered the book for sale but is also subjected to a battery of publicity about its message and its author. In addition to the work itself, a sizeable penumbra of influence can reach many people who never buy or read a book.

This is true irrespective of the quality of the work. Rachel Carson's *Silent Spring* (1962) led to restrictions on use of dangerous insecticides. However, equally influential are books such as Judy Mazel's *The Beverley Hills Diet* (◆ page 82) and David Rorvick's *In His Image*, an account of the alleged cloning of a human being. Scientists who immediately dismissed Rorvick's work as fiction masquerading as fact when it appeared in 1978 were later vindicated. Four years later, publishers J.B. Lippincott conceded that the book was a fraud when they settled out of court with biologist Derek Bromhall. He had sued for defamation because Rorvick had cited his name as authority for the supposed cloning techniques. Yet despite this ignominious end, the publicity surrounding *In His Image* was so powerful that many people have probably accepted its central claim as genuine.

◄ Rachel Carson (1907-1964) influenced an entire generation of citizens by describing the ill-effects of pesticides in "Silent Spring", based in part on material from articles she had written for the "New Yorker" magazine. Legislation to restrict insecticide use in several countries can be traced to the book.

▼ Best known for his co-authorship of the Stanley Kubrick movie "2001", Englishman Arthur C. Clarke (b. 1917) is not only an influential science fiction writer but also a trained scientist whose predictions include satellite communications, long before they became a reality. Clarke now runs a center in Sri Lanka devoted to Third World science.

Microbiology is one science that has been reflected accurately and vividly in the movies

◄ *Paul Muni played the title role in the 1936 movie "The Story of Louis Pasteur". Together with successes such as "Dr Ehrlich's Magic Bullet" (1948), it set a trend in bringing to the silver screen the exploits of the "microbe hunters" who, beginning in the latter half of the 19th century, first incriminated microbes as agents of human disease and pioneered ways of combatting infections by vaccination and drug treatment. Although somewhat larger than life, and using artistic licence to give dramatic color to developments which often depended upon hard, meticulous work, these films were also effective in portraying the methods of science. They had a significant influence on health education too.*

Science in the movies

A successful film, or one judged to be unusually significant or important by its makers, is publicized and exposed in a variety of ways over a considerable period of time. TV repeats ensure that the motifs, characters and ideas pass across the public consciousness many times over, like the tunes and harmonies of oft-played music. This is true of the images in Stanely Kubrick and Arthur C. Clarke's *2001: A Space Odyssey* (1968), for example, and of Kubrick's black comedy *Dr Strangelove* (1963). Just as pervasive is the stereotype of the bomb disposal "boffin" in *The Small Back Room*, made in 1949 but screened repeatedly on television across the continents of the world in more recent years. *The Dam Busters* (1954), another film that continues to receive frequent TV showings, was based on the real-life story of British inventor Barnes Wallis and adds another ingredient to the public stereotype of the scientist: a hint of eccentricity or even madness. More recently came the cinematic world of aliens and androids – ideas and artefacts of science which virtually dominated the entire cinema industry at times during the 1970s.

From its very inception the movie business has, of course, been glamorous and larger-than-life. And many people can easily distinguish fact from fantasy. But for others the two worlds easily become confused. This was clear from public opinion surveys conducted in the United States in 1979 soon after the reactor failure at Three Mile Island (which caused no casualties) and the 1979 premiere of the movie *The China Syndrome*, which was based on a potentially disastrous reactor flaw (◆ page 57). Some American citizens felt that they had learned as much about the perils of nuclear power from the film as from the real life accident.

◄ *Written and directed by George Lucas and starring Mark Hamill, Carrie Fisher, Peter Cushing and Alec Guinness, "Star Wars" (1977) was a spectacular and highly profitable science fiction movie whose central plot was an unsophisticated fairy story. In a distant galaxy a rebellious princess escapes and, aided by two robots and an heroic young man, manages to overcome the forces of evil that threaten to destroy her. The dramatic dogfights in space can be criticized for contravening Newton's three laws of motion, although paradoxically the title of the film was subsequently taken up as a popular label to describe President Reagan's "strategic defense initiative" (◆ page 34), which in time will supposedly banish nuclear weapons from space.*

The influence of films was discussed during the annual meeting of the American Association for the Advancement of Science in 1978. According to reporter Thomas Maugh, participants agreed that the overall impression created by the movies and other media was that "scientists are frequently foolish, inept, even villainous. This portrayal, critics contend, is eroding public support for science and may be turning away many potential Einsteins, Paulings and Pasteurs before they are mature enough to appreciate the joys and wonder of science". Ben Bova, the science fiction writer and then editor of *Analog* magazine, claimed that the movies were the worst offenders in suggesting that scientists had "moral sensitivities no higher than a Hollywood producer's own sensitivities". Bova traced much of the public's apprehension about science to its capacity to make changes to the world.

"Science fiction – the predominant form in which science is displayed in movies and television – is primarily a drama of ideas," said another SF author, David Gerrold. "But ideas do not in themselves photograph well. Most science fiction stories in movies and on television are thus westerns, soap operas and other conventional plot forms to which science fiction trappings have been added almost as an afterthought...The primary qualification for success as a movie or television scriptwriter is the ability to turn out 56 pages of typewritten dialog in 10 days," he said. "Producers and directors also suffer from an impoverished world view: they do not even have an idea of Newton's three laws of motion, which is why we have such spectacular – albeit nonsensical – dogfights in *Star Wars* (1977). It is not surprising that there are so many inaccuracies and errors in science fiction dramas – errors that give the lay public a warped sense of science."

▲ *Edward G. Robinson played the leading role in the Warner Brothers movie "Dr Ehrlich's Magic Bullet", which told the story of the German physician who not only developed many of the key techniques used in bacteriology but was also the prime mover behind three branches of science – immunology, chemotherapy, and hematology. Paul Ehrlich was played with great panache, reflecting his rumbustious portrait in Paul de Kruif's "Microbe Hunters". Yet his achievement in suggesting the possibility of drugs targeted to particular tissues came across clearly.*

Educational movies

More consciously educative "motion pictures" were made in America by Thomas Edison between 1910 annd 1914 for the National Association for the Study and Prevention of Tuberculosis. A re-examination of these films by Martin Pernick many years later showed that they were major innovations in the popularization of modern scientific ideas about health and hygiene. With the conquests of Pasteur, Koch, and their fellow microbe-hunters as background, the opportunities and obligations facing public health crusaders in the early part of this century seemed clear. In 1905 the US Supreme court ruled that citizens could be forcibly and involuntarily vaccinated. Mandatory premarital blood tests for syphilis and the sterilization of "hereditary idiots" came next. At the same time, with the inception of commercial movies in 1905, physicians saw the possibility of reinforcing the threat of physical coercion with propaganda. The resulting films were highly popular, some being seen by several million people. According to Pernick, "audiences of 10,000 packed the parks and vacant lots of New York's Lower East Side to watch tuberculosis movies flicker across the side walls of their tenements. Specially designed movie trucks and railroad cars toured rural areas. For some rural dwellers, such health trucks provided their first exposure to *any* motion pictures".

Typical was Edison's *Hope*, produced in 1912, which dramatized the need for sanatoria in small towns. The movie showed a country girl whose family is helpless to deal with her tuberculosis. She has to leave home and go to Bellevue Hospital in New York. Heartbroken, her wealthy father awakens to the cause of building a local sanatorium and rallies the townspeople to that end.

The Temple of Moloch, made two years later, has as its hero a scientifically trained public health doctor who visits a worker's tenement and lectures his family about the need for open windows. But when he suggests sending the baby to a fresh air camp, the terrified wife grabs the child back, and as soon as the doctor has gone the family forgets his exhortations. The well-meaning doctor also fails to make

◀ *David Shale of Oxford Scientific Films working with a battery of equipment at the optical bench. The making of educational movies has been radically transformed from primitive origins over the past three decades. Wildlife programs on television, for example, now use many of the same techniques, such as ultra high-speed photography, which have been developed as research tools.*

▼ *Technicians from Oxford Scientific Films prepare to film Elf owls at nest in Saguaro, Arizona. Natural history offers film-makers great opportunities for combining stunning visual effects with colorful, graphic detail upon which to base explanations of phenomena ranging from animal behavior and plant development to the rich subtleties of evolution and ecology.*

any impression on the man's employer, who runs an unventilated, dusty pottery. Only when the worker's children develop tuberculosis and pass it on to the employer's children do both families realize something must be done.

The literature of the period confirms that no one was troubled about movie-goers being manipulated by these simplistic exercises. H.E. Kleinschmidt of the Tuberculosis Association (forerunner of the March of Dimes and the American Cancer Society) wrote in 1919 that good propaganda was "mental inoculation", the goal of which was "will-control...through education". Most health propagandists avoided discussing the morality of their craft. They confused ethics with effectiveness and assumed that anything that worked was, by definition, proper. And such films certainly had deep, widespread influence. Martin Pernick located several dozen people, then aged over 75, who remembered accurately specific scenes and information from pictures seen during World War I. Such memories confirm that the producer's original hopes were fulfilled. American psychologist J.B. Watson (1878-1958, the founder of modern behaviorism), and Carl Lashley conducted a government-funded survey in 1919 which concluded that over the long term venereal disease movies could revolutionize American health habits.

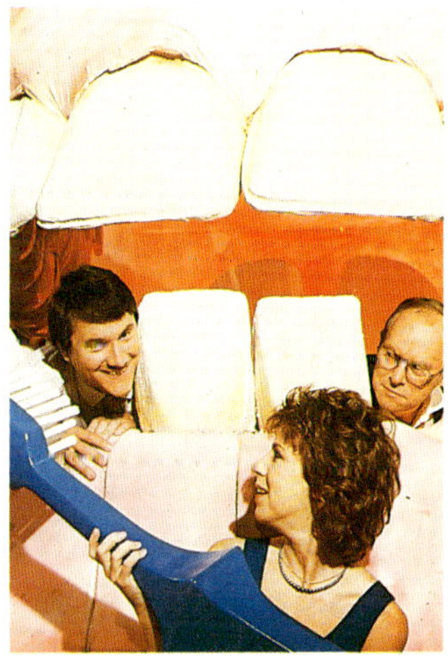

▲ *A modern counterpart of Thomas Edison's early health education movies – the three presenters of BBC Television's "Body Matters" show the importance of good dental hygiene and effective teeth-brushing technique. The Health Education Council in Britain believes that programs of this sort are among the most effective vehicles for explaining both elementary and more complex health matters.*

The sci-fi movie – a potent force

Scientists, businessmen, and science administrators recognize that movies have the power to shape public opinion. At a time when public clamor and controversy about technical issues (such as nuclear power and genetic manipulation) often ranges well ahead of public understanding, they believe that films have far-reaching influence, for good or ill, in determining which developments will be welcomed or resisted. An example of such concern is Twentieth Century Fox's science fiction movie *Warning Sign*, which is centered on an ill-fated experiment in which genes are transferred between one organism and another. Starring Sam Waterston, it was directed by Hal Barwood and produced by Jim Bloom, whose earlier SF movies include *Invasion of the Body Snatchers*. According to Twentieth Century Fox publicity agent Ted Hollis, the movie deals with "the raw emotions of scientists and technicians who suddenly find themselves sealed in a fortress-like laboratory with an experiment that has gotten out of control. It is a consciousness-raiser, like *The China Syndrome*." Barwood evolved the idea after reading about Legionnaires' disease, combined with his interest in medical mysteries and the way people behave under stress.

Late in 1984, when biotechnologists in the United States began to hear about plans for *Warning Sign* (originally to be called *Biohazards*), their first reaction was dismissive. But gradually, the emerging businesses in this field started to realize that the movie posed a potentially serious threat to public confidence in their work. By early the following year one company, the Cetus Corporation, had become so alarmed that it had agreed to serve as an anonymous consultancy on the project, in exchange for an early preview. Another biotechnology company, Monsanto, which was then developing genetically altered bacteria with a view to releasing them into the environment for

▼▶ *Made in 1983, "War Games" tells the story of an American teenager who accidentally taps into the Pentagon through his home computer, and convinces the authorities that the Soviet Union is about to launch an attack with nuclear missiles. Although overburdened by technical jargon and hardware, the movie both exploited and encouraged the notion that hackers can gain access to major computer systems.*

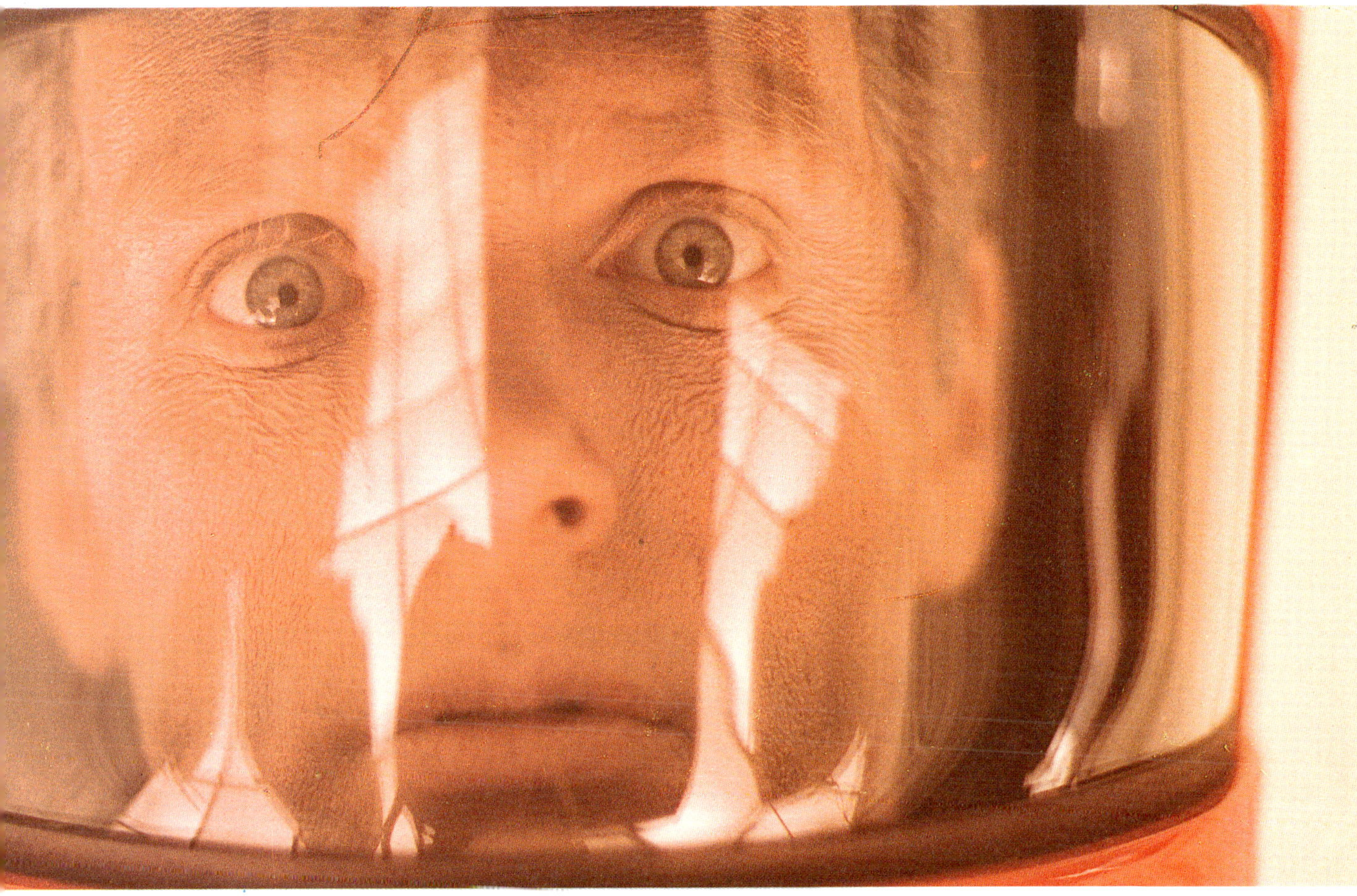

▲ *Stanley Kubrick and Arthur C. Clarke's "2001: A Space Odyssey", which was released in 1968, is a classic of science fiction in the cinema. The character HAL suggested that computers might eventually be "personalized" and share or even improve on the properties of human minds. Another idea highlighted in the film is that of suspended animation, with crew members kept on ice to pass the years until they are required. Although scientifically implausible, this has since become the purpose of several US companies established to preserve cadavers until their aging or terminal diseases can be conquered (♦ page 121).*

beneficial purposes (♦ page 69), launched a public relations campaign directed at public reassurance about biotechnology. Although Monsanto denied that this was related to the imminence of *Warning Sign*, the timing of the company's efforts appeared significant. The movie was certainly a subject of anxious discussion among industrialists attending biotechnology conferences at that time.

By the time a general preview of *Warning Sign* was held on August 12, 1985 and attended by several company representatives, it had become clear that the US Army, rather than industry, was a more likely target for public disquiet. As described by Marjorie Sun in *Science*: "In the opening sequence, a crop duster sweeps down over the Utah countryside. The film then goes on to show the military conducting secret biological weapons research in a small Utah town, using an agribiotechnology company as a cover...The movie's last line is meant to evoke outrage. 'I'm a scientist,' insists one of the characters. 'I know what I'm doing.'" According to Sun, several US Army representatives at the preview were highly critical of the movie – screened at a time when steps were being taken, against some political opposition, toward the building of a new laboratory for biological weapons research at the Dugway Proving Ground in Utah. They pointed out factual errors to reporters – for example, that only unbreakable test tubes would be used in the sort of laboratory shown in the movie, and that protective helmets could not, as in the movie, be raised, thereby exposing the wearer to infection. But the fact that Army representatives attended at all was highly significant. Even a decade earlier, they would have considered this laughably unnecessary.

See also
Social Relations 5-20

The Kalinga Prize

The Kalinga Prize for the Popularization of Science (named after the ancient Kalinga empire in India) is presented each year by UNESCO. The winners of the prize are writers and broadcasters who have helped to promote public understanding of scientific ideas and developments.

The winner of the Kalinga prize in its fifth year (1956) was a distinguished practitioner as well as a popularizer of science. George Gamow (1904-1968) was born in Odessa in the Soviet Union but became a US citizen in 1940. He was a nuclear physicist whose "Mr Tomkins in Wonderland" (1939) and "Mr Tomkins Explores the Atom" (1944) are two still hugely successful efforts to explain arcane ideas to nonspecialists. As a young man, Gamow worked with Niels Bohr in Copenhagen and Ernest Rutherford in Cambridge, England, and later made major contributions toward our understanding of radioactivity. In one of his books, "The Birth and Death of the Sun", he made a dazzling triumph of presenting for a lay audience ideas that were not yet familiar to many scientists.

Reaching the world of popular science by a very different route, Ritchie Calder (1906-1982) was a lawcourt reporter by the age of 15, yet subsequently became one of the creators of science journalism in Britain. Through the "News Chronicle" newspaper and "New Statesman" magazine and books such as "Birth of the Future" (1934) and "Common Sense about a Starving World" (1962), he used his felicitous style and wry humor to explain science and its relevance to human need. He was awarded the Kalinga Prize in 1960. Lord Ritchie Calder's credo was: "Science is knowledge. Wisdom is knowledge tempered by judgement. The promotion of the common understanding of science is essential to its wise use for the benefit of mankind."

The following year's Kalinga laureate was Arthur C. Clarke (b.1917) (◆ page 84), best known as one of the great science fiction writers. Clarke has also made considerable contributions to the popularization of science, through books such as "Interplanetary Flight" (1950) and "The Treasure of the Great Reef" (1964). Born in England but now a resident of Sri Lanka, he has lived to see his idea, published in 1945, of satellite communications become practical reality with the Early Bird satellite (1965).

Luis Estrada Martínez (b.1932) is famed as the catalyst of the "systematic vulgarization" of science in Mexico and of measures to promote scientific understanding in the Third World. Founder of the periodical "Físicia" (now named "Naturaleza"), he has promoted science clubs, fairs, exhibitions and "coffee house chats" to bring scientists and nonscientists together. Formerly a physicist at the National Autonomous University of Mexico, he now works for the university's Directorate General for Cultural Propagation. Luis Estrada became the youngest-ever recipient of the Kalinga Prize in 1974.

▼ Mexican physicist and magazine editor Luis Estrada Martínez (right) receives the 1974 Kalinga Prize for the Popularization of Science from UNESCO's Director-General, Mr M'Bow. Established by Mr Biju Patnaik, founder and chairman of the Kalinga Foundation Trust in the state of Orissa, India, and awarded for the first time in 1952, the prize recognizes distinction in interpreting science for the public.

Global Change

A shrinking planet...The world's harvests...Manmade disasters – desertification and deforestation...Species conservation – a luxury issue?...Natural disasters... Countering pollution...Health campaigns...PERSPECTIVE ...Scientists North and South...Feeding the world... Tackling AIDS...The Gaia hypothesis

As the planet grows larger, in terms of human numbers, it is shrinking in terms of the effects people and events can have over great distances: across national boundaries, across oceans and across cultures. A decision taken in a boardroom in New York may lead to the clearing of rainforest and the uprooting of an entire indigenous tribe in Brazil; pollution from British factories kills fish in Sweden; a civil war in Central America threatens to involve superpowers far from the scene of the fighting.

Human activities have affected the lives of others far away since the colonial era, but today technology makes the effects quicker and larger – often too large and too quick for the slower-moving, often smaller-scale checks and balances of politics – and certainly those of science – to guide and channel effectively. The greatest political problem is perhaps the deep split between the "developed" nations of the "North" and the "developing" countries of the "South".

Where scientists are

Most of the world's scientists work in the North, on "Northern" problems. There are 28 scientists, engineers and technicians doing research and development for every 10,000 inhabitants in the developed market economies, and an even higher ratio in eastern Europe. In the Third World, there are only 2.5 such researchers and developers per 10,000 inhabitants. Not surprisingly, little of the world's technology is particularly suited for Third World problems. Nor is much of the research in either the North or the South on key Third World problems such as dryland agriculture, tropical diseases or low-energy industrial development.

It is not just a matter of training scientists in the developing nations, for the best tend to leave for the North, where salaries are higher, communications with other scientists easier, and sophisticated equipment more widely available.

There are encouraging signs of change. The umbrella organization for tropical agriculture, the Consultative Group on International Agricultural Research (CGIAR), is financed with northern money but has established institutes throughout the South. For instance, the center for the study of semiarid crops is in India, that for the study of animal diseases in Kenya. These act as centers of both research and training for local scientists. African scientists have formed an African Academy of Sciences. But it remains difficult to see how the "developing world" can develop.

◄ M.V. Greenpeace off Ross Island, Antarctica. Greenpeace is one of several thousand environmental pressure groups whose numbers are growing, especially in developing nations. This growth reflects the widespread concern that man is impoverishing future generations by squandering environmental resources, but their activities are no match for present political and economic systems which often undervalue such resources, be they seals or clean air. Such groups are working closely with scientists to add rigor and data to their argument.

Has science been "let down" by political and economic systems?

The distribution of the world's harvests

The case could be made – though it would be hotly argued – that science has been let down by political and economic systems. Thanks to the development of new crop varieties, fertilizers, chemicals and better irrigation techniques, foodgrain production, for example, for some time has been rising faster than world population. Yet there are more hungry people on the planet today than ever before, and their numbers are growing, not shrinking.

This "unfairness" is not the fault of of science. Science has made possible the "Green Revolution" based on new, high-yielding varieties of wheat, rice and corn (maize). The results have been most profound in increasing wheat and rice production in south Asia and India. Yet 470 million of the 730 million people said by the World Bank to be not getting enough calories for an active working life in 1980 live in South Asia; 42 million of them live in India. In emphasizing high yields, plant breeders have not "designed" the new strains to be hardy, so they rely on large doses of chemicals and irrigation. This puts them out of the range of poor farmers, who can afford neither the agricultural "inputs" nor the food eventually harvested.

▲► Low-tech versus high-tech. A peasant farmer in Ethiopia's drought-prone Tigray province winnows sorghum from his tiny plot using techniques thousands of years old. In Kenya, barley fields farmed by mechanized equipment stretch to the horizon at 2,600m on the slopes of Mount Kenya. This can produce more grain, but much of Africa's soils are unsuitable for tractor plowing. And growing crops by high-cost techniques can not only displace small farmers, but may produce food which few can afford. The challenge of science is to make high-tech farming systems more suitable to the African environment, and low-tech systems more productive and more reliable.

▲ Planting corn and beans together, Guangtong Province, China. Much western agricultural teaching insists on "monocropping", one crop in a field; but peasant farmers have long mixed crops, a practice called "intercropping". Recent studies show that the peasants were right all along. In this case the beans fix nitrogen in the soil. The nitrogen increases the productivity of the corn. Studies in Africa have found that intercropping the cereal sorghum with groundnuts, also a nitrogen-fixing plant, give a combined yield 25 percent higher than when the two crops were planted separately. Intercropping can also prevent pests or disease from running through an entire field. And by mixing crops which are drought-resistant with those that require much rain, farmers can ensure at least some harvest in times of poor rains. Intercropping is a low-tech practice, requiring no new machinery or chemicals.

▲ The "Triticale" hybrid of wheat (Triticum) and barley (Secale) grows in a greenhouse lab, while at a UN crop research station at Kamboinse, Burkina Faso, a technician studies a sorghum strain (its flowers bagged to prevent cross-pollination). Crop research in the Third World has gradually been getting out of the lab and into the research station. The next step is from the research station into the farmers' fields. For only by understanding farmers' needs and conditions can researchers produce suitable crop varieties. Too often lab research has produced crops requiring more labor than farmers can provide. But when science gets it right, African farmers are quick to take up the new hybrids.

The "haves" and "have-nots"

Thirty percent of the gross domestic product (GDP) of "developing" countries comes from agriculture and mining, while for the "developed" countries with their industrial market economies the figure is only seven percent. About one-fourth of the world's people live in the industrialized nations, but because of their styles of living and producing, they consume about three-fourths of the world's resources used annually. The three-fourths of the planet's people living in the developing world consume only one-fourth of the world's resources.

While the economies of most developing nations have grown, those of the developed nations have grown faster; so the split between "haves" and "have-nots" grows bigger. According to Sir Sridath Ramphal, secretary general of the Commonwealth secretariat, "At the end of three decades of international action devoted to development, the result, by 1985, is likely to be an increase of $50 per capita in the annual incomes of the poorest groups over 1965 incomes, compared with an increase of $3900 per capita for those of the richest."

In 1950, there were about 2.5 billion people on Earth; some time in 1986 world population probably passed 5 billion. Most of this growth is happening in the poorest countries. Some 95 percent of the increase in population between 1980 and the year 2050 will take place in the Third World, according to UN estimates. Thus the poorest and most densely populated regions of the world depend most on resources such as soil, water and forests, which support agriculture. Getting the best use of these "environmental" resources offers tremendous scientific challenges. But the political and economic challenges are greater, in that the poor in the Third World have neither political nor financial power to seek scientific solutions to these problems.

Desertification and deforestation

Many of the people hungry for food are also hungry for land; thus poverty encourages families to overuse their own land, or common land, or to seek more land by the clearing of marginal areas. These are the root causes of the global syndrome of "desertification". About 30 million square kilometers of drylands – over 20 percent of the Earth's surface and home of some 80 million people – are under direct threat of desertification, according to UN estimates in 1977. Every year some 200,000 square kilometers of land deteriorates to the point of economic worthlessness at an annual cost in lost agricultural production of $26 billion. The syndrome affects about 100 nations: some 10.5 million square kilometers of the threatened land is in North America, 7 million in South America, 6.9 million in Africa south of the Sahara, 1.3 million around the Mediterranean, 1.7 million in India and Pakistan and 2.6 million in Australia and Asia.

The famines affecting more than 20 African nations and 30 million people in 1984-1985 intensified the debate over relationships between human activities and climates. Clearing the land of trees not only opens it to the forces of wind and water erosion, but it also increases the reflectivity of the land, decreases the amount of water evapotranspiration from vegetation and puts more dust into the air. All these factors can prevent the formation of clouds. But since climatologists only have data from one planet on which to base their conclusions, they have no way of comparing variables.

Deforestation is, like desertification, closely tied to growing human numbers' needs for more farmland. Trees are also cut by companies seeking timber; by governments clearing for roads, dams and mines, and by the 2.5 billion people in the world who rely on firewood for cooking and heating. But the greatest cause of loss is forests cleared not for the wood in the trees but for the land beneath them. The world is losing about 7.3 million hectares of tropical forest per year according to a 1981 UN study – most of it in Latin America.

The open, dry forests are relatively easy for peasant farmers with machetes to clear; their loss increases erosion and desertification. The loss of the dense, tropical moist forests (TMF), the "jungles" of the world, raises other issues. Brazil, Indonesia and Zaire contain more

▼ Young trees, drip-irrigated and protected from the winds and animals by sacking, hold the desert in check in Dubai, United Arab Emirates. Science has the technology to control desertification, but politicians often have trouble finding the cash and the motivation to spend it on projects that may not show profits for years, and then will benefit small farmers and nomads more than the powerful urban elite. In 1977, the livelihoods of 80 million people were directly affected by desertification; by 1984, this figure had jumped to 230 million.

◄▲ Short-term goals can mean long-term environmental problems; spectacular erosion (left) the result of road building in Rondônia province and (above) a logging camp, both in dense Brazilian rainforest. Roads also bring in settlers unused to difficult forest soils, and their farms quickly go bankrupt. Tropical forests which could produce valuable timber indefinitely are often logged out in years by governments hungry for foreign exchange.

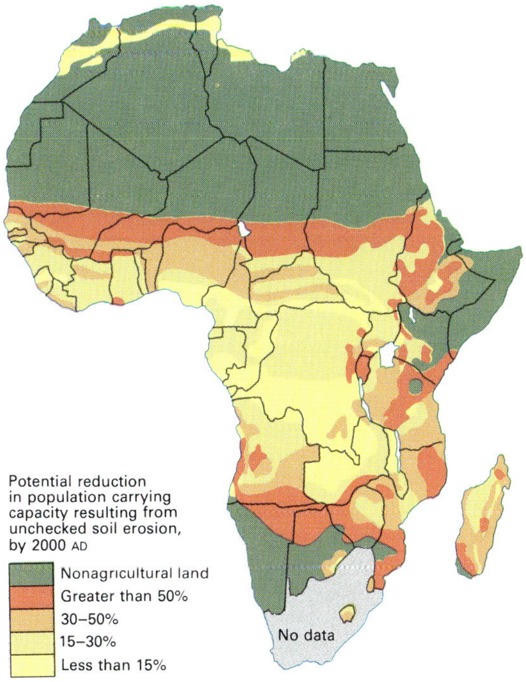

◄ *The center of Africa gets heavy rainfall almost all year round. But the closer one gets to the Sahara Desert in the north and the Kalahari in the south, the more prone to erosion the soils become, and the more the scant rainfall is confined to cloudbursts within a few months. Thus erosion is a threat to the Sahel region, and to Zimbabwe and Botswana. There, unless it is checked, erosion could reduce population-carrying capacity by over 50 percent by the year 2000. But productive areas of East Africa, where population growth rates are high, are also under severe threat.*

▲ *Erosion can be controlled by picks and shovels and hard work, as shown by these terraces in central Java, Indonesia. The ditches catch the rainfall and put water into the soil, while the trees planted among the crops help to anchor the soil on the slope. There are myriad such anti-erosion techniques in the Third World, but farmers cannot undertake the hard labor required unless they get reasonable prices for their harvests. Poor crop prices discourage such work in much of Africa.*

than half the world's 900 million hectares of TMF. Most of the soil underneath TMF is poor in nutrients, so when the forests are cleared, the land quickly loses its fertility and often bakes hard in the sun. Many settlers in Brazil and Indonesia have needed food relief one year or so after beginning farming, and many have given up.

Though TMF covers only six percent of the Earth's land surface, it is believed to contain 40-50 percent of the planet's 5-10 million species of plants and animals. Already tropical forest plants have provided chemicals and drugs, and foodstuffs as yet untried under large farming methods may ease the world's reliance for 85 percent of its food supply on only eight plant species. According to the "Global 2000" report of the US government (➧ page 110), some one million TMF species could become extinct by the end of the century.

Species conservation – a luxury issue?

The problems of deforestation and species loss raise the general issue of species "conservation". Formerly, conservationists tried to preserve plants and animals for their own sake, because the planet seemed a richer place for them. Yet this was seen by many, especially in the Third World, as a luxury issue, a concern for the rich. Thus conservationist organizations like the World Wildlife Fund have gradually made conservation more "scientific" by referring less to beautiful animals and more to "genetic resources". However, this still does not solve the problem of poor southern nations being asked to forego the development of regions because they host rare species which might be of value to agriculture and industry, when that agriculture and industry lies in the North. Some southern leaders have thus called for a system of payments for genetic resources found in the South and developed in the North, and a few southern nations have even banned the export of all genetic material.

These developments in the South have coincided with increased patenting of seeds in the North and the movement of big petroleum companies into the seeds business. These companies are already making agricultural chemicals, so their incursion into the seeds business is logical and potentially very profitable, as farmers worldwide spend some $7-10 billion a year on seeds. Seed-patenting, or the guaranteeing of "plant breeders' rights", are seen by many to be the only way to motivate scientists and companies to go through the long, laborious process of producing new crop strains. But there are drawbacks. The existence of relatively short lists of patented, approved seeds means that long lists of unpatented seeds disappear – with their genetic material. Farmers want the latest and the best, which means that most corn or rice growers in one nation or region may be planting the same variety, creating one vast, uniform medium for a disease or a pest to attack.

► African cheetahs such as these are listed as "vulnerable" by conservation groups, while Asian cheetahs are "endangered". In the 1980s, some 5,000 skins were still being traded annually. Yet the destruction of wild habitats by Man takes a bigger toll of rare animals than does hunting and poaching. Citizens of wealthy industrialized nations want the Third World to conserve its rare and beautiful wildlife. But should poor southern farmers be kept off land to satisfy northern nature lovers? When people living near Third World parks receive a percentage of the revenue from foreign tourism, poaching declines.

► This western swamp tortoise of Western Australia is the world's rarest reptile, with only 50 left in the wild. Is it of any value, besides being a curiosity? The answer for most rare species is that we simply do not know. The more plant and animal species which science studies, the more new food crops and new medical and industrial chemicals are discovered. But the northern nations derive the most benefit from these discoveries. New techniques in genetic engineering will make more wild genetic material commercially valuable. How can the North repay the South, where the species are found, for its conservation work?

Beyond the realm of applied science

The oil companies entering the seeds business are beginning to produce complete "packages" of seeds designed to be used with the company's fertilizers and pesticides. Even fewer farmers can afford the whole package than can afford high-yield seeds. Most important, the key issue with patented seeds is that some of the genetic material going into these seeds comes from southern nations who are asked to conserve their land and thus their wild plant varieties in the name of science, but then get no recompense for doing so. The money goes to northern companies.

There still remain conservation issues which fall outside the realm of applied science. We conserve rainforest to conserve valuable genetic material; even wild and endangered large mammals like the wild Asian buffalos may contain genetic material which could prove valuable in improving domestic cattle breeds. But will we ever need genes from rhino, elephants or tigers? It seems unlikely, though there is no way of foretelling what genetic materials the very new science of genetic engineering will wish it had access to next century.

Conservation of large animals

Science works at conserving big and exotic species because many people want them around. And there is the "piggyback effect", in that conserving one tiger requires many square kilometers of relatively unspoilt forest and all of the other species in it. In India "Project Tiger" focuses the need to protect many other threatened species, including gaur, rhinoceros, wild buffalo, the mugger (a crocodile) and golden langur.

Nevertheless, arguments will continue to rage between those who say it is all right to hunt whales on a sustainable basis and those who claim that it is stupid, greedy and immoral to turn these intelligent and majestic animals into oil and meat, no matter whether the particular species is endangered or not. The gradual change in the membership of the International Whaling Commission (IWC) from mainly whaling states to – after 1979 – mainly nonwhaling states, may have been as responsible for the decision in 1985 to impose a moratorium as were the available scientific data, always very controversial, on the state of the various populations.

► *Scientists are now better able to predict volcanic eruptions – by measuring earth movements and changes in gravity, or by studying gas samples, as here (inset) on Mt Etna. The eruption of Armero in Colombia in 1985 was predicted but the death toll was high (right). Warning procedures must keep pace with predictability.*

▼ *Hurricane Elena, taken from the US Space Shuttle on September 2, 1985. As prediction methods based on radar and satellites have improved, the death tolls have fallen dramatically in the United States. But such storms are still major killers in poor nations such as Bangladesh, where people have no shelter strong enough to withstand the winds.*

Statistics of natural disaster

The erosion, desertification and deforestation of poor lands are slow, grinding, manmade disasters. But recent findings have shown that, worldwide, poorer people are closely associated with "natural disasters". A 1984 study by the Swedish Red Cross found the numbers of people affected by the major natural disasters – droughts, floods, tropical cyclones, earthquakes and tsunamis (tidal waves) – were increasing each decade, though the basic climatic and geophysical mechanics behind these events do not seem to be changing. For instance, 2.5 million people were affected by cyclones each year during the 1960s, 2.8 million each year during the 1970s. The study attributed this jump largely to the increased numbers of poor people living in dangerous housing on dangerous ground. Rich nations may be "disaster-prone", but their people are not as "disaster-vulnerable" as those in poorer countries. In 1960-1981, Japan lost 63 people killed per disaster, while Peru suffered 2,900 deaths per disaster.

But there are two other major disasters, both associated with the way people use their land. Stripping the vegetation from dry ground makes droughts worse and makes the land more drought-prone; clearing land which gets tropical storms make floods worse and the land more flood-prone (◂ page 96). Thus not surprisingly, droughts are the "biggest" disasters in terms of numbers affected: 18.5 million per year in the 1960s, 24.4 million in the 1970s. Floods are the fastest-growing disaster in terms of numbers affected: 5.2 million in the 1960s, 15.4 million in the 1970s. Events in the 1980s – the African and Indian droughts and floods in all Andean and Himalayan nations – seem to be carrying on this disastrous trend.

Three serious pollution threats to the planet all relate to energy and industry: the "greenhouse effect", acid rain and ozone depletion

The threat of pollution

Desertification and deforestation are threats to the human environment at the "front end" of the resource pipelines; pollution still provides several threats at the back end of the line. Three of the most serious pollution threats to the general health of the planet are all related to energy and industry: the "greenhouse effect" and the associated threat of planet warming; acid precipitation, and a diminishing of the layer of ozone surrounding the planet in the stratosphere. While the science of none of these three phenomena is well understood, any "solutions" to these threats are more likely to be political and financial than wholly scientific. In the late 19th century there were about 280 parts of carbon dioxide in the atmosphere for every million parts of air (by volume); this ratio rose gradually to about 343 parts per million (ppm) in 1984. CO_2 is put in the atmosphere by burning fossil fuels and vegetation, and thus this presence has been rapidly increased by industrialization and the burning of forests. CO_2 allows short-wavelength radiation from the Sun to pass through, but it traps longer-wave radiation leaving the Earth's surface. Thus it can act like greenhouse glass, warming the Earth's surface and lower atmosphere. Sometime in the 21st century, the 19th century level is expected to double to 560 ppm, and is expected to be accompanied by a rise in the global mean equilibrium temperature of 1.5-4.5°C, according to a meeting of experts from 29 nations in Villach, Austria, in 1985. The meeting found that CO_2 buildup was implicated in the general rise of 0.3-0.7°C over the past 100 years or so.

But there are other "greenhouse gases" besides CO_2: chlorofluorocarbons (aerosol propellants, refrigeration and foam-producing chemicals), methane (produced by microbes and by burning biomass, and producing coal and natural gas), nitrous oxide (produced by the burning of biomass and fossil fuels and by fertilizer use) and ozone. Already the role of these gases in changing the climate is about as important as that of CO_2; thus an increase in these gases could have the same effect as a doubling of CO_2 concentrations long before CO_2 amounts actually doubled, perhaps as early as 2030.

▼ Smog in Los Angeles. Though such photos are still possible, smog and air pollution have diminished in most northern cities following various clean-air acts. The banning of the use of coal in London has rid the city of the killing fogs that affected it as recently as the 1950s. And buildings once cleaned of Victorian soot stay clean. The problem of urban air pollution is now largely one of poorer countries. In such metropolises as Mexico City and Calcutta, discharges from the smokestacks of unregulated industries, old and poorly maintained vehicles, and the cooking fires of the shanty towns kill the very young and the very old. Some 60 percent of Calcutta's population suffers respiratory diseases because of air pollution.

◀ *Dying trees in France's Vosges Forest. The burning of fossil fuels releases into the atmosphere sulfur dioxide and nitrogen oxides. In Europe and North America, about one-third of this acid is traced to nitrogen and about two-thirds to sulfur. The problem is not only acid "rain", but acid fog, dew, mist, snow and even solid particles which attach to vulnerable buildings. The tall smokestacks meant to reduce local pollution send acid far across national boundaries. Some 58 percent of the sulfur landing on Sweden comes from abroad: for Czechoslovakia the figure is 56 percent and for Finland 55 percent. But Britain receives only 12 percent of its sulfur from abroad, which may explain why it has been slow to become involved in international efforts to control the pollution. Science has yet to explain exactly how and which pollutants damage forests. But by 1985, some six million hectares of trees were affected in only five countries: West Germany, Austria, Czechoslovakia, Poland and Yugoslavia. There was also damage in the United States and Canada.*

The warming of the Earth's surface would be least near the Equator, greatest nearer the poles, and the effects there are expected to be greatest in late autumn and early winter. But that is about as far as predictions go. The increases could make some dry climates of the tropics and subtropics – such as the Sahel – drier still. Temperature rises within the Villach predictions would cause sea levels to rise 20-140cm, the conference reported. A sea-level rise in the upper range would flood many low-lying cities and floodplains. This would be caused mainly by the increased melting of land ice.

The acid rain issue is more immediate and perhaps even more complex than the "greenhouse effect". Burning coal and oil and gasoline releases into the air sulfur dioxide and nitrogen oxides, which can turn into sulfuric and nitric acids. The cause-and-effect links between increased acidity and degraded forests have proved so far impossible to pin down. The *World Resources Report* (1986) identified ozone and nitrogen compounds as the top two villains in North America; ozone and acid deposition, particularly fogs and mists, as the top two factors in western Europe; and gaseous sulfur dioxide and nitrogen oxides, plus ozone and other photochemical oxidants, as the two chief factors in eastern Europe. Research will doubtless reveal much more about the mechanics of water acidification and forest death, but most "solutions" will probably come in the form of laws and subsidies and loans to force and encourage the use of such things as low-sulfur oil and coal; methods which clean coal and oil before they are burned; "scrubbing" systems which clean sulfur from flue gases; new technologies to burn fuel cleaner, and catalytic converters to reduce nitrogen emissions from cars.

Ozone is a pollutant near the Earth's surface, but in the stratosphere forms a layer which absorbs ultraviolet radiation at wavelengths harmful to life and which plays its own complex role in weather systems. The chemicals known as "chlorofluorocarbons" (CFCs) – used as aerosol propellants, in making foam, in solvents and in refrigeration systems – react with the ozone (and other chemicals) and reduce it. A rough consensus has it that emissions of CFCs at current rates will diminish the ozone layer by 3-5 percent over 100 years. In October 1986, ozone levels over the Antarctic were half that of the lowest readings of 1985. Preliminary reports from an expedition to study the phenomenon dismissed several natural causes, such as changes in solar radiation. An ozone depletion of 2.5 percent could increase the cases of certain, usually nonfatal skin cancers by 470,000 per year, according to the US Environmental Protection Agency. It also may increase cases of melanoma, an often fatal skin cancer; damage some plant species; increase cases of eye cancer in cattle; damage the plankton in the ocean which form the basis of most marine food chains; and degrade polymers.

Science has much to do in coping with these three main pollution threats to life on Earth. It can monitor effects; it can explain effects; and it can develop techniques to limit negative effects. But in coping with the threats, science will also have to cope with the illogical way in which politicians have approached these and other environmental degradations. They have given these problems largely to bodies which have no control over the mechanisms causing the problems. Ministries regard this pollution as "side effects" of their energy and industrial policies rather than direct effects, and they are not held administratively responsible for the costs of the damages. To a scientist, it makes little sense.

▲ *Testing a catalytic converter meant to limit exhaust emissions. Science has developed a wealth of such technical fixes to acid pollution: ways of "washing" the sulfur from coal, fluidized bed combustion systems to burn fuels more cleanly, and techniques to "scrub" the gases leaving stacks. But industry has been slow to spend the money to convert to the new technologies, especially when other nations decline to go along, and cleaner industries are thus rendered less competitive. Eastern Europe has taken the odd approach of trying to breed trees resistant to acid, but there has been no real evidence of success.*

Smallpox, eradicated by 1980, killed two million people as recently as 1967

▲ ***Indian schoolchildren on World Health Day as the World Health Organization (WHO) begins its successful 10-year campaign to banish smallpox from the face of the Earth. The success is thought to be permanent, in that animals cannot carry the disease. WHO chose one of the few, if not the only, major disease, we may be capable of eradicating. A similar effort to rid the world of malaria failed. Every day some 13,000 African children die, usually of chronic conditions such as malnutrition and diarrhea rather than acute illnesses such as smallpox. Thus WHO and governments are now concentrating on "control" rather than eradication – through campaigns of public education and vaccination.***

World health campaigns

In May 1980 the annual assembly of the UN's World Health Organization (WHO) declared that the world and all its peoples had won freedom from smallpox, which, as recently as 1967, had been endemic in 33 countries, killed two million people and infected 10-15 million, severely disfiguring many of those that did not die. But the world, largely through the efforts of WHO, decided to banish the disease from the planet. Between 1967 and 1977 some $33 million were spent in a worldwide vaccination program toward this end. As the cost of vaccine and of quarantine measures around the world before the campaign came to $1 billion yearly – leaving out all cost of treating cases – then the campaign was extremely cost effective.

The success raised hopes of banishing other diseases. But hindsight showed what an easy target smallpox was. The variola virus lives only in humans; it has no animal hosts. Humans cannot be "carriers"; you either have it or you do not, and the disease is easy to spot. If you die, the virus dies with you. If you survive, you do not get it again. The virus also dies out when it is surrounded by vaccinated people and has nowhere to go. The vaccine, made from "vaccinia virus", is cheap and easy to manufacture and can be dehydrated, packed in bags and stored for more than a month without refrigeration.

There is no other obvious disease candidate for elimination. But there is much scope for the improvement of vaccines and vaccination programs. It has been found that the vaccinia virus which gave people immunity to smallpox has some "blank" spaces on its genetic coding. These spaces could perhaps eventually be coded through genetic engineering to produce a multi-purpose vaccine against the viruses behind flu, herpes infections, rabies and hepatitis.

Other less futuristic multipurpose vaccines have had great success against polio, measles, mumps, diphtheria, tetanus, cholera and whooping cough. A vaccine against malaria, which at any given time probably infects 160 million people worldwide, is expected before the 20th century ends, though making it cheap enough to reach the poor who need it may be a harder problem than creating it in the first place.

It is probably just as well that the UN are moving more toward very long-term, multifaceted health campaigns. For instance, for as little as $5, a child can be immunized against six key childhood killers: diphtheria, measles, tetanus, whooping cough, tuberculosis and polio. The first four kill 352,000 children every year in Nigeria alone. UNICEF is also encouraging mothers, especially in the Third World, to return to breast feeding to give their children natural immunities; it is establishing programs to monitor children's growth, and it is encouraging the use of Oral Rehydration Therapy (ORT), a mixture of water, sugar and salt which has the effect of getting water into the systems of children suffering from diarrhea. It is a cheap "medicine"; almost all mothers possess the ingredients and the implements to make the mixture. If it spreads, it may save more lives in a year than penicillin does in a decade.

The drawback to these grassroots approaches is that they are not as glamorous as banishing a virus. They will require much more money over many more decades; and much of the money will have to come from the rich countries and benefit poor countries. While the northern nations could see the benefits for them in banishing smallpox, with its two million deaths in 1967, they have been less interested in programs to control diarrhea, which kills six million Third World children yearly and contributes to the deaths of another 18 million.

Medical care

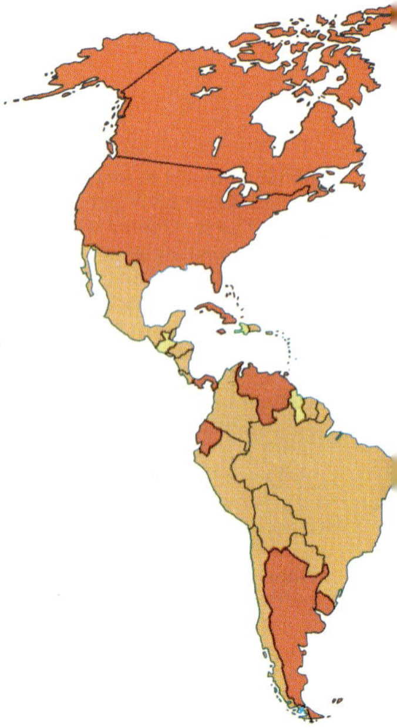

Persons per doctor
- Less than 1,000
- 1,000 – 5,000
- 5,000 – 10,000
- 10,000 – 25,000
- Greater than 25,000

▲ ***Hospital beds are fewest where disease and mortality are highest. But the answer is not necessarily more hospitals. Improved sanitation, safer water supplies, better nutrition, sounder housing – all these reduce mortality rates faster and more cost-effectively than increases in the numbers of staff.***

► ***"Formula" baby milk is on sale throughout the Third World; this stand is in Managua. Babies drinking such products do not get their mothers' resistance to diseases; but they may get dirty water and over-diluted mixtures. One Cairo study found that bottle feeding increased babies' mortality risks by as much as 30 percent. The code on advertising such products forbids the suggestion that they are healthier than mothers' milk. But it is widely flaunted by northern multinational companies and local firms. UNICEF has made a return to breast feeding one of the main thrusts in its program for mother-and-child health care, launched in 1982.***

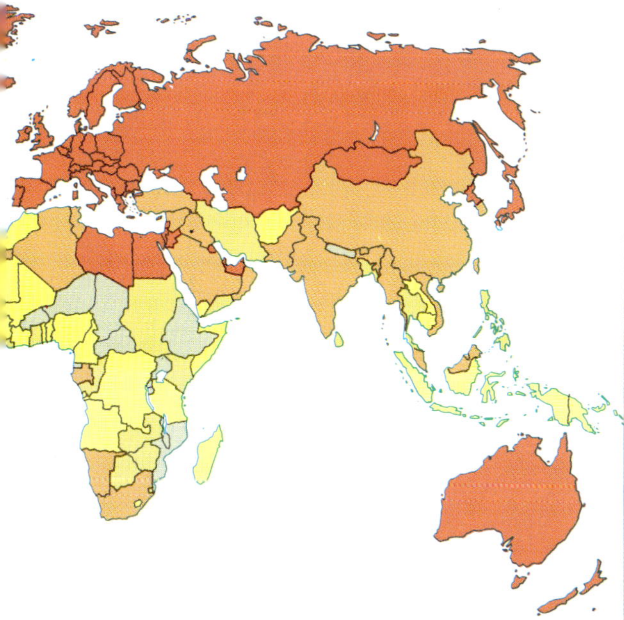

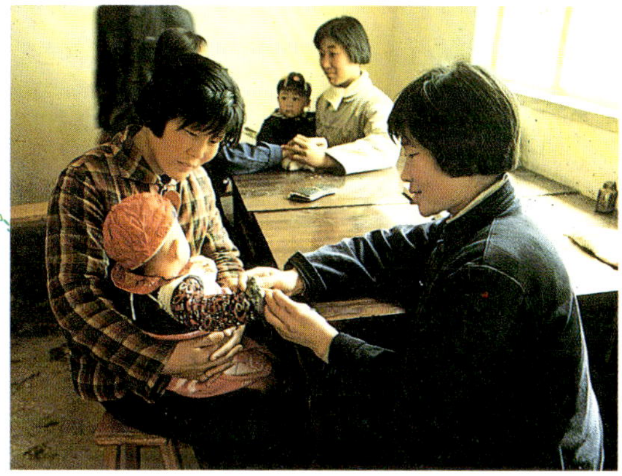

◄ *A "barefoot doctor" at work in a Chinese commune. These are really community health workers, not "doctors". Their job is to educate, advise, treat where they can and send patients to doctors where they cannot. More than 100 such workers can be trained and equipped for the cost of educating a single doctor. And these workers carry health to the countryside, while doctors tend to stay in city hospitals. The task is to convince governments of the effectiveness of such workers.*

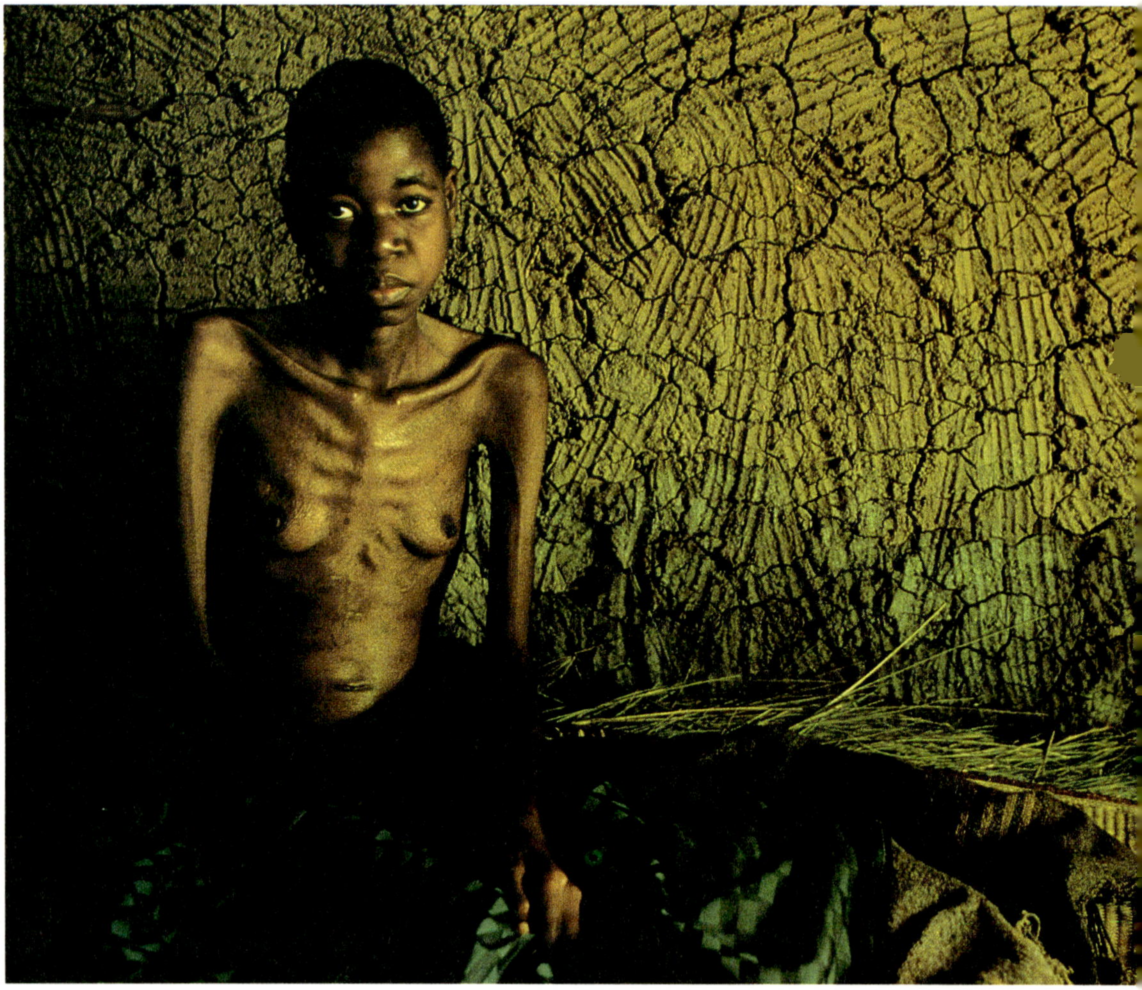

► *Yeta is a 24-year-old Ugandan woman who had been suffering from AIDS for two years when this photo was taken. She is doubtless dead by now. At Uganda's Nsambia Mission Hospital, 20 percent of blood donors under 30 years of age were found to be infected by the AIDS virus, as were 20 percent of pregnant women in the hospital. AIDS is more than a killing disease in Africa; it could become a development disaster, taking funds from Africa's fledgling primary health care efforts in the countryside. But there are signs that African governments are becoming more frank both in providing statistics about the disease and in educating their people about how to avoid it.*

The fight against AIDS

Just as medical scientists were basking in the triumph of smallpox eradication (◀ page 104), an even more fearful epidemic disease came to light: acquired immune deficiency syndrome (AIDS), the virus of which wrecks the immune system and thus renders the body vulnerable to a wide range of potentially fatal infections and to at least one form of cancer. It also behaves like a "slow virus", infecting the brain and nervous system. But human immunodeficiency virus (HIV) was not identified until the early 1980s – nearly a decade after the infection seems to have begun to move, unseen, around the world.

Only in the mid-1980s did the international dimensions of the problem become clear, and by 1987 the World Health Organization announced that over 40,000 cases had been reported in North America, Europe, Australia and New Zealand. But infection with HIV does not necessarily result in AIDS, and there are divisions of opinion over what proportion of HIV-carriers are likely to become ill and die. The WHO estimated that between 10 and 50 percent of those infected would develop AIDS within five years of acquiring the infection. By 1987 some 1.5 million people seemed to be infected in the United States – at least 100 times the number of those actually with the disease. The likelihood that an infected mother will transmit HIV to her newborn child is thought to be about 50 percent – so that in parts of the world where 8-10 percent of pregnant women are infected, up to five percent of newborns may become infected. The

► *A human T-lymphocyte (a kind of white blood cell) infected with the AIDS human immunodeficiency virus (HIV), the virus particles appearing as small blue, rounded dots. The virus is very fragile outside the human body, which explains why AIDS cannot be passed by casual contact such as shaking hands. But inside the body, the virus attacks the T-lymphocytes, which guide the body's defenses against invading organisms. Thus in an early stage of AIDS, the lymph glands are enlarged and the patient suffers fever as the lymphocytes are attacked. Later, with the immune systems disabled, the patient suffers "opportunistic infections" – including those by common organisms which do not usually cause disease.*

virus is more commonly spread through sexual intercourse, however, particularly when this is sufficiently violent to rupture blood vessels. In the developed world most AIDS transmission has been among male homosexuals, bisexuals and intravenous drug users. In Africa and the Caribbean, AIDS is predominantly spread via heterosexual contacts. Screening programs have virtually eliminated the problem of HIV being transmitted through blood.

Screening – for example, among patients attending hospital for other reasons – will undoubtedly bring HIV carriers to light and help to curb the spread of the disease. But it can also be seen as an infringement of personal liberty. The WHO and other organizations have also considered the possibility of screening international travelers, but concluded thus far that the ensuing legal, ethical and other problems would outweigh the likely returns in briefly retarding the spread of AIDS. Measures such as compulsory quarantine have also been considered but rejected.

Likewise, some experts have felt that governments in parts of central and western Africa have been insufficiently helpful in permitting thorough investigation of the disease in their countries. In 1987 the WHO claimed that while 36 African countries had reported a total of 3,538 cases, studies in several cities had shown an AIDS incidence at least as high as that in New York and San Francisco. Estimating that 1-2 million Africans were infected, WHO warned that a minimum of 10,000 new cases could be occurring each year.

The major strategy by health education agencies has been to encourage the use of condoms, which while not 100 percent effective do reduce considerably the chance of HIV transmission. One drug, azidothymidine, has helped to ameliorate the symptoms of AIDS, but causes toxic side effects too. And progress towards immunization has been bedeviled by the difficulty of developing a vaccine against a virus which attacks the immune system that usually repels infection.

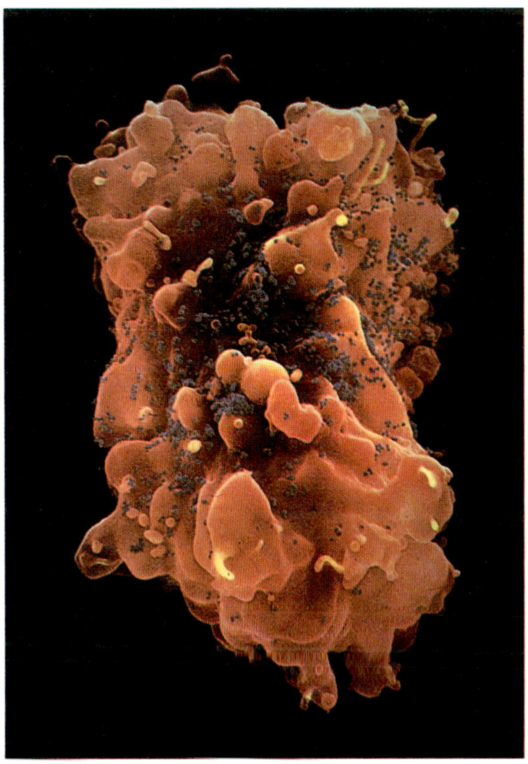

◄ *"International AIDS Day", London. Such events are part of a worldwide campaign to educate people about the disease – and how to prevent it. Condoms are key to the notion of "safer sex", as is the limiting of the number of one's sexual partners in general, and specifically not having sex with those known to be at high risk of carrying HIV; prostitutes – male and female – and intravenous drug users. Prudery has helped the spread of AIDS, as governments have been loath to speak openly about condoms and sexual practices, or to teach drug users safer techniques. But such shyness has been disappearing rapidly, and educators are now keen to teach children how to protect themselves.*

See also
Social Relations 5-20
Paymasters 21-40
Nuclear Power and Radiation 57-64
Genetic Engineering 65-76

Diagnosing planetary "illness"

The environmental debate has raised many questions and given few answers. To understand the global consequences of our activities we need to find out much more about how the essential "life-support" systems of the Earth work.

In 1986, British atmospheric chemist James Lovelock proposed a new scientific discipline, "geophysiology", derived from his Gaia theory. Geophysiology is the study of the systems by which the entire living community of a planet, the "biota" maintains living conditions, the climate in particular, favorable to itself.

Carbon dioxide is a "greenhouse gas": it traps heat radiated from the warmed ground surface, so forming a "blanket" that warms the air and the ground beneath. During the last four billion years the Sun is believed to have been growing steadily hotter, yet the temperature at the ground has varied little. This climatic stability has been achieved by the removal of carbon dioxide from the air and its burial eventually in ocean sediments well away from the processes that might liberate the captured carbon. Carbon dioxide released from living organisms reacts with the calcium silicate in weathered rock to form calcium bicarbonate, a soluble substance. This is taken up by marine organisms, which convert it to calcium carbonate, and make into their shells. When they die the shells drift to the sea bed, where they accumulate as sediments. Thus the process by which the temperature on Earth remains fairly constant is controlled biologically.

This is not the only way in which our climate is being regulated. When the temperature rises, more water evaporates, especially from the oceans. Water vapor is also a greenhouse gas, and increases the warming effect, but when it condenses to form clouds, the surface is cooled, partly by being shaded and partly because white clouds reflect incoming solar radiation back into space. Water vapor will not condense, unless there are microscopically small particles to act as "cloud condensation nuclei": the vast majority of them are made from sulfate formed from dimethyl sulfide, which is emitted by phytoplankton.

The Gaian theory and the new science of geophysiology derived from it allow scientists to study the Earth as though it were a single living entity. Although the patient is shown to be inherently robust it does not follow that its natural resilience licenses humans to overexploit the planet with no thought for the consequences. Gaian theory leads its supporters to refute the old idea of organisms adapting to environments over which they have no control. It substitutes a more profound study of the Earth.

◄ Rainforests trap and recycle moisture, thus making rain. They remove carbon dioxide from the air, and their plants store it. We do not know to what extent their now rapid destruction will alter climate and carbon cycles, but it seems wise to proceed with caution.

Futurology

8

Chance as a principle of science...Predictions by organizations...The nuclear winter debate... Microelectronics and information technology...The prospects for limitless energy...Visions of the future ...The prospects of immortality...Doom and Utopia... Escape to the stars?...PERSPECTIVE...Time travel... Criticisms of economic forecasts...**Brave New World** ***and*** **1984**

Attempts to forecast the future are based on the mistaken belief that if we collect enough information about how things are today, then plot graphs of the current direction and speed of change, then it is possible to predict exactly where the world will be at a given tomorrow. Some blame the mechanistic world views encouraged by the work of such mathematicians as Isaac Newton (1642-1727) and Pierre-Simon, Marquis de Laplace (1749-1827) for making us believe there is a scientific – as opposed to visionary or magical – system for predicting the future. The work of Albert Einstein (1879-1955) on relativity heralded a less mechanistic world view by suggesting that if everything were in fact relative to everything else, then one could never describe enough variables to determine future events. The "uncertainty principle" enunciated in 1927 by the German quantum physicist Werner Heisenberg (1901-1976) states that – in the world of subatomic particles at least – it is impossible to determine accurately the position and momentum of a particle simultaneously; the more accurately you know one, the less accurately you know the other. In as far as this suggests that uncertainty is now not only a part of science, but a "principle" of science, it is a radical departure from the days when scientists thought that, given enough data and enough time to calculate, they could predict the future of any system. Yet these lessons have been slow to filter outside of physics, and until recently some organizations, encouraged by the rapidly-growing power of computers, appeared willing to try to look into the future from an 18th-century perspective.

Traveling into the future

Before this century time was regarded as simply "there" – "absolute, true and mathematical time, flowing equably" to use the words of Isaac Newton. Then, with Albert Einstein's theory of relativity, our view of both space and time was transformed. Suddenly time became part of the physical world, rather than a mere backdrop to it.

Relativity weaves space, time, and matter into a unity and leads to a number of effects that cause distortion of time. Perhaps the best known is the "twins effect". An astronaut who leaves Earth and travels at high speed to some distant star finds on returning that he/she has aged less than the twin sibling left behind. What has happened? During the journey, time passes more slowly in the spacecraft than on Earth. However, the astronaut is quite unaware of this, because thought processes – and everything else – are equally slowed: time passes "normally", and the returning traveler is surprised to find that events on Earth have "got ahead".

The size of the effect depends on the spacecraft's speed. In the theory of relativity the speed of light plays a key role, and the magnitude of the time-stretching effect being described here is determined by how close the spacecraft can approach the speed of light. To take an example, at 99 percent of the speed of light, a journey to the nearest star and back takes about nine years as far as the Earth twin is concerned, but to the astronaut the round-trip time is only about 16 months. If the speed is 99.9 percent of the speed of light the journey time from Earth remains more or less the same, but for the astronaut it is reduced to about five months.

In effect, the returning astronaut has traveled into the future. In principle, by extending the journey time and getting very close to the speed of light the astronaut could travel hundreds or even thousands of years into the future. A trip around the galaxy might take ten years of spacecraft time, but the astronaut would return to Earth one million years after leaving it!

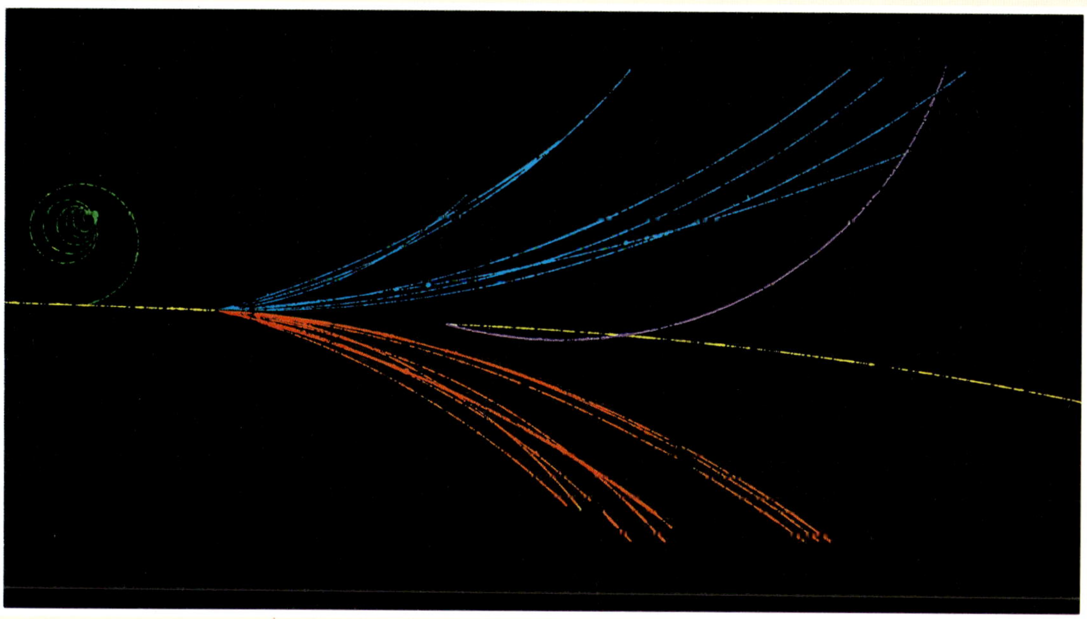

◄▲ Newtonian physics suggested that the future could be calculated from the present position and velocity of every particle. Werner Heisenberg showed that, in the subatomic world, shown (left) by lambda particle decay, only one of these quantities could be accurately known.

The wealthier nations' "Club of Rome" called for "Limits to Growth" in 1972; in the late 1980s a UN commission called for a return to vibrant economic growth

Predictions by organizations

One of the best known of efforts to forecast the future development of the world was the computerized study carried out by the Massachusetts Institute of Technology's Systems Dynamics Group and sponsored by the Club of Rome; the resulting study was published in 1972 as *Limits to Growth* and has had a deep influence on people's view of their environmental resources. It analyzed five variables – technology, population, nutrition, natural resources and environment – and concluded that if current trends continued, various global systems would collapse under the strain over the coming 100 years and the Industrial Revolution would collapse. Thus it called for efforts to sharply limit both population and economic growth. Even when it was published, *Limits to Growth* was criticized as being overly pessimistic, and since then it has been even more heavily criticized for presuming to predict not a future but *the* future based on current trends. One group of critics maintained that even a modest rate of discovery of substitute resources and invention of pollution-control devices would head off the catastrophes foreseen by the Club of Rome. Another group ran the original computer model backwards in time and found that it showed an infinite world population before 1880. But the report did serve two very useful purposes: it analyzed resource problems and environmental problems as two sides of the same coin, and it helped to introduce the idea that "development" ambitions must be limited by environmental and resource realities.

Other models followed quickly during the 1970s. The Czech *Strategy for Survival*, published shortly after the Club of Rome report worked on similar assumptions but stressed alternative strategies for the ten regions of the world which it analyzed. (Czech scientists had become carried away with futurology in the 1960s, and used its apparent "scientific" approach to show that industrial progress would require decentralization and increased rewards. This was all part of the liberalizing process which Soviet tanks suppressed in 1968.)

The Bariloche Foundation in Argentina developed the "Latin American World Model" in the mid-1970s, and this remains the only major Third World model of the future. It predicted that the world could be provided with adequate diet, education and housing. The Organization for Economic Cooperation and Developments "Interfutures" model of the late 1970s did not predict, but instead imagined different futures based on different development strategies. In 1980, the again much criticized *Global 2000* report to United States President Jimmy Carter was not a model but an attempt to analyze and forecast what would happen if present trends in population growth, natural resource use and environmental protection remain unchanged. It has been criticized both for its methods and for trying to draw graph curves into the future. But it also had great influence.

The Club of Rome's dire scenarios and the criticism they drew have made such work unfashionable. In 1984, the United Nations established the "World Commission on Environment and Development" to come up with ways to guide the world into the 21st century in ways that would allow "development" to continue in both rich and poor nations, but without destroying the environment in the process. After two-and-a-half years of hearings and expert advice around the world, the 22 commissioners predicted only that for the condition of the majority of the world's poor to be improved, the world must return to vibrant economic growth, but a "quality" of growth which respected ecological realities.

▶ What is the real future of these children playing in the polluted water of an Ecuadorian shanty town? All present trends are against them, in that each year the gap between the rich and the poor nations increases. Despite technological improvements, rapid population growth means that every year there are more – not less – people on the planet who are hungry, ill-housed, illiterate, without safe water, sanitation and adequate health care. The 1972 Club of Rome report "Limits to Growth" called for limits to both population increase and economic growth. But the 1987 Brundtland report, "Our Common Future", argued reasonably that the only way out of poverty is increased economic growth – unless, that is, the North is willing to redistribute its wealth southward.

Criticisms of the approach of the 1970s

At the end of the 1970s, the authors Frank and Fritzie Manual wrote that "the present day world is teeming with futurologists. We are drunk with the future, as 19th-century romantics were drunk with the past." But they accused the futurologists of leaving out crucial unknowables and befuddling us "with inconsequential knowables".

Since the 1970s, the hubris associated with such exercises seems to have died as the sheer pace of change in the world seems to have picked up. The United Nations Environmental Program (UNEP) in 1982, in publications to mark the 10th anniversary of the UN Conference on the Human Environment in Stockholm, looked forward to the next decade, and criticized several of the 1970s models as being "simplistic, inadequate, based on faulty understanding of the problem and on limited and even faulty data".

It said that the exercises were asking the wrong questions. The problem was not so much what would happen if the current trends were to continue, but how to change those trends to make a better future.

The global models and predictions of the 1970s were perhaps really meant to serve more as warnings to the present than as predictions of the future. This brings up one of the key problems about predictions of the future: most, if not all, are made by people who have axes to grind in the present.

▼ These charts show the growth paths of world population and resources projected by the MIT model. The vertical scales have been left blank to admit that the forecasts are numerically imprecise. (1) shows what happens if we do not change our ways: a population peak in 2050 as resources plummet. (2) imagines unlimited nuclear power, but here pollution and dwindling food cause a similar population peak. Increasing capital investment, cutting pollution, reducing birthrates and increasing agricultural production (3) gives stability for much of the 21st century, but then pollution soars and industry and farm production plummet. Long-term stability was only found (4) by raising food production by 20 percent, while cutting pollution, capital investments and birthrates.

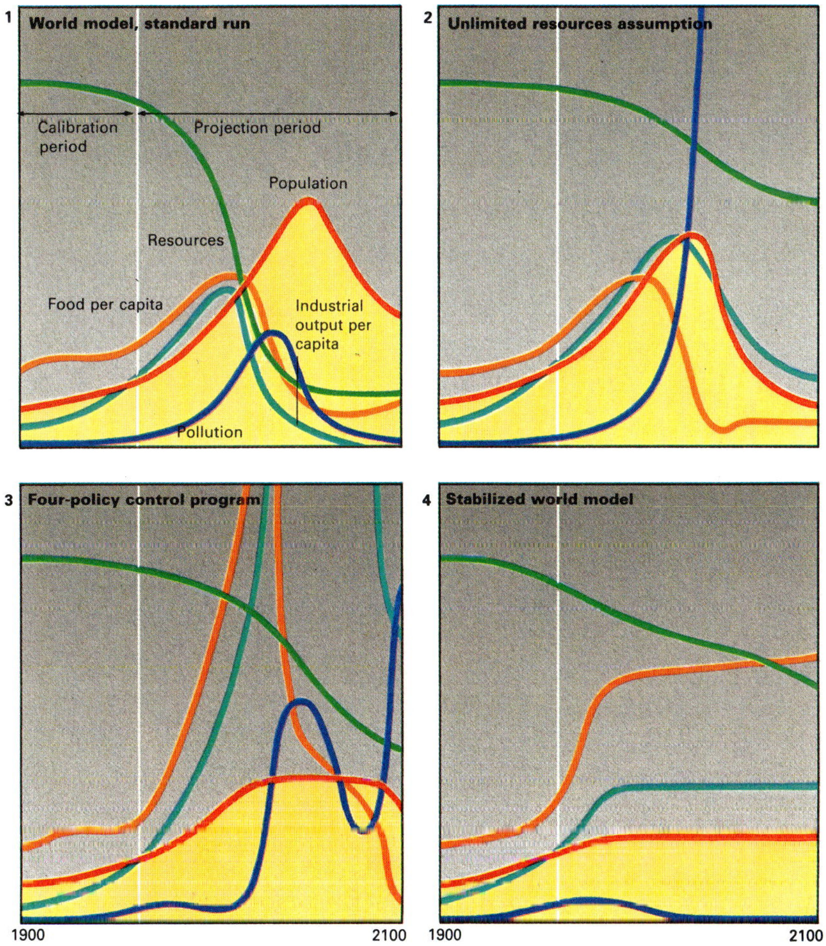

1

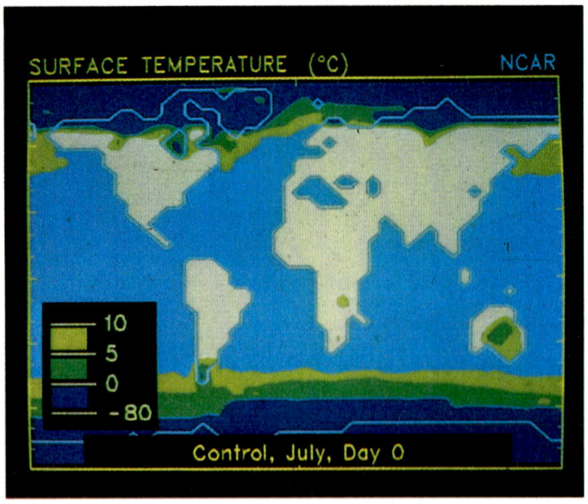

► *Data from erupting volcanoes, such as Mount St Helens in May, 1980, are used to help predict the cooling effects of a nuclear war. Scientists have also studied forest fires, some set for just this experimental purpose, and atmospheric nuclear tests. The smoke which would have the greatest cooling effect is the black, sooty smoke from burning cities, military bases and oil refineries. Computer simulations predict how high this smoke will rise. If much of it goes up above the water-vapor level, then effects will be severe and long-lasting. If it stays lower, it could be washed out of the atmosphere very quickly.*

The "nuclear winter" scenario

Some predictions by scientists may be intended as warnings to the policy-makers of today, rather than as forecasts of what will happen in the future. By 1986, nuclear powers had stockpiled in their strategic arsenals around 12,000 megatons in 24,000 warheads – equivalent to the destructive power of about 300,000 Hiroshima bombs and enough to allow the United States and the Soviet Union to destroy each other's cities 50 times over. This stockpile worries most world citizens and scientists alike, many of whom feel some responsibility for the development of such weaponry.

In the early 1980s, two chemists – Paul Crutzen of West Germany and John Birks of the United States – were estimating the amount of pollution which would be generated by a nuclear exchange. They realized that one of the greatest contaminants would be sooty smoke of the sort which effectively absorbs incoming solar radiation. Much work since then – using data from forest fires, volcanic eruptions and atmospheric nuclear tests, and running such data through computer models of weather systems – has built a scenario describing how much smoke there might be and what might be its effects. One of the fullest reports on this scenario was produced in 1986 by the Scientific Committee on Problems of the Environment (SCOPE) of the International Council of Scientific Unions.

The SCOPE-ENUWAR (Environmental Effects of Nuclear War) results are not a prediction of what will happen, but a prediction of what might happen given a 6,000-megaton "nuclear exchange" at varying times and varying places. The science is complex and controversial, but essentially it is envisioned that such an exchange might have 250,000 square kilometers of urban and industrial regions burning and put 50-150 million tonnes of fine smoke particles into the atmosphere, about half of which would be the sooty, carbon-based variety which effectively absorbs solar radiation. This absorption warms the smoke and surrounding atmosphere, but cool's the planet's surface and the air near it. Radiation from the Earth's surface outward is of a different wavelength, and would escape relatively unhindered. Because the air near the Earth is no longer warmer than the air high in the atmosphere, the lower air would not rise to replace the higher air.

The result would be a long-term "reverse-greenhouse effect" with an acute, an intermediate and a chronic stage. The acute stage would last for days, weeks or even months, with temperatures over northern continental interiors down by 20-30 degrees centigrade. The next

2
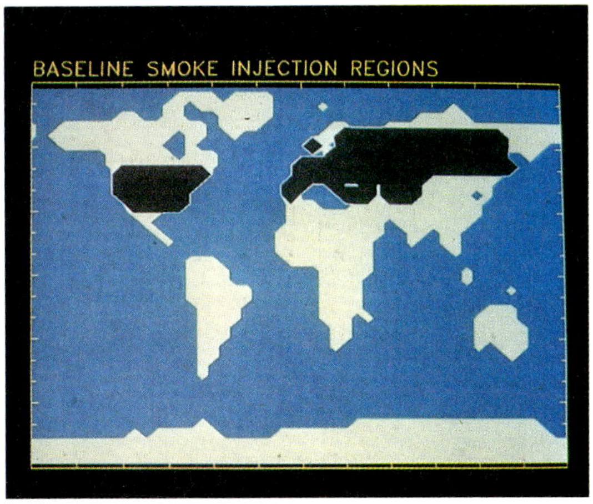

3
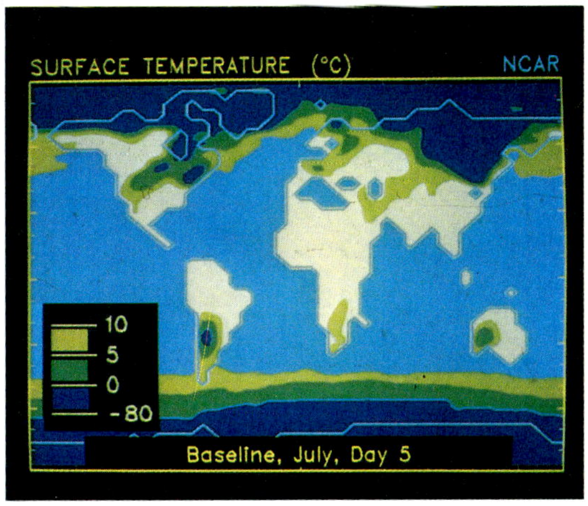

◄ *The US Navy Cruise missile being tested off California is real but the three maps are only computer simulations of the "nuclear winter" expected to follow a nuclear war. Map 1 shows typical northern hemisphere July surface temperatures (°C). Map 2 shows the regions that would produce 180m tonnes of smoke over two days between ground level and 7km high, assuming major nuclear strikes involving 6,000 megatons of bombs targeted only in NATO and Warsaw Pact nations. Map 3 shows the surface temperature five days after the nuclear "exchange". Such computer exercises can never forecast temperature changes for a specific time or place, but rather the type of changes a nuclear exchange would bring. Only a real war would provide exact, uncontroversial data. This simulation was done by Stanley L. Thompson of the US National Center for Atmospheric Research and Stephen H. Schneider.*

phase would last from one to six months, with temperatures still below normal. But there might still be a final "chronic" stage whereby, if earlier cooling had altered snow and ice boundaries, the lower temperatures could persist for years.

The nuclear winter scenario goes on to describe the destruction of entire ecosystems, especially in the tropics, and a resulting world in which famine was more a threat to survivors worldwide than was radiation.

Critics of the scenario, scientific and otherwise, attacked it for not having been scientifically rigorous in its release for peer review, claiming that the essential elements of nuclear winter were being promoted in the early 1980s by the antinuclear lobby before scientists had had a chance to check the results. The United States Defense Department dismissed the SCOPE report because it said it had not been subject to peer review, even though it was compiled by 300 scientists in 30 nations, East and West. In 1986, scientists at the United States National Center for Atmospheric Research (NCAR) published the results of their own computer study which showed temperature drops of 10-15° in the center of continents for anything from a day to a month. The press referred to this as a "nuclear autumn". Some critics of the SCOPE report took the NCAR work as the "refutation" of SCOPE, even though the NCAR group write in their own study of the climatic changes producing "unprecedented worldwide human misery".

Even before the NCAR report, policy makers associated with the superpowers' military efforts tended to ignore or discount nuclear winter, while arms protestors championed its "science". The nuclear winter scenario is still controversial. But perhaps the controversy shows that even when "science" does come up with a fairly well-researched future probability, it catches only the attention of those already so disposed. But then we are rarely rational about the future. No one disagrees that modern nuclear weapons can destroy northern cities many times over, and there is a strong historical backing for the fear that every efficient weapon ever invented is eventually used in large quantities, yet most major cities have ridiculously inadequate shelters and civil defense measures and only a few of the thousands of burns-treatment facilities which would be needed. No nuclear-armed nation has assigned its best minds to the chore of assuring that such weapons are never used. If we are so irrational when faced with a real and present danger, how can we be expected to take heed of other, less palpable, future threats?

Opinion is divided over prospects for a "global village" or a world of "information-haves" and "information have-nots"

► Early science fiction writers tended to err on the side of caution in their prediction of future technological marvels. Reality has outstripped imagination. One spot-on prediction came from Frenchman Jules Verne. In his book "A Trip to the Moon" (right, Georges Méliès' 1902 movie version) he had a rocket manned by three men take off from Florida, orbit the Moon but not land, and then splash down in the ocean – exactly what happened a hundred years later. Unfortunately he had the rocket fired from a huge cannon by a private club of Civil War veterans, an approach to escape velocity which would have crushed all of the passengers to death. "Futurology" may be the most inexact of sciences, in that it is based on all the variables of all the others.

► A robot is serving customers in a California restaurant. The future of both services and industry depends largely on advances in information technology. But events over the past decade show how inaccurate we are at predicting the speed and direction of developments in both fields. Rapid change increases future uncertainties, and technological leaps may widen, not narrow, the gaps between industrialized and developing nations. The prospects of a "Global Village" in which the most remote African farmer can have instant satellite-generated information about local rainfall patterns, and of a world of "information-haves" and "information-have-nots", are presented with equal certainty by those presenting the extremes.

Microelectronics and information technology

In the late 20th century, uncertainty over the future dominated peoples thoughts, and this uncertainty has been increased, rather than decreased, by scientific and technological advances. Most observers agree that both microelectronics and advances in information technology are keys to the futures of both industry and services. But, this being true, should governments push ahead in these fields as rapidly as possible to stay competitive, while disrupting employment patterns, or adapt gradually to the new technologies, thus falling behind the faster-moving countries? Will the technologies create more humane, interesting jobs or make growing numbers of people unemployable? This question should be answerable, but it is not. Most observers believe that the middle-level jobs, between unskilled and top management, will be most affected. But will people at this level have to learn new jobs or will they have to learn to live without jobs? One school of thought holds that the Protestant work ethic must be eased out of existence, and nations concentrate on creating wealth and not jobs. Another holds that new technology will mean new wealth which will mean new demand which will mean new jobs – as has always been the case when new wealth was created.

On the international level, will these technologies result in a "global village", in which the most remote African farmer can have instant satellite-generated information about local rainfall patterns, or will they create "information-haves" and "information have-nots"?

New information and computing technologies cut both ways in the realm of national politics also. Governments could use them to find out what future their citizens want. Through interactive cable-television, instant rates could be cast on all issues, and such polling – on a "for information only" basis – has been tried in the United States. On the other hand, governments may find it more efficient to seek decisions on future use of resources from such machines than from a less well-informed electorate. And of course the information technologies allow governments to keep much closer tabs on the actions of their citizens, an ability which could threaten traditional liberties in traditionally libertarian societies.

▲ *A panel of solar cells at the experimental solar power station at Vignola, on the island of Corsica. The cost of solar cells, which convert sunlight directly into electricity, has been falling dramatically. So these cells are already cost-effective for remote communications or irrigation needs and for that remotest of all locations – outer space. But it could be decades – if ever – before every African hut has its own solar panel, eliminating the smoke, dirt, burns and environmental destruction associated with burning wood.*

► *This reactor produces "cold" nuclear fusion in the gold-lined hemisphere (top) measuring 5cm across. Deuterium and tritium are fed into the chamber. Electron-like muons are beamed in through the vessel's steel casing, causing the hydrogen atoms to fuse and release energy. This device was developed by Augustine J. Caffrey and Kenneth D. Watts of the Idaho National Engineering Laboratory.*

Nuclear fusion

Will we ever possess limitless sources of energy? With the risks associated with nuclear power becoming ever more apparent (♦ page 57), future possibilities may depend upon exploiting other renewable resources when fossil fuels such as oil and coal eventually run out.

Research by scientists and technologists in a number of fields – ranging from nuclear physics to simple techniques of harnessing solar radiation stored in the sea or vegetation – may achieve commercially viable energy resources of infinite capacity by the beginning of the next century.

Nuclear fusion – deriving energy from fusing the nuclei of two atoms – is one long-term hope for a safe and virtually infinite source of energy. Its main attraction is the prospect of an inexhaustible source of fuel, deuterium, a heavy isotope of hydrogen, which exists naturally in water. In addition, there are no long-term problems of nuclear waste disposal, the reactors are incapable of radiation leaks, and there will be no need for reprocessing plants. If the inherently difficult challenges of producing an economically viable power source from this process are met, fusion reactors will be a practical option in the 21st century.

Current plans for fusion energy involve two alternative approaches: magnetic confinement and laser implosion. In the first, the hydrogen isotopes exist in a plasma, a gas of such high energy levels that the electrons separate from the nuclei. At sufficiently high temperatures the hydrogen isotopes will collide and fuse to form helium, giving off energy in the process. The temperature required is at least 100,000,000°C, at which all metals would be vaporized, so the plasma must be contained within a magnetic field or "bottle". The second concept uses powerful beams of laser light to compress and heat a pellet of deuterium and tritium to cause fusion. The first approach has received most support, and the race is on to contain tiny portions of matter for several seconds at the necessary temperatures and pressures. By the mid-1980s scientists had succeeded in generating temperatures well over 100,000,000°C, but not simultaneously with other required conditions.

Major fusion research has been going on in Europe, the United States and the Soviet Union, and there is much international co-operation. Japanese experts were hoping that their toroidal JT-60 machine could achieve "break-even" – giving more energy than it consumes – by 1990. Scientists are also collaborating on the International Thermonuclear Experimental Reactor (ITER).

Power from the sea

The largest store of solar energy is found in the world's oceans. If a tenth of one percent of the energy stored as heat in tropical waters was converted to electricity, it would amount to more than twenty times the generating capacity of the United States. The technology to achieve this is still in its experimental stages. Known as OTEC (Ocean Thermal Energy Conversion), it exploits heat differentials in the depths of the sea to produce power. In the most common type of OTEC system, the warm surface water evaporates ammonia and the expanding gases drive a turbine generator. The vapor is then condensed by the cooler, deeper water. The only geographical requirement is a temperature differential of 18°C between surface water and water 1,000 meters down, a requirement met in virtually all of the world's tropical seas and within reach of 99 nations.

The benefits appear enormous. The technology is said to be no more than "sophisticated plumbing" OTEC can produce electricity where it is scarce – in the energy-poor tropical Third World. The process raises nutrient-rich deep waters which can be used for fish farming, and the possibility of freshwater production also makes such schemes attractive.

Power from plants

In the most fertile regions, plants capture and store the equivalent of one and a half times the total world human energy demands each year. Attempts to make use of this vast reservoir of stored energy began in the 1970s, when production of ethanol (ethyl alcohol), directly from sugar by fermentation or indirectly from starches, was developed. Many Brazilians are already running their cars on ethanol. But scientists are also coming up with efficient methods of converting ethanol into hydrogen.

▼ This odd piece of plumbing is actually 1,000m long. Cold, deep water is pumped up the heat exchanger in the warmer water near the surface, where it is used to evaporate and condense ammonia as part of a cycle to drive turbines and produce electricity.

Ocean thermal gradient plant

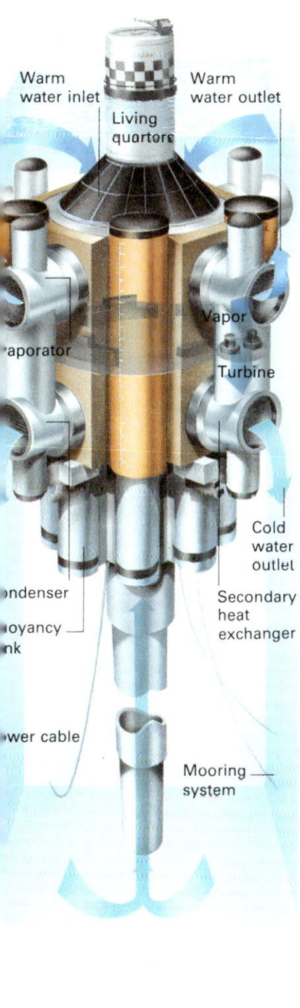

◀ A massive wind turbine. Wind has powered human activities for centuries, and is producing electricity in both developed and developing nations. But the need now is to find ways of getting as much electricity as possible, so that the land does not become covered with unsightly, whirring structures more intrusive than the largest power lines. One solution might be to put the "wind farms" at sea. They must be kept as simple as possible. As one energy expert said about Africa: "Any mechanic skillful enough to keep a wind turbine working could probably spend his time better keeping lorries on the road". Better batteries will also be needed to store the wind electricity.

► *A still from the 1926 movie "Metropolis" illustrates a recurring pessimistic view of the future. For planners always come up against the fact that society would be easier to manage if people were more like machines. But this approach leaves out human individuality, spirituality, creativity and plain old eccentricity. Worse, it has humans serving machines rather than machines serving humans. People once did the work of animals: during the Industrial Revolution and until recently they did the work of machines. Now machines can "think" and robots are moving into factories. So human thinkers are busy trying to decide what the proper work of humans really is.*

Visions of the future

A few thinkers have pointed out the great flaw in being able to foresee the future: it would not give us new freedom, but would almost certainly cost us our freedom. If we knew what developments were in the offing, we would doubtless feel the need to organize ourselves to meet them. This organization could well require authoritarian governments – or perhaps one world authoritarian government. In 1974, McGeorge Bundy, former United States White House adviser, predicted the establishment of a world "authority" by the year 2024 to control nuclear weapons and enforce population quotas on nations by withholding food from those which exceeded the limits.

Gerard O'Neill, professor of physics at Princeton University, New Jersey, attacked the apparently innocent report *Limits to Growth* (1972) (◀ page 110) for its recommendations "that all of humanity should make the transition to a globally managed static society in which the individual could move and use energy and materials only within tightly circumscribed limits; those constraints would bind not only those of us alive now, but our descendants to the end of time." He derided its authors for "urging us once again to surrender freedom for 'a greater good'". (O'Neill published his own best guess at the future in 1981 in *2081: a Hopeful View of the Future*, which showed that even in the 1980s a physical scientist could conceive of a well-ordered planet 100 years hence, but there is little discussion of social tension or social change.)

The threats and promises of such developments as artificial intelligence, interplanetary flight, nuclear weapons stockpiles, genetic engineering, automation, acid pollution, ozone depletion, acquired immune deficiency syndrome (AIDS), or "testtube babies" do not point to one future. They point to many, many possible futures. The trick is to organize political, economic and scientific systems so that humans can go on striving toward the futures they want.

However, giving humans choice is messy – involving strife, argument, disagreement and confusion. But it might be better than boring certainty. In the words of W.R. Inge (1860-1954) the "gloomy dean" of St Paul's cathedral in London: "The effect of boredom on a large scale in history is underestimated. It is the main cause of revolutions and would soon bring to an end all the static Utopias..."

▲ *The totalitarianism of Orwell's "1984", in the movie version of the same year. Those concerned with human freedom and creativity are relieved that our governments cannot see into the future with any certainty. For then they would organize to meet perceived threats, and that organization could well mean an elimination of the messiness and strife which is inherent in freedom and democracy. Rapid changes in technology do not point toward one future, but many possible futures. And new forms of communications can also allow people ever more freedom to chose the future they want.*

Brave new world

Two of the century's most popular visions of the future – Aldous Huxley's "Brave New World" (1931) and George Orwell's "1984" (1949) – reach very different views of the future. It is hard to know which came closest to getting it right.

Orwell's view is of a totalitarian government which outlaws human freedom and turns language against itself so that humans will lack the power to think for themselves and threaten the state. Though the book is far more about Orwell's fears for Britain in the late 1940s than a serious attempt at prediction, many see the accuracy of his prophecy in the nature of some authoritarian states of the late 1980s.

Huxley portrayed a static Utopia whose affluent citizens are discouraged against thinking for themselves and interfering with the status quo by the availability of mind-easing drugs and mind-numbing televised entertainment.

In his 1985 study of the negative effects of television on social discourse and its ability to trivialize the most serious political and social issues ("Amusing Ourselves to Death"), Neil Postman argued strongly that – certainly as far as the United States of the 1980s was concerned – Huxley's view was far more accurate than Orwell's.

Few if any statements about the future have proved accurate, and those are praised only when hindsight is possible. Fewer still have been siezed on by national electorates and leaders and used as guides for action. Perhaps the British writer C.S. Lewis (1898-1963) said as much about the future as it is possible to know today: "The Future is something which everyone reaches at the rate of sixty minutes an hour, whatever he does, whoever he is."

◄ Utopia can be boring. Social scientists are better than physical scientists at predicting the future, as psychology changes more slowly than technology. Predictions gathered by the British writer Nigel Calder in 1964 of the world in 1984 were accurate about the increased acceptance of homosexuality and improved rights for women. But the physical scientists promised widespread rocket transport systems, the phasing out of stones, bricks and concrete as building materials, along with the disappearance of books and newspapers.

Science has offered encouraging possibilities of increasing the human life span

Will science cancel death?

Improved health care has led to an increase in life expectancy, but this has not been accompanied by an increase in the maximum life span of individuals. All the indications are that this maximum has not changed over the centuries. In other words, a barrier to further life extension appears to be present.

In practical terms this means that the major causes of death are age-related disease or the process of aging itself. It is easy to see why many people have been fascinated by the possibility of simply preventing the aging process. In this way the problem of debilitating disease would disappear and individuals would be able to enjoy the retention of all their faculties for a much longer period or even indefinitely.

In order to decide whether halting the aging process may be a reality in the future or is merely a fictional scenario, it is necessary first to understand why aging occurs in humans and all other mammalian species.

Why we age

The British evolutionary biologist George Williams (b.1930) has pointed out that if organisms have evolved the seemingly miraculous process of development from egg to adult, then they should have solved the much lesser problem of maintenance of the adult. Such maintenance might involve continual replacement of cells and tissues by regenerative mechanisms, repair of damage and so on. The crucial problem, therefore, is to understand why successful maintenance of an adult animal does not occur.

Almost all offspring are produced by young adults, very few from middle-aged animals and almost none from old animals. It therefore becomes a pointless strategy for an organism's genes to invest resources into continual maintenance of the adult body, when that body is likely to die from some other cause. It is much better strategy to divert resources which might otherwise be used for the avoidance of aging to rapid growth to adulthood and reproduction.

► Californian Mary McKinney, aged 112 and reputedly the oldest woman in the world when this photograph was taken in March 1986. There have been reports of people (particularly those living in remote communities, unaffected by civilization, stress and pollution) who have lasted appreciably longer than this, even into their 130s. But the absence of reliable records usually makes the authentification of such claims impossible.

◄ Mike Darwin, President of Alcor Life Extension Foundation of Riverside, California, displays his "neuropatient storage vault". Inside are six aluminum cannisters, each carrying a human head, which are submerged in liquid nitrogen. Mr Darwin believes that his deceased subjects can be thawed out at some time in the future, when medical science has advanced sufficiently for their former illnesses or malfunctions to be cured.

▲ HeLa cells, which originated with tissue taken from an American victim of cervical cancer in 1951, have proved extremely useful for cultivating viruses and other purposes. Potentially immortal, the cells have continued to replicate and are now found worldwide in laboratories. Our understanding of aging would be advanced if we knew why some cells divide indefinitely when grown in tissue culture, while others soon die out.

Germ line cells are potentially immortal

Animals have evolved as efficient mechanisms for reproduction, not mechanisms for achieving immortality of the body. It follows from this that germ lines which transmit eggs and sperm from generation to generation must never age: in fact germ line cells from all extant species are, indeed, potentially immortal. The aging process is seen in wild animals when they are placed in a protected environment such as a zoo, where starvation and predation does not occur and disease is controlled. The maintenance of the adult animal begins to fail after a given life span and the same applies to humans in any society with appropriate health care.

From the organism's point of view, it is clearly pointless to invest resources for the efficient maintenance of any individual tissue or organ system, while allowing others to degenerate: many body functions tend to deteriorate together. Of course, there is not complete synchrony; for example some older individuals retain an excellent mind and memory as their body deteriorates, and others are physically strong but have become demented, and so on. But in general the synchrony in all age-related processes is quite striking and certainly supports the view that fundamental defects in cells and macromolecules are accumulating in all parts of the body.

Increasing the human life span

It has been shown many times that rats kept on a low-calorie diet are known to increase their life span by about 50 percent: the same might apply to humans. Another approach is to study human cells in culture. Some types of cell which can be grown successfully in the laboratory have a finite life span. On the other hand, cancer cells will grow indefinitely. So far, however, the way in which cancer cells escape from senescence is not understood.

Nonliving cells cannot survive for ever and many essential parts of the body consist of such cells and therefore have a low capacity for repair and renewal – the brain and sense organs, and to a large extent muscles and connective tissue, and therefore the heart and circulatory system. We can nevertheless imagine a complex organism which is capable of continual regeneration and renewal in all parts of its body. It would have pools of stem cells to replace nerve cells in the brain, and many other essential organs would also have to be in a "steady state" with continual turnover of cellular and structural components. In addition, the design of skeletal structures would have to be entirely different, with built-in maintenance mechanisms. This organism would not be an improved version of a human being, but rather a different organism altogether.

Utopian visions are out of vogue – end-of-the-world scenarios exert much greater fascination

Doom and Utopia

The future holds a fascination for all, not just for those playing the horses or the stock exchanges. But what does it say about human nature that the two most popular futures are the Utopias and the disasters, with the end-of-the-world scenarios exerting far greater fascination over the humann imagination than the Utopias?

Consider such films as Stanley Kramer's "On the Beach" (1959), in which Australia waited to be wiped out by nuclear fallout, or Stanley Kubrick's "Dr Strangelove", in which a United States nuclear bomber manages to drop its bomb on the Soviet Union, and in the process sets off a planetary doomsday device, and then try to think of a popular film depicting a happy and peaceful future world.

► *An abiding image that continues to haunt deliberations over our planet: "The Four Horsemen of the Apocalypse" by the German artist Albrecht Dürer (1471-1528). Like his Italian contemporary Leonardo, Dürer was a man of considerable intellectual curiosity and what we would now call scientific insight.*

Visions of the Apocalypse

The Christian Bible manages to squeeze both disaster and Utopia into one chapter. St John of Patmos tells in his book of Revelation of the final battle, Armageddon, in which the powers of good will do battle with the powers of evil and which will be followed by the construction of the new Jerusalem, a Christian Utopia. (Some of St John's descriptions of the battle – including forces able "to scorch men with fire" – have led fundamentalists to see this as a prophecy of a coming nuclear war.)

Many prophecies of doom center at the turning-points of millenia – thousand-year periods. St John of Patmos himself may be largely responsible for this doomsday pattern, as he wrote of the Devil being bound for 1,000 years and Christ reigning for 1,000 years. This idea so exercised European Christians of 1,000 years ago that as the end of the year 999 approached men and women confessed sins, gave away land and property, forgave debts and generally behaved very respectably toward one another. Many were said to have died of fright as the bells rang out at midnight on the eve of the new year, 1000.

► *Australia waits to be annihilated by radioactive fallout, following a series of nuclear explosions in the Northern Hemisphere. In this scene from Stanley Kramer's movie "On the Beach", which was based on Nevil Shute's novel, the commander of a submarine, Dwight Towers (Gregory Peck), sends Lieutenant Sundstrom (Harp McGuire) ashore in protective clothing to investigate a garbled radio message.*

Year 2000

Year 2000 is already sparking the same sort of fascination as the year 1000. Charles Berlitz, writer on the alleged mysteries of the "Bermuda Triangle", has assembled in his book "Doomsday 1999 AD" all the prophecies which hold that the world will end in or around that year. They range from the Buddhist prophecy that Buddhism would last for 2,500 years, to the precisely-timed vision of the 16th century prophet Nostradamus:

"The Year 1999, month seven,
From the sky shall come a great king of terror."

Not all doomsday warnings are from nonscientists, nor are they all based on ancient prophecies. British science writers John Gribbin and Stephen Plagemann published in 1974 a book called "The Jupiter Effect" explaining how the major planets would be in rough alignment in 1982, and this would affect both ocean tides and flows of the Earth's molten inner core, causing floods, earthquakes and other disasters. The Earth passed through the alignment unscathed, but the two noted that there would be an even more direct alignment of large and small planets in May, 2000.

▼ *One artist's impression, from early this century, of "how the world will be saved from starvation" by means of grandiose technology, bullishly applied. The July, 1907, issue of "Sphere" magazine presents a typical wheatfield in 1970.*

Visions of Utopia

Utopian scenarios go back to Plato's "Republic"; the name "Utopia" comes from the 1516 book by Sir Thomas More describing a benign state governed entirely by reason, a state More held in sharp contrast to the conditions of his own time. "Utopia" comes from the Greek "ou" ("not") and "topos" ("place") – "nowhere".

Utopian literature had its high-point in the 18th century Enlightenment in Europe, when humanity's reason and abilities to control fate were predominating ideas. Today, such literature is very much out of vogue, both because an account of a world of sweetness and light makes boring reading, and – given the modern threats of nuclear war, overpopulation, and a bankruptcy of environmental resources – such visions strike many as naive.

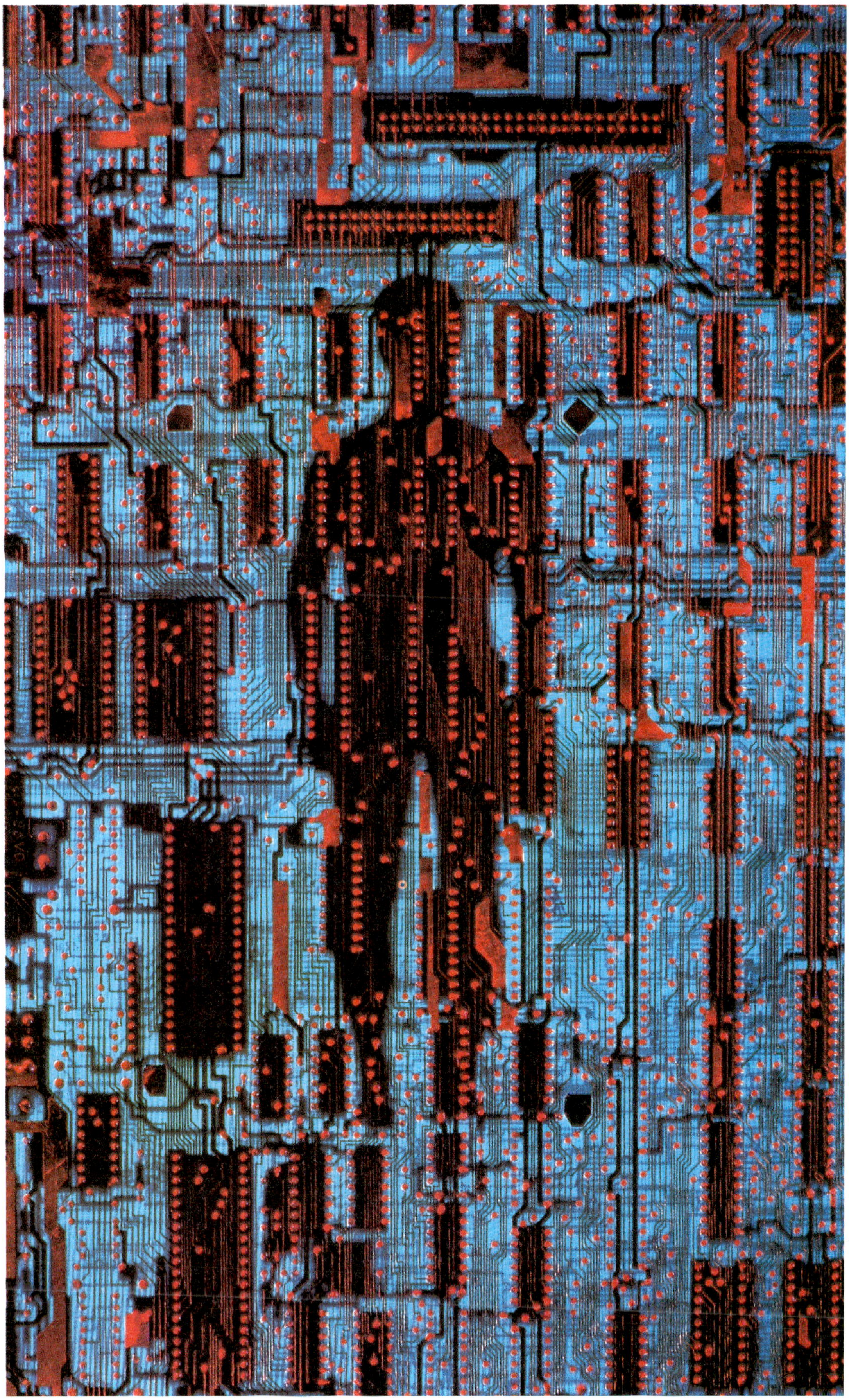

◀ *As humanity approaches the year 2000 nothing is certain, except that the future holds a fascination for all. It seems that at present, as at many times in the past, the scenarios which hold the greatest sway over our imagination are the disasters and catastrophes, not the Utopias and ideal blueprints. Utopian literature attained its greatest popularity in Europe during the Enlightenment of the 18th century – when confidence in humanity's reason and in scientific progress were characteristics of the age. Today such visions may strike many as naive, but if the potential for the products of science and technology to do harm is unprecedented, equally the capacity of science for good has never been greater.*

See also
Paymasters 21-40
Nuclear Power and Radiation 57-64
Genetic Engineering 65-76
Global Change 93-108

Escape to the stars

What is the probability that mankind will one day, out of either choice or necessity, acquire the capability to travel to and colonize distant parts of the universe?

It is certain that true interstellar exploration and colonization will demand the most powerful and ambitious propulsion methods known to science. The ultimate rocket propulsion system is the photon rocket, where matter is completely annihilated and the resultant energy is radiated away to produce thrust. There is no possibility, within our present day knowledge of physics, of a vehicle containing its own energy source and propellant being better than this system.

Another vehicle potentially capable of relativistic speeds is the interstellar ramjet, conceived as a way to avoid vehicles having to carry their own fuel and propellant. All the propulsion system consumables come from outside the vehicle. Interstellar space contains a certain amount of hydrogen gas, some in the neutral and some in the ionized form. This gas is collected by an intake on the ramjet and is fed into a reactor, which converts some of the mass of the hydrogen into energy in fusion reactions. This energy is used to accelerate the unconverted matter rearwards to provide thrust. With its range and speed unlimited, the interstellar ramjet has enormous potential.

World ships

The use of fast starships for interstellar flight has received a good deal of attention, but an alternative is the use of much slower vehicles. Such a vehicle would leave its planetary system carrying a community whose objective was simply to live a normal existence, such that future generations would have the option of exploring or colonizing other planets as they were encountered. These vehicles would have coast velocities of a fraction of the speed of light, and to compensate for the resulting long journey times they must increase in size to such an extent that they should be considered to be small worlds in their own right.

A vehicle which would be in operation for perhaps many millenia must be capable of providing a stable environment. The inhabitants of the starfaring "planet" would wish to take their culture and basic environment with them, and to do this they would build the largest ships practicable.

The simplest structure capable of providing these conditions is a rotating cylinder with the occupants on the interior. It would have a radius of at least 10 kilometers and a length of about 115 kilometers. The ship would rotate to give a gravitational attraction at the inside surface equal to that of the Earth. The mass of the world ship structure, the soil and the atmosphere could be some 550 billion tonnes, and the population around 700,000.

▼ A NASA painting of a "space colony". In order to propel a vehicle the size of a "world ship" the engine power would need to be about a million times the artificial power output of the Earth. Since a world ship must be able to command such power at any time, even when light years away from home, the power source must be on-board. The only practical mechanism currently known is the external nuclear pulse rocket. It is clear that the capability of building several hundred world ships should not represent a strain upon a Solar System-wide community. The fuel is abundant, and given a stop in any planetary system it would be possible to refuel.

Glossary

Absolute zero
The temperature at which all substances have zero thermal energy.
Academy
Plato's Academy was named for the garden where he taught; medieval academies were schools; new academies of the 15th to 18th centuries were associations promoting science, literature and technology.
Accelerator
In particle physics, a research tool used to accelerate subatomic particles to high velocities.
Acid rain
Precipitation, in rain and mists, that bears sulfuric and nitric acids formed in the atmosphere from sulfur dioxide emitted by burning coal, oil and gasoline; it can severely damage plant (forests) and animal (fish in lakes) life.
Acquired characteristics
It was the view of Jean Lamarck (1744-1829) that changes which took place in a plant or an animal in its lifetime could be passed on to later generations.
AIDS
Acquired immune deficiency syndrome, an epidemic disease whose virus wrecks the immune system, rendering the body vulnerable to potentially fatal infections.
Amino acid
A basic chemical unit, from which proteins are synthesized by the body.
Anomie
Term applied by Émile Durkheim to social instability stemming from a breakdown of generally accepted values accompanied by widespread personal feelings of alienation and uncertainty.
Antibiotic
A chemical produced by a microorganism and used as a drug to kill or inhibit the growth of other microorganisms.
Antibody
A defensive substance produced by the immune system to neutralize or help destroy a specific foreign substance or ANTIGEN.
Antigen
A foreign substance that provokes the body to produce ANTIBODIES.
Applied science
Science intended to produce clearly identified returns, as opposed to PURE SCIENCE.
Astrology
The science-art of divining the future from study of the heavens.
Atomic clock
A device using the constant frequencies of electron spin reversals of the cesium atom to define an accurate and reproducible time scale.
Bacteria (singular bacterium)
A large and varied group of MICROORGANISMS, unicellular and 0.3μm-2μm in diameter, classified by their shape and staining ability. They live in many environments; only a few are PATHOGENS.
Bacteriophage
See PHAGE.
Binomial system
The system of NOMENCLATURE introduced by Carolus Linnaeus (1707-1778) comprising two Latin names, generic and specific, for each plant (or animal), e.g. *Homo sapiens*.
Biometry
The statistical analysis of biological observations and phenomena.
Bubble chamber
A device used to observe the paths of subatomic particles, by reducing pressure as the particles pass through so that bubbles form along the paths.
Calculus
Mathematics dealing with continually changing quantities.
CAT
Computed axial tomography; a diagnostic use of X-rays, which scan the body, the data being computer-stored to build up the image of a "slice" which is color-coded to show up slight differences between different parts of the body.
Cell fusion
A technique of fusing different types of cells together in order to combine their genetic material; it has led to the creation of HYBRIDOMAS.
Chlorofluorocarbons
Gases used to propel aerosol sprays; they are accumulating in the atmosphere, where they appear to be destroying the protective layer of ozone.
Chromosome
A thread of genetic material contained in the cell nucleus and duplicated when the cell divides.
Citation
The reference in one scientific paper to another; co-citation is the citation together of papers in a third paper.
Classical science
Generally taken to be that period in western science between the publication of Isaac Newton's *Principia Mathematica* in 1687 and the discovery of radioactivity and the overthrow of Newton's ideas on time and space, by Albert Einstein and others, in the years around 1900.
Classical world
The Mediterranean civilization centered first on Greece then later on Rome between about the 8th century BC and 4th century AD.
Control
In scientific experiments, a group or individual (animal, plant or inanimate) that affords a standard of comparison with a similar item subject to a variablle to which the control is not.
Creationism (creation science)
A form of FUNDAMENTALISM, emerging in the USA in recent years and claiming equal time with evolutionary biology in school curricula.
Deduction (deductive method)
A form of logic in which particular conclusions are reached by reasoning from certain general principles assumed to be true. An alternative process is INDUCTION.
DNA
Deoxyribonucleic acid; its structure contains the blueprint that contains genetic information.
Electromagnetic radiation
RADIATION consisting of an electric and magnetic disturbance which travels in a vacuum at a constant speed known as the speed of light (about 300,000 km/s). Visible light and radio waves are examples.
Electron micrograph
A highly magnified image obtained by using a beam of electrons rather than light.
Element
Defined in 1787 by A. Lavoisier as a substance that was chemically "simple", i.e. could not be decomposed; 2,000 years earlier, Empedocles defined four elements: earth, fire, air, water.
Empiricism
In philosophy, the view that knowledge can be derived from sense experience. Empirical: relying on experience, observation and experiment.
Enzyme
An organic catalyst, composed of a protein.
ESP (extrasensory perception)
Perception using senses other than those generally recognized.
False-color photography
The processing of special photographic or other emulsions to display information, using added or "unnatural" color.
Falsification principle
As suggested by Karl Popper: a single unambiguous piece of evidence against a general statement is enough to destroy its credibility; scientific laws cannot be proved, only tested; much of science is devoted to systematic attempts to refute or falsify laws and hypotheses.
Fission
In nuclear physics, the changing of an element into two or more elements of lower atomic weight, with the release of energy.
Fundamentalism
A religious movement developed in the USA after World War 1; fundamentalists insist on the absolute truth of the Bible, including the Creation story.
Fundamental science
Pure science.
Fusion
In nuclear physics, the merging of two nuclei to form a new element of higher atomic weight, usually resulting in the release of energy.
Futurology
The study of what developments, particularly on a global scale, are possible or likely in the future.
Gene
The unit of heredity, made up of DNA and located on a CHROMOSOME in a cell nucleus.
Gene-splicing
A method of taking a piece of DNA-carrying hereditary GENES from one living organism and inserting it into another organism.
Germ theory
The theory pioneered by L. Pasteur (1822-1895) and Robert Koch (1843-1910) that diseases are spread by living germs (microbes).
Gravitation
The force of attraction existing between all matter.
Green Revolution
The use in the 1960s and 1970s of high-yielding varieties of grain (notably wheat and rice) developed by scientists, and the ensuing changes in agriculture, society and food output.
GUT (grand unified theory)
An attempt to explain theoretically the forces of nature in terms of one underlying force.
HeLa cells
Cells which originated with tissue taken from a US victim of cervical cancer in 1951 (HeLa being the first two letters of her first and family names). Potentially immortal, the cells are widely used for cultivating viruses.
HIV
Human immunodeficiency virus, infection with which may result in AIDS.
Homeopathy
The treatment of medical symptoms by giving minute amounts of a drug which produces similar symptoms.
Humanism
The individualistic and critical spirit, and emphasis on secular concerns, that was a characteristic of, for example, the RENAISSANCE.
Hybridoma
A fusion of malignant and ANTIBODY-generating cells, with wide pharmaceutical, medical and research uses; can produce MONOCLONAL ANTIBODIES.
Ice-minus
A strain of the BACTERIUM *Pseudomonas syringae* bred to remove the GENE responsible for producing a substance that triggers ice nucleation when the bacterium is present on the leaves of crop or other plants.
Induction
a) The process of reasoning from particular instances to make general propositions; as a scientific method, it requires accumulation of quantities of information in the hope or expectation that conclusions will emerge.
b) The phenomenon in which an electric current is generated when a conductor passes through an electric field.
Industrial Revolution
The major change in national economies which began with the introduction of power-driven machinery in the late 18th century in England, and continued through the 19th century.
Integrated circuit
A structure on which a large number of electronic components are assembled on one SEMICONDUCTOR wafer; has largely replaced the TRANSISTOR.
Intercropping
A "low-tech" farming practice whereby two (or more) crops are grown together; it can increase yields, and limit pest damage.
Irradiation of foods
The exposure of foodstuffs to ionizing RADIATION to preserve the food and/or destroy microbes responsible for causing food poisoning.
Isotopes
Atoms of an element with the same number of protons in the nucleus but a different number of neutrons.

Laser
Light Amplification by Stimulated Emission of Radiation; a device producing a very intense beam of parallel light with a precisely defined wavelength.
Macrophage
A white blood cell specialized to circulate through body tissues and consume foreign bodies and cell debris.
Magnetohydrodynamic generation (MHD)
A procedure in which electric current is created by passing high-temperature ionized gases through a magnetic field.
Mechanics
The study of the action of forces on bodies.
Meltdown
An accident in a nuclear plant in which (as at Three Mile Island), following failure of cooling systems, core fuel rods and grid spacing melt down.
Metaphysics
The study of or speculation on the fundamentals of existence or reality.
Meteorology
The study of the atmosphere, weather and climate.
Microbe
MICROORGANISM.
Microorganism
A living organism too small to be seen without a microscope.
Monoclonal antibodies
Extremely pure versions of ANTIBODIES assembled by the body in response to infection; produced by HYBDRIDOMAS.
Mutation
A change in genetic material (GENE or set of CHROMOSOMES).
NASA
National Aeronautics and Space Administration, the US government agency responsible for space exploration, artificial satellites and rockets.
Natural philosophy
Until the 19th century "natural philosophy" meant something similar to our word physics.
Natural selection
The mechanism of evolution discovered by Charles Darwin (1809-1882).
NMR
Nuclear magnetic resonance; technique of imaging the interior of the body using the magnetic resonance of the atoms comprising the elements of the tissues.
Nomenclature
In biology, an internationl system of Latin names used for plants and animals. See BINOMIAL SYSTEM.
Nuclear winter
The lower temperatures, and their consequences, forecast as following on a nuclear war and the consequent absorption of solar RADIATION by smoke from fires.
ORT
Oral rehydration therapy; administration of a mixture of water, sugar and salt to children suffering from diarrhea.
Paleomagnetism
The study of past changes in Earth's magnetic field by examining the magnetic properties of old rocks.
Panspermia theory
An explanation of the origin of life according to which the Earth was initially seeded with living organisms from space.
Paranormal
Describes a phenomenon that is not explicable in terms of acceptable science.
Parascience
A loose term covering the study of PARANORMAL phenomena.
Pasteurization
A technique of heating milk, beer, wine etc. to destroy bacteria it may contain; named after L. Pasteur (1822-1895).
Pathogen
An organism that produces disease.
Peer review
The process by which scientific papers are assessed by REFEREES or members of advisory panels of periodicals, also, the assessment of grant applications by fellow experts.
Periodic table
A table of elements arranged by atomic number (the number of protons in the nucleus) to show similarities and trends in physical and chemical properties.
Phlogiston
One of three varieties of "earth"; a combustible material lost by the substance that burns (18th century).
pH
A measure of the acidity of an aqueous solution.
Phage
A VIRUS that attacks BACTERIA; also known as a BACTERIOPHAGE.
Pneumatic chemists
Chemists of the 18th century who studied airs released from solids and fluids, including J. Black, J. Priestley, H. Cavendish, C. Scheele.
Priority
The condition of publishing or announcing a scientific discovery before anyone else.
Protozoa
The single-celled animals.
Pure science
Also known as basic or fundamental science; the disinterested quest for information to compile and the process of compiling, accurate pictures of the physical and biological world (also called "curiosity-oriented").
Quantum theory
A theory developed at the beginning of the 20th century to account for certain phenomena that could not be explained by CLASSICAL physics.
Radiation
The emission and propagation through space of ELECTROMAGNETIC RADIATION or subatomic particles.
Radioactivity
The spontaneous disintegration of unstable nuclei, accompanied by the emission of RADIATION of alpha particles, beta particles or gamma rays.
Rationalism
A theory that reason alone, unaided by experience, can arrive at basic truth; in the 17th century the rationalism of R. Descartes, G. von Leibniz and B. Spinoza stood in opposition to the EMPIRICISM of J. Locke.
Reductionism
A viewpoint expressed by, for example, J. Monod (1910-1976), that life's mechanisms, including apparently goal-directed behavior, can be explained in terms of physics and chemistry.
Referee
One of a panel of advisors who help a periodical editor to assess the quality of submitted papers, a process known as PEER REVIEW.
Relativity
The theory of space, time and matter, enunciated by A. Einstein (1879-1955).
Renaissance
The transition between medieval and modern times in Europe, beginning in Italy in the 14th century and continuing to the 17th century, marked by a HUMANISTIC revival of CLASSICAL learning, and the beginnings of modern science.
Research front
A cluster of co-cited papers. See CITATION.
RNA
Ribonucleic acid; a single-stranded nucleic acid that cooperates with DNA for protein synthesis.
Scanning electron microscope
An electron microscope in which the electron beam scans the specimen's surface; this emits secondary electrons that are focused as a three-dimensional image, a scanning electron micrograph or SEM. See TRANSMISSION ELECTRON MICROGRAPH.
Scholastics
In western Christendon in the 9th-17th centuries, a movement combining religious dogma first with the mystical and intuitional tradition of philosophers such as St Augustine (354-430) and, from the 13th century, with the ideas of Aristotle, mainly translated into Latin.
Semiconductor
A material whose electrical conductivity is intermediate between that of an insulator and a conductor at room temperature and increases with rising temperature and impurity concentration. See TRANSISTOR.
Spectroscopy
The production, measurement and analysis of SPECTRA, much used by astronomers, chemists and physicists.
Spectrum
The distribution of the intensity of ELECTROMAGNETIC RADIATION with wavelength. The visible spectrum encompasses those wavelengths to which the human eye responds, the different wavelengths corresponding to the different colors.
Staphylococcus
A BACTERIUM responsible for many skin, soft tissue and bone infections.
Strategic science
Basic science carried out because its results may help solve foreseeable practical problems in the future.
Strata
The various layers in which sedimentary rock is formed. The singular "stratum" is rarely used.
Stratigraphy
The study of the chronological sequence and the correlation of rock STRATA in different districts.
Superconductor
Material which, when cooled to low temperatures, conducts electricity with little or no resistance.
Teleology
The use of predetermined purpose to explain the Universe.
Thermodynamics
The science of the interconversion of heat, work and other forms of energy.
Transistor
An electronic device made of SEMICONDUCTOR materials used in a circuit as an amplifier, rectifier, detector or switch. See INTEGRATED CIRCUIT.
Transmission electron micrograph
Or TEM; an image from an electron microscope based on the notion of replacing light with electrons, focused by magnetic fields rather than through glass lenses.
Transmutation
Alchemists believed that one substance could be transmuted into another – hence their efforts to transmute into gold. The same term was used by Darwin to label the process of one species giving rise to another.
Trigonometry
The study of the ratios of the sides of right-angled triangles.
Uncertainty principle
A principle of subatomic physics, enunciated by W. Heisenberg (1901-1976), that it is impossible to determine simultaneously the position and the momentum of a particle.
User pays
A system whereby the cost of research and development is borne by their beneficiaries rather than by government or another public funding agency.
Vaccination, vaccine
Originally, the introduction of matter from cowpox pustules to lessen the danger of catching smallpox; by extension, vaccines. Vaccines contain attenuated (weakened) or killed microbes or their fragments, which are used to confer immunity but do not cause disease.
Virus
A submicroscopic parasitic MICROORGANISM comprising a protein or protein/lipid sheath enclosing nucleic acid (DNA OR RNA); those that attack BACTERIA are BACTERIOPHAGES.
Vitalism
A once-popular theory that cells depend for life on a mysterious force that cannot be analyzed in terms of physics and chemistry.
Vitamin
An essential nutrient found in low concentration in food. Vitamins are organic substances which perform vital functions in the body.
X-ray diffraction.
The process by which the X-ray diffraction patterns of crystals are translated into pictures showing the relative positions of the atoms in a crystal, as in a photomicrograph of very high magnification.

Index

Page numbers in *italics* refer to illustrations, captions or side text.

Credits

Key to abbreviations: AP Associated Press; ARPL Ann Ronan Picture Library; BCL Bruce Coleman Ltd; BHPL BBC Hulton Picture Library; FSP Frank Spooner Pictures; MEPL Mary Evans Picture Library; OCD Oxford Chemical Designs Ltd; RFL Rex Features Ltd; SPL Science Photo Library; TCL Telegraph Colour Library; TPL Topham Picture Library; b bottom; bl bottom left; br bottom right; c center; cl center left; cr center right; t top; tl top left; tr top right; l left; r right.

5t Mansell Collection **5b** M. Fielding/SPL **6-7** Camera Press **7t** IPPF **7b** Photosource **8tl** AP **8-9** B. Longcore/ SPL **8b** Premier Brands **10** TPL **11** Biophoto Associates **12t**, **12b**, **13l** ARPL **13r** TCL **14-15t** BHPL **14b**, **15br** Thorn EMI Research Laboratories **15tr** EMI Electronics **16** TPL **17t** Photosource **17b** American Institute of Physics **18t** Lowell Georgia/SPL **18b** Ford Motor Company **19t** RFL **19b**, **21** FSP **22tl** Camera Press **22tr** Popperfoto **22b** D. Parker/SPL **22** inset Tony Stone **24t** European Space Agency **24b** FSP **25t** Jerry Maso **25b** ESPRIT **26tl** Bell Laboratories **26-7t** Dr. R. Damadian/SPL **26-7b** New Scientist **27tr** W. McIntyre/SPL **28** Professor T.A. Mansfield **28-9** Shell Photographic Library **29t** OCD/SPL **30** Giraudon/ Musée Marmottan **31l** ARPL **31r** Keystone Collection **32** Ron Church/SPL **33** NASA/SPL **34-5** Lawrence Livermore Laboratory **35** Popperfoto **36** University of Warwick **37** FSP **38**, **39bl** Hutchison Library **39t** FSP **39br** International Center for Theoretical Physics **41** J-L. Charmet **42t** Bridgeman art Library **42b** ARPL **43l** MEPL **43r** Mansell Collection **44** MEPL **45l** ARPL **45tr,br** BHPL **46l** Henry Morris/Presbyterian and Reformed Publishing Company **46-7t** TPL **46br** Sinclair Stammers **47tr** BHPL **47b** Popperfoto **48bl** TPL **48br** Novosti **48-9** Lenin Library, Moscow **50l** AIP Niels Bohr Library **50r** TPL **51** Popperfoto **52** FSP **52-3** Xinhua Press Agency **53tl** Hutchison Library **53tr** S. and R. Greenhill **54-5**, **55tl** FSP **55r** Novosti **56** Derby Museum and Art Gallery **57** Columbia Pictures Industries Inc./National Film Archive, London **58t** Format Photographers **58-9b** RFL **58** inset AP **59** UKAEA **60l** AP **60r**, **61cr** FSP **61tl**, **61br** Novosti **61tr** Camera Press **62** Tass **62-3** London School of Hygiene and Tropical Medicine/SPL **63b** U.S. Dept of Energy/SPL **63** inset Leatherhead Foods R.A. **64** South California Edison Co. **65** Camera Press **66t** News and Publication Service, Stamford University **66b** SPL/Alexnder Tsiaris **67l**, **67r**, **68** New Scientist **69t** Tony Sleep Photography **69bl** Dr. D.H.L. Bishop **69br** AP **70** BCL **70-1** Susan Griggs **71c** Dr. J. Burgess/SPL **71br** BCL **72l** Dr. J. Burgess/SPL **72-3** CNRI/SPL **73t** BHPL **74-5** Dr. G. Murti/SPL **75bl** A. Tsiaris/SPL **75br** C. Raymond/ SPL **76l** Jerry Mason/New Scientist **76r** Dr. J. Burgess/SPL **77** Hutchison Library **78-9** The Exploratory, Bristol **82** P. Biddle and T. Malyon/SPL **82-3t** S. and R. Greenhill **83r** D. Parker/SPL **84bl** New Scientist/ Edwardo Castaneda **84tr** AP **84-5** TCL **86t** Warner Bros./Kobal Collection **86-7b** Lucas Films/National Film Archive, London **88l** Warner Bros/Kobal Collection **88r**, **88-9** Oxford Scientific Films **89r** BBC Enterprises **90bl**, **90-1t** MGM/Kobal Collection **90br** MGM/National Film Archive, London **92** UNESCO/ M. Claude **93** D. Allan/SPL **94l** M. Goldwater/ Network **94r** BCL **94-5** S. and R. Greenhill **95tr** Zefa **95br** Panos Pictures/Sean Sprague **96bl** Tropix **96br**, **96-7** Hutchison Library **97r** BCL **98** Geoscience Features **98-9** Ardea **100** NASA/ SPL **100-1** FSP **101** inset Geoscience Features **102t** FSP **102-3b** Zefa **103** Johnson Matthey Ltd **104** World Health Organisation **105t** S. and R. Greenhill **105b** J. Matthews/Format **106-7** M. Goldwater/Network **107bl** Böhringer Ingelheim **107br** S. and R. Greenhill **108** OSF/G. I. Bernard **109l** Brookhaven National Lab/ SPL **109r** Camera Press **110-11** Hutchison Library **110tl**, **111tl**, **111tr** National Center for Atmospheric Research **112tr** TPL **112-13b** Frank Lane **114** Melies/ Kobal Collection **115** Lowell Georgia/SPL **116t** P. Plailly/SPL **116b** Idaho National Engineering Laboratory **117** Jerry Mason/New Scientist **118** National Film Archive, London **118-19** Virgin/Kobal Collection **119b** Image Bank **120** FSP **121l** Alcor **121r** SPL/E. Gravé **122bl** Illustrated London News **122tr** British Museum **122br** United Artists/Kobal Collection **123** Image Bank **124** NASA

Artists Alan Hollingbery; Kevin Maddison; Colin Salmon; Mick Saunders; David Smith; Del Tolton
Production Joanna Turner, Clive Sparling
Index Barbara James and John Baines
Media conversion and typesetting Peter MacDonald, Ron Barrow